Testimonials

George Browning is a public theologian. From its inception, Christianity has been both a personal and a public faith. In the majority world, it continues to be a public faith. However, in the west, self-appointed cultural manipulators, both within and outside the church, are increasingly determined to drive Christianity from the public realm. Yet Christianity will always remain at its heart a public faith. If you want to understand Christianity in its personal and public implications, then read this inspiring, poignant, insightful, challenging, and, most of all, truthful book.

Reverend Professor Emeritus James Haire AC
Past Executive Director, Australian Centre for Christianity and Culture
Past President, National Council of Churches in Australia
Past National President, Uniting Church in Australia

Speaking truth to the power of Empire in whatever its multitude of manifestations has never been easy. The prophets of ancient Israel knew its disappointments and dangers. It requires a good deal of resilience and tenacity and commitment to a vision of the truth.

Moreover, those to whom truth is addressed will respond in a variety of ways— not all capitulating as did David to the prophet Nathan's 'You are the man'. Consider the cynical nihilism of Pontius Pilate. Power is likely to claim the right to define truth in ways that suit those who would wield it. The recent history of the United States of America is replete with stunning examples. George Browning provides us with examples of the rejection of politically inconvenient truths closer to home.

Thankfully, George has the courage and tenacity to speak truth to power. His vision and commitment is clearly based in the mission of Jesus, coming out of Jesus' own experience of God's overwhelming love for all. That mission calls for the denunciation of the religion of Empire, and the demonstration of the way of Jesus, living in harmony with God, one another, and all creation. George Browning's book is an inspiring collection of his work over many years which will encourage us all to respond.

Bishop John Noble (Brisbane, North Queensland and Melbourne)

Not afraid to speak truth to power, Bishop George Browning is a prophet of our time. He sees with great moral clarity some of the major issues facing humanity, including the catastrophic existential threat posed by global warming. As a tireless champion of the common good and the Gospel values of justice and compassion, he has also fearlessly warned of the dangers of free market economics and unrestrained capitalism that lead to deep and widespread injustice and unrest, and a dehumanising and insecure life for many. We owe him a great debt of gratitude for his passionate commitment to a vision of society which values all equally and seeks the wellbeing of all.

Roland Ashby (Immediate past editor *Melbourne Anglican*)

Here, in the best prophetic tradition, are melded heat and light and deep humanity. To those in power with vested interests, it is bound to be received as 'Not Helpful'.

Father Bruce Henzell Brisbane

"Not Helpful"

Tales from a Truth Teller

George Browning

First Published in 2021 by Echo Books

Echo Books is an imprint of Superscript Publishing Pty Ltd, ABN 76 644 812 395

Registered Office: Suite 401, 140 Bourke St, Melbourne, VIC, 3000

www.echobooks.com.au

Copyright © George Browning

Creator: Browning George: Author.

Title: Not Helpful: Tales from a Truth Teller

ISBN: 978-0-6488546-1-6

NATIONAL LIBRARY OF AUSTRALIA

A catalogue record for this book is available from the National Library of Australia

Book layout and design by Peter Gamble, Canberra.

Set in Garamond Premier Pro Display, 12/17 and Bon Vivant Serif

Cover Image: Shutterstock.

www.echobooks.com.au

Contents

The Front Cover

Graffiti artists have found their own way of truth telling. Amongst them the English artist Banksy is arguably the most well-known and effective. In Sydney, Australia, Arthur Stace, Mr Eternity, etched his own place in Australian folk lore.

The front cover is one of Banksy's most well-known images. It has appeared in many places, but most famously on the separation wall in Bethlehem near Rachel's tomb. Facing the wall, Banksy has established his hotel/art museum of the occupation, the 'Walled Off'.

The context in which the art finds itself on the wall is the prolonged occupation of Palestinian Territories by the Israeli government and the consequent suffering and loss of human rights endured by the Palestinian people. It is one of many pieces of art together with quotations from inspiring people that can be found along the length of this 708-kilometre wall.

Like all good art it does not match oppression with counter threat or violence, but with an image of liberty and freedom. The message of the art is that external constraints cannot contain the human spirit, Palestinians will not remain silent, invisible, or caged, even a little girl with balloons can scale this wall.

The image has been chosen for the front cover in part because it speaks directly to the Israeli/Palestinian catastrophe, one of the issues addressed in the book, but more especially as an image to confront every situation of injustice. Like the girl with the balloons the human spirit, energised by justice and equity, trust and respect, can scale any wall.

Walls will not protect injustice from justice.

Acknowledgements

Few thoughts are original, and few experiences genuinely unique. While this book flows out of my lived experiences and conversations, some intensely personal, the unfolding pages are shaped by hundreds, probably thousands of fellow travellers who have blessed me through the intersection of their lives with my own.

I owe an immeasurable debt to Margaret, companion, partner, friend, wife for 56 years. Margaret has shared a deep understanding that our marriage and life of ministry have been inextricably woven together. They have been part of a single vocation. If there has been anything of value, anything commendable, anything of lasting effect, she has been responsible for at least half, and in some situations, much more than half.

I am in debt to three children and nine grandchildren whose lives of faith and sharpness of conversation have been an endless source of inspiration. So much so that I am now not sure whether thoughts and insights for which I claim ownership, were in fact theirs. Have they humoured me by allowing me to think insights were mine?

I am especially grateful to Canon John May of St John's College Morpeth, Archbishop Sir John Grindrod of Brisbane and the Diocese of Canberra and Goulburn for their unwarranted investments in me.

Being notoriously inattentive to detail, I remain in debt to staff in Morpeth, Singleton, Woy Woy, Brisbane, and Canberra who have made me look more competent than I deserve and for whom mutual respect has endured.

In the production of this book I am very grateful for the encouragement and care afforded me in the writing by Stephen Pickard, Bruce Henzell, Richard Edwards, John Noble, Roland Ashby, Richard Refshauge, and particularly by my friend and colleague Alan Wilson whose eagle eye has saved me from many embarrassments.

Foreword

Bishop George Browning, ninth Bishop of the Anglican Diocese of Canberra and Goulburn, appointed me as Chancellor of the Diocese in 2000. In Australian Anglican ecclesiology, the Chancellor of a Diocese is the confidential legal adviser to the Diocesan Bishop. Accordingly, I had a close relationship with Bishop George until he retired in 2008 and we dealt with many things together, not strictly limited to the somewhat arcane Anglican canon and ecclesiastical law.

In that time, it became clear to me that his commitment to the gospel of Jesus Christ was not just directed to the making of Christian believers as people who accept faith in Jesus as God, which he pursued devotedly, but also accepting that the Christian faith brought obligations to much besides, especially to the world that God had created and pronounced as good (Gen. 1:31) and to the people who inhabited it, who had been made in the divine image (Gen. 1:27).

Bishop George was active and passionate in all his concerns and not afraid to engage in the public space to address the ways in which society had failed to respect these things. Thus, for example, he was the force behind the creation, with Sir William Deane and Professor Lowitja O'Donoghue, of the Australian Centre for Christianity and Culture, where the interface between the Church and society and the Christian faith and other faiths can be developed in a thoughtful, respectful and influential way.

This book, essentially of essays, shows many of the concerns of Bishop George and exposes his passion and dedication to them and his views on how we should behave when we come to live a life that affects the creation that has been entrusted to us and the neighbours whom we are exhorted to love.

It is a fascinating personal autobiography of his boyhood and youth in his family in the United Kingdom and then his transplantation, with his family, to Australia, initially to the regions, which was somewhat of a culture shock, but filled with great agricultural experiences, and through the Church to the urban Australia and finally to Canberra.

He is also reflective in the essays which form something of a philosophical autobiography. He shows how his youthful experiences were so formative. He also shows how the title to Chapter 10, 'We are the Company we keep', has been so true for him. The quote from Archbishop Desmond Tutu, 'A person is a person through other persons', is so exemplified in his life and in forming his thoughts and passions.

The intense commitment he has for the Jesus he knows is evident, perhaps for me particularly beautifully expressed in his 2007 Synod Charge, his final Synod Charge, which he sets out in full in Chapter 4.

In contradistinction to many of the modern Christian apologists, he has on display here his humility and the advantage that failure can bring in moderating and reshaping, and thereby often strengthening, the concerns one has and the appropriate approach to them. He makes a virtue of vulnerability and provisionality, both of which I see as great Christian virtues, neither of which are inconsistent with the formation of opinions, which he has on an amazing array of subjects.

Thus, he can express forthright opinions but only where he can find them rationally and theologically based. This enables him especially to engage with society in a way that brings a generous perspective to the debate, addressing some of the huge problems we face with an insight underpinned by Christian perspectives, especially with an Anglican grounding.

The book also shows his strong biblical theology and draws on the personal experiences he has had and the stimulation he obtains from others. A great example of this are the stories of the youth pilgrimages that he created and lead for some years.

The story of the amazing institution, the Australian Centre for Christianity and Culture, is here wonderfully told and shows the essentiality of the Centre and how it has already shown its worth. All in all, this is a fascinating book.

I found it educative, stimulating, thoughtful and inspiring. As is obvious, I thoroughly enjoyed reading it and found it difficult to put down.

The Hon Richard Refshauge SC

Chancellor, Anglican Diocese of Canberra and Goulburn

Retired Judge, ACT Supreme Court

November2020

Preface

In our era, the road to holiness necessarily passes through the world of action.

Dag Hammarskjöld.
2nd General Secretary
United Nations, 1953—1961)

We are living through a very troubling period of history when voices of reason seem muted and trust is in short supply. Political leadership feeds on conflict and division, little energy is invested in global consensus, service or servanthood seems to have slipped from the lexicon of potential leaders. In this context where is the voice of faith?

In his, *Who rules the world*[1], the prolific and courageous commentator, Noam Chomsky, champions intellectuals who can be relied upon to use their knowledge and expertise, as well as their passion for the good of fellow citizens in the context of global humanity, to 'speak truth to power'. He says they fall into two categories.

First, there are those members of foreign regimes, who bravely speak against the excesses of their leaders and are championed by the West—as if they champion western values. Such voices might be heard from within Russia,

1   Noam Chomsky. *Who rules the world?* (London: Hamish Hamilton, 2016).

Iran, or China. Similarly, there have been voices that suit the West's economic or colonial aspirations from South and Latin America, from many Islamic countries, and from Asia. It is salutary to note that western voices, political and intellectual, unequivocally backed the 'Arab Spring'. Unbiased commentary might argue that this intervention has resulted in a less free, democratic, and secure existence for those who live throughout the Arab world.

Then there are those who have spoken critically from within the West, like Chomsky himself, against excesses of their governments—US, Australia, or Israel. The former are persecuted, imprisoned and possibly tortured by their regimes while lauded in the West, while the latter, not facing the same physical fate, are nonetheless pilloried at home. The pillorying has reached extraordinary heights in the US where any criticism of President Trump is labelled 'fake news'. It is also shrill in Israel where any criticism of Netanyahu's government is labelled either anti-Semitic or self-hating Judaism, depending upon the source of the critique. The pillorying is also shrill against voices of environmental justice who are perceived to be opponents of individuals' rights. In Australia, Newscorp has been at the forefront of this pillorying which has included attacks on Greta Thunberg and any who have dared to speak for a carbon neutral economy.

While I am gratefully aware of these champions of free speech and their commitment to justice, respect, and equality, and as deserving as they are of much attention, they are not my focus in the pages that follow. I want to focus attention on speaking truth to power from the perspective of faith, from a theological position, and more specifically from a Christian position. I will be speaking out of my own experience.

In his *Truth speaks to power*[2] Walter Brueggemann insists on the radical and subversive political implications of the Bible. He says 'occupants of power are of necessity always seeking out versions of truth that are compatible with their present power arrangements. Conversely, outsiders present power

2   Walter Brueggemann. *Truth Speaks to Power* (Louisville, Kentucky: Westminster John Knox Press, 2013).

(especially Scriptural narrative) as counter truths that will permit and legitimate counter arrangement of power.'[3]

The Christian alternative or counter truth is founded in trinitarian belief that community is everything, and that everything and everyone relates, therefore all must be interested in the good of the other for we all rely on good being shown to us. In the economy of God, relationship is the ultimate truth.

On the one hand Christian truth emphasises that individual humans have a unique status to know and be known, to choose life or to destroy; while on the other, to realise we are all part of an integrated, intentional, created order, in which everything and everyone relates to everything else, for blessing or curse. Because of this mutual interdependence, everything, and everyone, human and nonhuman, is to be accorded respect and honour. Attributing respect or honour is recognising beauty and value in that which is other than self. In this spirit, as sentient beings, humans have the capacity, indeed the vocation, to act as stewards of harmony, wholeness, and well-being. 'The hope which is set before us' is that this harmony, wholeness, and well-being ultimately transcends temporal existence. Through the incarnation of Jesus what is temporal has been absorbed by what is eternal.

Because shalom (peace and well-being) must always be the focus of people of faith, it is inevitable that brokenness in a transient world must be taken seriously. Speaking truth to power from a position of faith is therefore a focus on redeeming, making whole, restoring, and naming the cause(s) of brokenness.

Dualism is alien to Christianity which asserts, through the incarnation of Jesus, that taking spiritual values seriously means taking the world in which we live seriously—for good. Those who claim to be Christian and shun the world, or worse consider the material world to be inherently evil, have never read the Bible.

3   Walter Brueggemann. *Truth Speaks to Power* (Louisville, Kentucky: Westminster John Knox Press, 2013): 4.

Speaking truth to power from a Christian perspective assumes there is a life-giving, unifying energy which can be chosen and embraced by those who seek common good. Named 'love' in the Christian community, this energy can be understood by way of contrast with its opposite—fear. Human choices are made for one, or the other. It is well known that peace and contentment are associated with meaning and purpose found in the service of others, whilst restlessness, even emptiness, is surprisingly associated with accumulated power and wealth, without reference to altruism.

In the scriptures, the foundational authority of the Christian community, those who speak truth to power are called prophets. Jesus is considered the ultimate prophet, for in his living and dying, as much as in his words, he confronted power, turning its meaning on its head. Like Jesus, those who refuse to be intimidated by worldly wealth or power are the true victors, ones with real power—power to transform. Chomsky knows well that biblical prophets are the forerunners of his intellectuals. The question that needs to be faced is whether religious communities have now become so weakened that the voice of the prophet is only heard in the secular world, no longer in the world of faith.

The 21st century Western Church has significantly declined and acts as if it is permanently under siege. The Australian Royal Commission into child abuse has made clear the institutional Church can be relied upon to protect its institutional life and neglect the witness to love and justice for which it exists. With few exceptions, institutional Christianity appears to have lost its prophetic voice and failed its calling to be God's agent of transformation in the world. In the chapters ahead, I will use anecdotal material gained from ministry over the past 50+ years to encourage a new generation of courageous prophetic voices to rise from within the community of faith, especially the Christian faith.

Introduction

*Your life as a Christian should make non-believers question
their disbelief in God.*
Dietrich Bonhoeffer

In the biblical tradition, no one covets a prophetic role; speaking truth to power is uncomfortable, seldom appreciated, and at times downright dangerous. In the modern era this has been clearly demonstrated through the murder of Jamal Khashoggi in the Saudi consulate in Istanbul in 2018 for daring to critique the power elite of Saudi Arabia.

Religious prophets, past and present, have been associated with doomsday cults, the assertion that terrible foreboding is lurking just beyond plain sight! The 'end of the world' is the final and perennial foreboding prophesied repeatedly for 2000 years and beyond. Usually connected to an interpretation of current world events against the background of sacred text, the phenomenon is alive and well in the 21st century. Its purveyors are frequently syndicated TV networks and owners of large bank accounts. They are misusers of sacred text, charlatans playing on the gullibility of ordinary women and men.

True biblical prophecy is a much more serious matter. It is not about that which is beyond sight, but about that which is in plain sight, or at least that which should be in plain sight if ignorance, wilfulness, power, and greed were not being used to hide it. It is about pointing the world in the direction of life and away from choices that are destructive of harmony and wholeness.

Arthur Stace[4] who famously adorned Sydney sidewalks with *Eternity* from 1932—1967 is not normally associated with the prophetic vocation. Anonymously drawing the attention of passers-by to a vital and missing dimension in their lives obscured by the busyness of work and the allure of consumerism, he was a significant, Australian, 20th century prophet. Retrospectively his role has been immortalised. As a tribute to the man known as Mr Eternity, the Sydney Harbour Bridge was lit up with the word 'Eternity' as part of the celebrations for the beginning of the year 2000 Sydney New Year's Eve celebrations, as well as part of the Sydney 2000 Olympic Games Opening Ceremony, the celebration of the XXVII Olympiad. This was done to not only celebrate Arthur Stace's achievements, but to celebrate the new millennium. How extraordinary that Australia should greet the new millennium with this word, originally copperplated by a war veteran who became a drunk and then converted to Christianity. Most preachers covet, but never attain, such influence.

Early in his ministry Jesus rose in the Nazareth synagogue to read the jubilee passage from Isaiah 61 with the extraordinary inference that it was fulfilled in him. It is a passage that splashes eternity about, that daubs the walls with it. It is a passage that celebrates freedom, health, and wholeness which burst forth when earth is daubed with heaven, when what is physical and transient is imbued with the spirit of life. It is a passage that makes clear the creator's intention to redeem what has become marred. Brokenness is not supposed to be a permanent state, least of all passed on from generation to generation. Paradoxically, the passage conveys how difficult Jesus found it to communicate such exciting news: 'a prophet is not without honour except in his own country' (Mark 6:4).

4   Arthur Malcolm Stace (9 February 1885–30 July 1967).

David Attenborough, a man with little or any religious background, stands firmly in Chomsky's tradition of intellectuals who mirror the prophetic tradition by pointing to what is in immediate sight. He makes clear that human behaviour on a global scale has reached the point where our combined footprints detrimentally affect every other living species, animal and plant, threatening climatic stability (the Holocene) that has enabled human flourishing for the last 200,000 years. Since the onset of the industrial revolution, through our own actions, we now live in what the atmospheric chemist, Paul Crutzen, calls the age of the Anthropocene, the first moment in earth's history when the future of all life, is in the hands of just one species—humans. To speak of the possible end of life as we have known it within a few generations unless we change our behaviour, as Attenborough is calling us to consider, is audacious, but it is to stand in the tradition of Amos and Jeremiah whose messages were equally shocking. Attenborough's message is genuine prophecy, calling to account prevailing behaviours with the hope of change, because the price of no change is unthinkable. As a natural historian and an observer of the evolution of life, Attenborough takes for granted the reality that everything is related to everything else; alter the balance inherent in this web of relationships and there are consequences.

In 1980 Margaret I and our boys found ourselves in the UK for a short exchange. While there I had the opportunity of attending a lecture by the missionary, theologian bishop, Lesslie Newbigin.[5]

I have little recollection of the substance of his address, but I do have a vivid memory of question time that followed. During his address he had said: 'you don't really believe anything unless it makes a difference to the way you live your life'. A young student then stood and asked: 'bishop, in light of your statement about belief, you say you believe God is Trinity, could you say how this belief makes a difference to the way you live your life'? The bishop replied: 'thank you for the question, this belief affects my life profoundly, for through it I understand ultimate truth to be relationship'.

5   Lesslie Newbigin (1909–1998), author, theologian, bishop, missionary to India.

This simple exchange has had the most profound effect on my own life's journey. Not only did it turn Trinity Sunday from what had been a preacher's nightmare to a day of keen homiletic anticipation, but it has helped me to understand that God and truth do not reside in any particular reality, but in the space between—in the relationship. God is the energy, experienced by us as love, which holds all things together in unity. Every person, every cell, every moment, is distinct, but all are part of a wonderful whole.

This exchange was a piece of profound theology. Theology is not, or at least should not be, a dry piece of academic philosophy, but the dynamic of spirit and mind, from which the gut spontaneously utters 'aha now my eye sees you!' Theology is nothing less than doing business with God. After a long struggle with three comforters (tormentors) and then confronted with God's dressing down out of the whirlwind Job can say 'I had heard of you by the hearing of the ear, but now my eye sees you' (Job 42:5).

In the Newbigin exchange I learned profound, indeed eternal truth about God and the world. God is not an entity that/who can be described or imaged. Hence the second of the ten commandments—'Thou shalt not make for thyself a graven image or likeness ...'. Idolatry or image making is not restricted to art, it is most potently present in words. The Reformation witnessed the destruction of much religious art, but Protestantism has more than adequately replaced the art with image making words and catch cries. For example: to say God *requires* the death of Jesus to expiate sin, as expressed in the substitutional theory of the atonement, is idolatry. It images God after a frail human judicial system. Even more extraordinarily, some Anglican Dioceses require submission to this verbal idolatry before authority is given to minister in their Diocese.

God is the one who causes to be. God causes to be through love. Indeed, we can say God is love.

As long as we love each other, and remember the feeling we had, we can die without really going away. All the love you created is still there ... Death ends a life not a relationship.[6]

---

6 Albom Mitch. *Tuesdays with Morrie* (New York: Doubleday, 1997).

Theological understanding emerges out of a context—triumph or tragedy—more often the latter. Reflecting on the terrible suffering of the First World War, the bishops of the Anglican Communion meeting in London in 1920 were to say the great evil facing humanity is the dominance of self-interest, and the worst form of self-interest is national self-interest. These words, which I will come back to later, are profoundly theological and prophetic and most apt for our current age. Nationalism has become our current scourge.

The Newbigin encounter, focussing on relationship as the ultimate truth, has led me down a path of commitment to justice with those who have shared bread with me along life's journey.

Visiting a Karen refugee camp on the border of Thailand and Burma in the 1980s and enjoying their generous hospitality, then visiting many similar places since in Africa and the Middle East has helped me understand that citizenship is less about nationality, and more about common humanity.

Having my life enhanced through engagement with Australia's first peoples has opened my eyes to see that civilisation has more to do with culture, language, family ties and care of creation than it has with technology or monetary wealth. The latter only have value in service of the former, indeed if they are accrued at the expense of the former, they are more curse than blessing.

The privilege of teaching young Palestinian ordinands in the 1980s has taken me on nearly 40 years of engagement with one of the most extraordinary ethnic groups on the planet. Educated, generous, entrepreneurial, and with a history and culture on their land that can be traced for thousands of years, recent Palestinian history is of terrible suffering and privation. The injustice now perpetrated against them, an injustice funded and supported by the most powerful nation on the planet and vicariously imposed on them because of the holocaust, must be called out, notwithstanding the fact that the calling out is labelled anti-Semitic.

Growing up on a dairy farm and migrating to Australia to work on the land, my heart and soul are deeply rooted in the natural order.

This rootedness has deepened and not diminished as the years have gone by. Hence, relationship with the natural order, seen afresh through the eyes of faith, has led me on a path of deep knowing that human destiny is inextricably bound up with the health and well-being of the natural order and that the human footprint is now taking us and the planet on a path of serious diminishment, unless we alter course. The window of opportunity to alter course is closing, day by day, hour by hour.

This book is about prophetic engagement in the contemporary world. It reflects the realisation that this engagement is vital for the health, well-being, and sustainability of civilisation. It is also written out of the knowledge that exercising this role will always be resisted by those in power, by those who have vested interest in the status quo. In the late 1990s I gave an address in the Great Hall of Parliament, Canberra, sponsored by Australian Prayer Breakfast on the importance of investment in Indigenous reconciliation.[7] The talk received a standing ovation. The next day I was invited/summonsed to a meeting in the office of the Prime Minister. Not knowing what it might be about, but assuming it may have something to do with the previous night's address, I tucked a copy of the speech in my pocket. When I arrived in the Prime Ministerial suite, Mr Howard was not there. Without being invited to sit, I was addressed by senior members of his cabinet and staff with, 'you have upset the Prime Minister'. When I asked why they thought upsetting the Prime Minister would worry me, they retorted that I might well think that what I had said was truth telling, but I needed to know *it was not helpful*—hence the title of the book. I left a copy of the speech with them, asking that they give it to the Prime Minister and assure him that I would be more than happy to talk over the contents when he had read it. I heard no more.

Truth is seldom if ever helpful to those for whom power is the reason for holding office. My dear friend Bishop Pat Power, auxiliary Catholic Bishop of Canberra and Goulburn once confronted Prime Minister Howard

7   Appendix 1: National Prayer Breakfast, 3 November 1996.

outside the Australian Centre for Christianity and Culture about the immorality of war in Iraq. This was clearly a meeting the Prime Minister found acutely unhelpful. Later you will read of an exchange between myself and the then Premier of Queensland, Sir Joh Bjelke-Petersen, which he also found unhelpful. Sir Winston Churchill found Bishop George Bell's critique of his blanket bombing of the civilian population of Dresden in the Second World War, extremely unhelpful. There is always a price to be paid in these exchanges. Because of the price, the contemporary Church has largely withdrawn from the primary prophetic reason for its existence—engagement.

In this void the secular world has, by default, taken the role of prophecy from the religious community. The general population is more ready to hear truth telling from taxi drivers and hairdressers than it is from men or women of the cloth. This is a small attempt to claim back some of the territory, to say that prophecy steeped in theology will be 'aha' for many, indeed it is just possible that those outside institutional religion are more likely to hear it than those within.

But first, a few insights into personal beginnings.

Part 1
The Formative Years

You can't go back and change the beginning, but you can start where you are and change the ending.

C S Lewis

Chapter 1
In the Beginning

You see, everyone has a point of view, but Mr God hasn't,
Mr God has a viewing point.[8]
Like Alice in Wonderland, Anna ate of the cake of
imagination and altered her size to fit the occasion—just like
Mister God.[9]

The biggest lottery of life is drawn before we are conscious of it. I was fortunate.

Timing was perfect. I was born early enough to remember the smell of horse's hooves being fitted with hot shoes drawn from the village smithy's forge, and to experience the saddling of our cart-horse, *Dobbin,* for his work in the fields; yet late enough to enjoy the benefits of antibiotics, and anaesthetics. (My first trip to the doctor was caused by inadvertently placing one of my little feet on a piece of hard ground on which *Dobbin* had chosen to place one of his substantial hooves).

Much later in life, I have enjoyed computers, Google, and relatively cheap air travel. I had the good fortune to live long enough in the UK,

---

8   Sydney Hopkins writing under the pseudonym of 'Fynn'. *Mr God this is Anna* (London: Harper Collins. 2005): 62.

9   Ibid, p80.

before coming to Australia, to be immersed in my English heritage and, although now an unrepentant Australian, it is a heritage that has shaped me and a deep well from which I draw water—the more so as I grow older. I am a staunch monarchist in the UK and an equally staunch republican in Australia. Being unequivocally loyal to the place you have chosen to live and yet investing it with the best of roots and origins is the secret of successful migration.

The place was perfect. I inherited the green, leafy country lanes of East Sussex where village life was rich and fulfilling, with a sense of belonging strongly rooted within a defined community. Life on a 78-acre dairy farm provided a childhood freedom which might now sound a little over romanticised, yet it was a blissful 12-year reality.

Family was ... well, no, no family is perfect. This book tells a great deal about me and them, about failures as well as successes, moments of greatness and moments which can best be described as profound learning experiences!

1942, midway point in the Second World War, the year of my birth, was in many respects a dark and desperate year. Allied victory was far from secure, despite the imminent threat of German invasion having been averted in the 1940 Battle of Britain and Britain stoically enduring the 1941 blitz. As children, we were taught to revere Churchill and learned some of his famous oratory by heart like: 'never in the field of human conflict has so much been owed by so many to so few'. Residents of Britain were sustained by devotion to their much-loved King and Queen, the oratory of their Prime Minister, and the extraordinary courage of their overstretched armed services. With dogged determination women and men at home stubbornly refused to entertain the possibility that they would be overcome. The songs of Dame Vera Lynn that sustained Britain during those dark days would later be seared into the memory of my elder brother David and I, because we heard them sung by my father in the dairy shed several days each week of our childhood.

I was born on 28th September 1942. I understand my father had leave for a mere couple of weeks over Christmas at the end of 1941. Clearly, I took advantage of this meagre opportunity, to make my debut appearance on the world scene!

I was named 'George' patriotically after the King, and 'Victor' in hopeful anticipation of the eventual outcome of the war. My father was by then serving in North Africa, and news of my birth probably did not reach him until after a battle that contributed to turning the tide and fate of the war, the unexpectedly successful battle of El Alamein. (Agreement on my name was obviously deferred until agreement between my father and mother could be confirmed)[10].

Brighton, on the Sussex coast, was home to both my mother and father. In 1942 it was not the safest place for a little baby, or indeed anyone else. Apart from the possibility of invasion, German bombers streaming across the Channel to drop their deadly cargo on Britain's airfields and industrial sites was a daily reality. Because of this and the eventual development in 1944 of the V-1, the infamous doodlebug, mother, David, and I saw out the latter part of the war in a lovely little cottage in the village of Hurstpierpoint. I am told that the nearest I came to personal engagement with Hitler was when one of the doodlebugs crashed near my pram. Mother was an avid supporter of an English tradition that you put your baby outside in the pram for a few hours each day, come rain, hail, or shine, to give them a bit of fresh air. I am sure it had the other advantage of giving the confined space of home a blissful couple of hours of quiet. I remember well going outside to shake the snow off the pram of later siblings who were enjoying their daily dose of fresh air!

I have no recollection of the Hurstpierpoint cottage, except through its photographs, but I know how important it was to my mother. She became

10 The Battle of El Alamein was fought between 23 October and 5 November 1942. My father had fought in Europe prior to the Dunkirk evacuation and was subsequently deployed in Africa.

an orphan in 1919 at the age of three as the ravages of the great Spanish flu epidemic struck first her father (on his return from service in the 1st World War), and a fortnight later, her mother.[11] Her early childhood, in the company of her sister (our beloved Aunt Joan), was an experience of being cared for first by grandparents and then more permanently by the much loved Aunt Gladys, her Mother's sister. This precious little Hurstpierpoint cottage was perhaps the home she loved the most, for it was her own. She later confessed she did not like the 'red house' at 'Sheeplands', the home of my childhood, probably because it was not hers. Although built for her and her rapidly expanding family, its detail was almost certainly dictated by others. Choice, let alone equality in decision making, was not a luxury she would know for the vast majority of her life, and yet she had the remarkable capacity of redeeming every situation, giving her best to every day, and finding good in it for all, especially those who in one way or another depended upon her quiet wisdom and simple capacity to cope.

My first years of marriage to Margaret were, I am ashamed to say, marked by similar male arrogance and intolerance, an attitude of which I am glad to say I have long since repented.

I was not to meet my father for the first time until I was three, his homecoming and welcome by my mother and David on the platform of the Hassocks railway station with his sausage bag on his shoulder is my earliest memory. My relationship with my father was always respectful, but equally, always fraught, becoming more so in adult life. I have wondered whether my three-year attachment to mother, his absence, and the inevitable change in the home dynamics made some unconscious, but indelible impact upon me. Perhaps I perceived him an intruder. I have often wondered whether he even harboured a doubt that my conception was his responsibility, hardly likely given my looks!

---

11 They are buried together in the old Brighton cemetery, Lewes road Brighton. The cemetery also contains the remains of her Penfold grandparents. Mother and Auntie Joan's ashes have more recently been interred in the same grave.

Following my father's eventual return from war, critical decisions needed to be made about his and our future. In one sense the war had been a convenient opportunity. Becoming an adult and looking for work during the Great Depression was a difficult, if not, a humiliating experience for him. With help from his father, Albert Quintus Browning, he had caught a boat to Canada where he had worked on a wheat farm. When work ran out there, he took an even more adventurous journey to Rhodesia (Zimbabwe) where he laboured on a tobacco farm. Inevitably work ran out there also. Before taking a ship back to the UK, he embarked on arguably the greatest adventure of his life when, equipped only with a compass, and the help of a carrier, he walked across country to the Victoria Falls. His diary indicates how foolhardy the trip was, made more so by the fact that he did little preparation and the gun he took with him must have had a loop in its barrel, he shot nothing to replenish supplies! Perhaps he was simply a bad shot. Years later a neighbour was to accuse him of shooting him in the backside with a few stray pellets from his 12-gauge shot gun when he had been aiming at a low flying pheasant! In September 1938 he journeyed to Australia where he worked on a sheep station near Roma, Queensland. In early 1939 it became obvious to all that war was inevitable. In February of that year he received a cable message from his father ordering him home to enlist in his father's newly formed 70th Searchlight Regiment.[12] He took the journey home by flying boat. Marriage with the lovely Barbara May Barnes was fitted into July, before war began.

While in Australia he had put his name into a ballot for a block of ground near Roma in Queensland and was fortunate enough to have his name pulled out. The war put an end to this dream which was perhaps no bad thing. With the benefit of hindsight, I have no doubt this avoided unnecessary dislocation at the wrong time. While Vicar of Warialda (1969–1973), I ministered to many parishioners, particularly around Yallaroi,

---

12 Father, John Russel Browning's own account of the early part of the war is at Appendix 2.

who were soldier settlement farmers. On blocks of about 1000 acres, many (in the early 1970s) were still living in a tin shed, lacking the means to build a house. Some were eventually successful, but success was possible if they were resourceful enough to buy out neighbouring, mostly failing properties. Many soldier settlements were places of dashed dreams and rural poverty, poverty that went unobserved because of pride and fear of failure. It is ironic that subdivision, the post war dream for a greatly increased regional population has now been universally reversed, with a successful farming economy being reliant upon large tracts of land. Technology has enabled labour to be replaced with machinery. The small rural village communities of Britain were never destined to become an economic, let alone a cultural, reality on Australian soil.

With the war over, a decision now had to be made as to the direction John Russel's life would take. It appears that dealing with authority was a difficulty for him. When as a captain he left his bride for the perceived glory and promotion offered in war, he had proudly proclaimed he would come back a colonel. As hopes turned to somewhat bitter reality, he spent much of the war sidelined in Tripoli, Libya, and returned as he had left, a captain. Fighting with authority figures, mostly through letters, was to be a hallmark of his life: local government, various instrumentalities, political leaders, or, notoriously, leading ecclesiastical figures were all recipients of largely unappreciated communication! Working for someone was therefore not likely to be a success. Whatever the reason, his father, my grandfather, bought him a small dairy farm of 73 acres (later 78 acres) within the boundary of the village of Ripe, nestling under the iconic South Downs, opposite Firle Beacon.

It is interesting to reflect upon the relative influence of 'nurture' and 'nature' that makes us who we are. Why my father appeared constantly 'at war' with himself and more obviously with others, including his children, is a bit of a mystery. His brother, Robert Frank Browning, says that the death of their elder brother Albert Sydney (Podge) Browning whom he adored,

Home on the farm with Firle Beacon behind.

when he has barely a teenager, had devastating effect. This was made worse by generational custom that such matters were not discussed with children.

He grew up without a paternal grandfather; indeed, this important figure was never mentioned, because of a mixture of unknowing, shame and resentment. Until his death in 1998 John Russel had no real idea what had happened to his grandfather, or indeed any sense of family pre-history past his own father. His grandfather, John Thomas Browning, had in fact abandoned his wife, my great grandmother, Annie Marie Dibley, when she was pregnant with her fourth child, Sydney John Browning. It was thought he had caught a boat to South America. In fact, he sailed for Australia on the '*Austral*' in April 1885, landing in Sydney. On the boat he met a 23-year-old Irish lass who was migrating with her family, Beatrice Elizabeth Jane McClean, whom he married at St Michael's Church Surrey Hills, inner Sydney, in February 1886. They gave birth to five daughters only two of whom survived to adulthood. Still lawfully married to Annie, John Thomas was charged with bigamy in a Sydney court in 1904. His life in Australia sounds somewhat fraught. In 1896 he was declared bankrupt.

He died on 1 June 1911 from injuries inflicted from a fall down a 'stoke hold' on a punt. He is buried in an unmarked, grave in the Gore Hill cemetery, North Sydney. I regret that John Russel did not catch up with this story before he died, nor indeed was he aware of the Browning pre-history which is traced back many generations in Devon.

I laid my father's ashes to rest on Firle Beacon, the observable feature of the South Downs visible from our farm, during the 1998 Lambeth Conference. Standing there with Margaret, Cousin Derek, and his wife Carol, on an August evening brought back evocative memories for me and hopefully ones of which he would have approved. Looking north from the Beacon you can easily pick out the farm, (which extraordinarily at that moment was bathed in a rainbow). It was an epiphany like moment. A storm threatened, but never materialised. From our vantage point on the beacon, with the farm and its surrounds bathed in light, it seemed as if a message of appropriate home dwelling was conveyed. Connections that had long been difficult to make, seemed at last to comfortably settle, nothing felt separated any more. Looking west from the beacon you can see the hills around Lewes where we sold week old calves at the market, where mother did her shopping and where we children went to secondary school. Looking south west you can pick out the town of Seaford where mother went to school (Seaford Ladies College). Looking south east, Cuckmere Haven[13] comes into view, my father's favourite swimming beach and the place we all enjoyed for our brief moments of recuperation on warm summer evenings, after haymaking.

The journey from Hurstpierpoint to look at the farm prior to our relocation in 1946, is the source of my second earliest memory. The little van with crank start in the front and two small, round windows in the rear, out of which David and I peered backwards at the disappearing hedgerows, ended in a roadside ditch. No one was physically harmed, although the driver

---

13 Cuckmere Haven is one of the first casualties of global warming on the English South Coast, a decision having been made not to protect the low-lying area that surrounds the Cuckmere's lazy approach to the sea.

was far from pleased. This was not the first time he had a close encounter with a ditch. Earlier he had come off his motorbike while en route to inspect the farm before its purchase. For the rest of his life he bore the battle scars inflicted that day with a right elbow which would not properly straighten. Seemingly this became a genetic deformity he then passed on, for I wear the same identifying badge when I fell from his shoulders stealing magpie eggs. My son Richard shares the same imperfection, the result of a tumble from monkey bars at Morpeth.

We arrived at 'Sheeplands' in time for the infamous winter of 1947. Our first meal, lunch, was a quintessential English fish pie, eaten on the concrete slab atop the well which would provide us with brown, peat tinted water for the next 14 years. As a child clear water seemed abnormal.

There are various reasons why Sussex is the least likely of English counties for snow to settle, however settle that year it certainly did. I have clear memories of the piles of snow on each side of the path to the front door that made you feel like you were passing the walls of water mounted on either side of the Israelites as they escaped through the Red Sea. When we first arrived, we lived in the little, white, Tudor style, cottage, three bedrooms upstairs, one living room, kitchen and pantry downstairs. Like mother, I loved the cottage and did not mind (with David) being moved back there when the expanding family (eight children) made it impossible for us all to squeeze into the red house. From its windows you could watch the cows calving, observe the seasons unravel their inexorable rhythm and, facing east, when English weather allowed, the sun would greet us with its morning warmth. The cottage garden was full of a lovely mix of apple and pear trees, with the occasional quince thrown in. Cox's orange pippin was our favourite. Mother was a wonderful gardener; she said it kept her sane. We would mostly eat home grown vegetables, enjoy our own berries (strawberries, raspberries gooseberries, red and black currants, and of course blackberries), and munch through our own apples. Harvested and laid out in rows in the loft, they would generally last us through winter.

The cottage had no inside lavatory, little boys coped with the lesser necessities in the orchard, always fun with snow or ice on the ground, details best left to the imagination. More serious matters requiring a seat were dealt with down the path towards the dairy where a little house could be found, if you knew where to look, for it was wonderfully camouflaged by a prolific overhanging plum tree.

The 1947 winter with all its snow was memorable. Undoubtedly it was a pain to parents, but for me it was a white wonderland, imprinted each morning with new paw marks of rabbits, stoats and weasels and decorated with innumerable bird tracks. No other winter matched that one; however, most winters we expected some snow to settle. Carrying hay bales to stock by sledge or riding a bike to school in the slush marks made by cars, was the stuff of childhood.

Growing up, I was familiar with the call of most local birds, knew where they nested and had a modest collection of blown eggs. I coveted grandfather, Albert Quintus', collection. Being in the fields was a never-ending delight, no matter what the weather. Hedgerow flowers reliably told of the month of the year without needing to look at any calendar. We nearly always had a brace of frozen rabbits hanging in the garage, and in season, the odd pheasant or two would join them.

I have a great deal of empathy for the Australian indigenous population and their identification with land, with country. However, I do not believe this instinct, even craving, is unique to them, nor simply to first nation people anywhere else. I believe this connection, love of one's own place, one's own land, is a human trait. That it is now considered a minority emotion is one of the signs of dislocation in the contemporary era. That we are all irreversibly connected to land is reinforced through the story of faith. The creation story tells us that our first name, all of us, male or female, is Adam; we are the *adam* from the *adamah* (the earth). Each time we return to the UK I feel a sense of identity with the English countryside that I can never quite replicate in Australia's sun swept and dusty plains.

As the family expanded, it became clear that there were two families within the family—the four eldest and the four youngest, who were perhaps somewhat patronisingly referred to as 'the little ones'. It is only relatively recently that I have become fully aware of the difficulties this has caused, especially for the four youngest. We have two perspectives. David and I, and to a lesser extent Rosemary and Nick have an experience of growing up in England while the 'little ones' experience is of having grown up in Australia and of the orchard at Uralla being their childhood home. While we remain a reasonably close family these two different experiences mean that our memories are not the same. The younger, to a greater or lesser degree, feel the loss of undeveloped British roots, while their older brothers were more like visiting uncles than brothers with whom they grew up.

Apart from Christmas, the most exciting annual ritual on the farm was the arrival of the threshing machine. It meant a hive of activity and work for all. The wheat cut by a binder, threw out sheaves which were built into stooks of six or eight in the field where they had been cut. There they stayed until they were dry, with no danger of heating or germinating in a stack. They were then thrown by pitchfork onto a trailer and carried to a place where they were made into a round stack with a pitched and temporarily thatched roof.

The threshing machine, looking like some wonderful prehistoric monster, was a source of enormous excitement. Parked near the stack the considerable workforce settled into its priority, tea and cakes provided by mother. Many hungry mouths needed feeding and appetites satisfying. One man stood on the stack pitching to the man on the threshing machine who cut the string and let the wheat fall into the beckoning jaws of the machine. One man (dirty job) had to make sure that the dust and chaff from the grain were kept away from the working parts. Another man hovered over the emerging wheat stalks making sure they were fed safely into the baler. Another man received the bales and began to make the new stack of straw with which to bed the housed cattle during winter. Most importantly another man kept the sacks up to the spouting grain, filling the two and one quarter hundredweight bags, which, when full, had to be sewn and carried by another man to a waiting trailer. My grandchildren love to mimic, with exaggeration, what I think is now a mild stoop. Pointing out that I carried these bags from the age of 12, garners no understanding or sympathy!

Finally, there were the mouse chases. I have happy memories of trying to catch the little furry fellows as they fled from the rapidly disappearing stack.

Financial anxiety must never have been far from father's mind. Seventy-three acres, even of rich Sussex soil, maintained a herd of less than 40 milking cows—not much to feed, house and educate a household of ten. The milk cheque was supplemented by the free-range eggs we sold at the gate, the turkeys we sold at Christmas, the sheep we agisted in winter, cash crops including a field of runner beans, but more regularly a field of wheat. In later years, the cottage was furnished, producing rent from a popular summer rural holiday let. However, when in the late 50s we started selling the pasture to a turf company it was clear that finances were very tight.

Some jobs on a farm are difficult to handle on your own, especially on a dairy farm, requiring twice daily milking. Regardless of how well you feel, or how dark, wet, and cold it is, the job needs to be done. Employed help was therefore a necessity even on such small acreage. In the early days, a German prisoner-of-war who had not been repatriated was employed. This abruptly ended following his hanging suicide. We children were shielded from the facts. However, coming home from the village school on my tricycle I passed near the offending hedgerow where this tragedy had happened. We later pulled the whole hedge out. I never knew how many Germans were left in the UK or why; I can only surmise that there was an unhappy reason why the man did not go home, unhappiness which eventually took his life. Later, a progression of young men whose lives 'needed direction and purpose' were employed. Most of these men stayed a short time. I was the last and stayed the longest when I left school two months before my sixteenth birthday in 1958 and stayed until we embarked for Australia just after my 18th birthday. I was employed at £2 10 shillings per week, with some being taken out for board and lodging. A modest start to a life career whose immense satisfaction has never come from salary or stipend! And yet through it all Margaret, I and the children have never wanted for anything or ever lacked anything good.

Village life profoundly shaped me. In 2008 Margaret and I went back to the UK to look for that which I had known as a child. We were not disappointed. Indeed, I think the experience was for Margaret, now a grandmother, as formative as it had been for me 50 years earlier as a child. I will always be immensely grateful for the extended family that was village life.

There was the shop. In fact, the shop came to us as much as we to it. Once a week Edgar would come and sit at the kitchen table where mother, after rattling though the pantry, would place her order for the week. Next day he would return with boxes of groceries and place them on the same kitchen table. Frozen goods were not an issue because we had no refrigerator until we arrived in Australia. The occasional ice cream treat was keenly anticipated. The family block, purchased from the store, was stored in a broad vacuum flask and when unwrapped on the table was ceremoniously cut into ten slices.

There was the church. I do not think we ever missed a Sunday. Mostly we attended matins, 11.15 on Sunday mornings at the flint walled St John the Baptist, right adjacent to the village school. I cannot say I found it at all enthralling and I was often relieved when the main markers of transition through the service, the hymn numbers on the board, were all finally ticked off. The services would also have been far less attractive were it not for some pretty village girls in the choir. I cannot remember much that I was taught, except that the clergy, Mr Goudge, Mr Baines (whose brother was one-time Bishop of Christ Church, New Zealand) were kindly men. I am sure they were at various times recipients of father's letters, especially Mr Goudge who was far too 'High Church' for him. At one Sunday lunch, always a roast and three veg with father at the head carving, he described our recent

Sunday morning experience as being more akin to watching the esteemed progress of an 'Indian Maharaja' than a Church of England vicar!

Mr Baines invited me to read in Church. Like most children of my generation, speaking for the first time in public was one of many moments of life graduation. The occasion was a Carol Service in our twin parish of St Bartholomew's, Chalvington. Mr Baines also prepared me for Confirmation. I was the only candidate from the parish that year. One evening a week, for six weeks, I rode my bike to the Rectory, where I was schooled in the Beatitudes.[14] He may well be proud of the journey in faith that his candidate subsequently took, but at the time his tuition pretty well went over the top of my head. Looking back, however, I cannot think of a more important subject to have been the focus of this rite of passage. Only later was I to begin to understand what 'to hunger and thirst after righteousness' might mean. I was subsequently confirmed by the Diocesan Bishop, the famous, redoubtable, and saintly George Bell[15] in the Alfriston Parish Church, along with candidates from other parishes in the Deanery.[16]

---

14 Sermon on the Mount, Matthew 5.1-10.

15 George Bell was Bishop of Chichester from 1929–1958. He had previously been Dean of Canterbury. It was under his leadership that 'Murder in the Cathedral' was conceived and written. As Bishop during the depression he walked and identified with the unemployed and homeless. During the war, his close friendship with Dietrich Bonhoeffer made him the natural recipient of many of Bonhoeffer's letters and appeals. He was a great ecumenist. Perhaps his moment of greatest moral challenge came when he criticised Churchill for the retaliatory bombing of Dresden following the blitz on Coventry. When William Temple died in 1944 many considered him the natural successor in Canterbury, his nomination was never going to succeed at number ten and he continued at Chichester until his retirement.

16 The clergy House at Alfriston was the first UK building to be classified by the National Trust. The church bells are housed in the central tower, above the crossing. The ringers take their place in full view of the congregation in the central aisle. My favourite English pub, the Tudor style *Smugglers Inn,* is a tantalizing feature of the village main street.

It is somewhat disheartening that today, rites of passage are mainly restricted to the driving licence, the first drink at the bar, or even worse, the moment of lost virginity. The world is in desperate need of inspiration and leadership from young adults whose significant moments of transition have been marked by rituals or challenges that have stretched physical endurance, that have explored meaning, value and belief, or that have involved acts of compassion generosity and respect through cultural exchange. It has been the desire to give young people an experience which could be called a 'rite of passage' that led me to lead five overseas youth pilgrimages when Bishop of Canberra and Goulburn, recounted in Chapter 10.

I am hopeful that all nine grandchildren will be stimulated and resourced by rites of passage such as these.

The Church was a focus of that great English cultural pursuit, campanology. Ripe only had five bells; however we had many wonderful moments under the tutelage of the Manor House resident, Major Sir Walter Scott.[17] We would not have been the best team in all England, or indeed in the local Deanery come to that, but it was fun. It was good to ring for special occasions in the Church, but equally it was fun to ring for significant occasions in the nation. We rang for the birth of the Queen's children and of course for her accession in 1953. Early in my learning period I broke a stay and found myself carried up through the ringing chamber and just before threading myself life a chipolata sausage through the first rope cowl managed to let go and landed with the small of my back taking my weight on the top corner of the choir robe cupboard. I received a little 'reviver' back at Manor House.

Childhood in the late 1940s and early 1950s was not a time to be cynical of symbols of national life, or to be embarrassed by patriotism; the memory of war and its cost was far too recent. As we listened to the home wireless we always stood for the national anthem, as we did before the film at the cinema. (My first film at a cinema was *Ivanhoe*).

---

17 Walter was not a descendent of the great Scottish novelist, poet and playwright, but of an industrialist who was rewarded with an hereditary peerage.

There was the village green (little circle in front of the shop and the larger field near the Church). The village gathered on the larger field for the annual fete to which everyone came. Every year we entered flowers and cabbages, carrots and drawings, collections of wild-flowers and pieces of craft. Every year we ran a stall and competed at them all. The tug of war rivalry between the villages was as intense as the Oxbridge rowing race on the Thames. I was always proud of father's tossing the sheaf ability. At the height of a reasonable pole vault the sheaf would sail skyward.

Every Christmas the village gathered in front of the shop for the singing of carols and the arrival of Santa Claus. This annual event was keenly anticipated, with a village family designated with responsibility. Each family set a standard that needed to be replicated, or surpassed, the following year. The year we Brownings took responsibility was exciting. An old chicken house was mounted over the Land Rover so that, when lit, it looked as if Santa's workshop was slowly gliding into the village. I was proud of our achievement. Some of my younger sisters were dressed as Santa's elves. Every child in the village was handed a present, (chosen and paid for in advance by their parents). I can remember every year holding my breath until my name was called.

There was the pub—the Lamb Inn. Unquestionably a major feature of village life. However, it did not feature for me, largely because Father, who enjoyed his regular drink of cider, was not a pub goer and not a social animal.

Then there was the school. The story of my education is not one of significant triumph, or even modest success. School and I never seemed to nestle into one another. Undoubtedly both parents and teachers held high expectations, because David set a high standard, one that sadly I was not motivated to match. The farm was approximately a mile and a half from the school, a distance I covered in the first instance on my tricycle, running the gauntlet of a verbal tirade from some of the young village boys. It was a two-teacher school run by Mrs Humphries and Miss Honneyset. I have few memories of these first three years of my schooling; I remember the chalk board and the abacus. I remember the corner in which you were stood when naughty. I remember more clearly riding to and from school, hopping into the shop to spend the halfpenny on sweets. Perhaps the bike flew at its fastest when passing the gypsy camp which regularly stood at the corner of our property. The gypsies generally only stayed for a day or so at a time, or until father rang the police and they were moved on. Looking back, I now regret not knowing more about the Romanies and their culture. I regret having been afraid of them, rather than learning from them. Minority groups the world over are very easily typecast out of prejudice and misinformation. I have no doubt that pheasants were taken and other minor crimes committed, but the world is no poorer because of its nomadic people, in fact the rest of us have a lot to learn from the light footprint they leave on the planet. Unbeknown to us at the time, the fifth child, Valerie was destined to live her life with a geographically distinct group of nomads, the Afar in Ethiopia.

Schooling took a major life determining direction in the form of the 11 plus examination when students transitioned from primary to secondary schooling. If you passed, you went on to the Grammar School and received an education that would equip you for a profession. If you failed, you went to a Secondary Modern School and were trained for a trade. It must have been clear to discerning parents from an early stage that their second son was not going to make it to the Grammar School on the performance shown at the village school. And so it was, at the age of eight, I was destined to join David at one of the prestigious Woodard Schools,[18] Ardingly College[19], to complete my primary education. To become a boarder at the age of eight was somewhat daunting. I remember well the trip to Gorringe's outfitters in London to be kitted out with my uniform. I also remember the tears when it was clear that they did not have a cap in stock that with some decency would fit my head!

---

18 The Woodard family of schools was founded by Nathaniel Woodard in 1848. Lancing College and Hurstpierpoint are two other well-known member of the family of schools in Sussex.

19 The school motto is *Beati Mundo Corde—Blessed are the pure in heart*, unbeknown to me at the time, but putting me in good standing for my confirmation lessons.

Being driven to school for the first time I am sure my heart was pounding its little self out of my chest cavity. The youngest boys were placed in Jericho House before graduating to Beattie, and finally to one of the three main preparatory boarding houses, Nelson, Drake and Granville. Jericho was situated directly above the house of the head of preparatory school. Receiving a beating was inevitable at boarding school, unless you managed to become one of teacher's pets, in which case the abuse of fellow students must have been infinitely worse. My first beating came immediately after a rather energetic pillow fight. The three on the backside was not too hard to take and could be managed without a tear; wearing it as a badge of honour back in the dormitory was always more than sufficient compensation.

Being at home has always been a place of security and peace for me; going away from home, has always carried more anxiety than it appears the same journey has meant for others. Perhaps this is one of the legacies of going away at eight. In later life mother observed how astonished she was at the frequency of my travel to third world destinations, given her knowledge of my earlier timidity about leaving home, even for a hiking holiday. Perhaps later travel had something to do with the need to face one's demons. Most first nights back in the school dormitory, I would vomit during the night. The experience was not ameliorated by the less than sympathetic response from fellow boarders and matron.

Once I settled, however, boarding school was a positive experience for me. David has told me in recent years he hated it. I am sure the difference is that while David was good at his studies, I was more than moderately competent at sport. Most weekends saw me in a bus heading off to play soccer or rugby against another town or school. I was not as good at summer sports, indeed for at least a couple of years I was not allowed to play summer sport until I had learned to swim one lap across the school pool. I eventually succeeded, under water!

Fagging was a feature of school life, but funnily enough I do not look back on it with loathing. The main task I can remember was cleaning

With brother David, in uniform ready for boarding school.

the shoes of the older boy. I do not remember bullying, either being on the receiving end, or shamefully on the serving end. There were various forms of initiation, but they were restricted to one's own age group. Similarly, I did not experience, nor was I aware of any sexual activity in the dormitory. There certainly was experimentation amongst peers, but not favours to any outside the age group. Fire drill punctuated sleep one night every term. If there ever was a fire I would have been burnt to death, because I would normally wake to the violent shaking of the house master and when my eyes focused, realise that everyone else had already left the dormitory.

Boarding school is essentially about fitting in. I enjoyed participating in almost everything: the cross country running, the boxing tournaments, the food fights, the conker fights, gardening, the chapel, and of course all kinds of sport. Skating on the frozen ponds and lakes in winter was a wonderful thrill, sadly something that is far less likely these days with more temperate winter weather. The cross-country run was a test of endurance that probably would not be contemplated these days. Sliding in and out of ditches, one felt as cold as the ice sheets cracked by our feet in the numerous puddles.

The local Southdown Hunt would occasionally meet at the school. One of my most amusing memories is of Jimmy Edwards[20] being hoisted by a harness attached to a tree and then lowered without too much ceremony into his saddle.

Chapel was always a space I entered with a sense of awe, but also with the warmth of home, it was a space I occupied with comfort. The Principal, the Reverend George D'Oyly Snow,[21] was a man of imposing stature, but also of warmth. He was clearly a man of faith and anxious that his charges were imbued with a clear sense that they were part of a world of wonder and delight, created by a loving God. Believing in God when the surroundings lift the spirits, when the music is inspirational and when the leadership is clearly of benign, intelligent, goodness makes the journey from a trusting childhood through questioning adolescence, to a foundational adult faith so much more likely.

Although David was at the school half the time I was there, I saw very little of him. I saw more of my cousin Derek, one week older than me, who was in the school while his father served in post-war Germany and then Egypt. Derek and I shared a small garden plot together on the slope leading down to the swimming pool.

As a young boy food is always an issue. The only food with which I found difficulty was tapioca pudding and stewed rhubarb embellished with curdled milk. The wooden tuck box packed with cakes and other goodies from home never lasted long. Various trips to the school tuck-shop compensated. In the first couple of years, these visits needed to be accompanied with the all-important post-war coupons, without which

---

20 Jimmy Edwards was a popular English comedian and script writer, perhaps best known for his role as the father in the *Glums*, played beside a young Ronnie Barker as his son Ron.

21 George Snow went on to become Bishop of Whitby. His son Jon, who grew up at the school is arguably the most well know face of British journalism today, being the main news reader at Channel 4.

you could not buy confectionery. Shortages caused by the war remained into the early 50s.

It was during my time at boarding school that I became consciously aware of the emotional distance between my father and myself. Of course, we always looked forward to mail from home. I was desperate to receive a letter with mother's scrawl on the envelope, but gradually came to hope there would not be one from Father. His letters were after the style of a Victorian authoritarian parent for whom emotional connection with his son was mamby pamby nonsense. After a while I did not read them and sometimes did not open them. He expected me to learn Rudyard Kipling's poem '*If*' by rote. I now like the poem, but then I was unreceptive to its poetry, let alone its message, because like a headmaster's stick, it was used as a hammer to crack open a most unwilling nut. These letters have created a problem that has remained in some form throughout my life. I find critical material received through the mail difficult to handle.

Correspondence sent in this manner, carries, in my case, a disproportionate weight. This was a grave difficulty in the crisis of 1999 and put enormous pressure on Margaret who read most of the accusatory material. Even to this day I have still read little of it, although of course I heard it presented in aggressive form on the floor of the tribunal, by then making any reasonable defence impossible.

I now wonder what it was that father found difficult, what was it about his childhood that caused him to be so seemingly authoritarian as an adult, paradoxically resistant to authority himself. This became a crippling situation for him. It denied him access to a healthy relationship with most of his children and prevented an intelligent and respectful, exchange with senior members of church and society. Looking back, I regret I lacked the wit to help him, always retreating, not finding the energy to engage, let alone confront.

I sat the 11 plus with all the other boys in the Ardingly classroom. The mixture of surprise and elation I felt on hearing I had passed has stayed with me.

I have to say I have always harboured a sneaking suspicion that they let me in because of David's reputation. Certainly, when I arrived at Lewes County Grammar School for Boys for the first time, I found myself in the lowest stream, a stream I am glad to say I managed to climb out of.

The years at the Grammar School were happy enough, but not memorable. While many who write of their school years, speak of the influence of particular teachers, I have no such memory. I am unaware that I received a certificate of achievement in academic study from any of the schools, but fortunately there is more to school than academic study.

We travelled to the Grammar School on the Eastbourne to Brighton bus (number 25) which passed the end of Ripe Lane every hour, approximately a mile and half from the farm, in the opposite direction to the village. Half-way along the lane we crossed the railway line where, in a neat row of four semi-detached cottages, our much-loved home help, Margaret Shoesmith, lived. Occasionally I missed the bus and then had to ride the bike the extra five miles to the school. The marks of war in bomb craters were still clear in the early fifties, as the bus passed them by along the side of the road. At school we used the old air raid shelter as our cadet shooting range.

The route to Lewes passed the lane into Glynde and *Glyndebourne*. During the opera season we frequently observed the long dressed and heavily furred women together with their bow tied and dinner coated male consorts arrive at Lewes railway station en route to their cultural if not somewhat elite experience. Curiosity got the better of me in 2009 when in the company of Margaret and our carefully packed cucumber sandwiches I finally joined their company. Apart from the occasional pantomime and father's imitation of Vera Lynn in the cowshed, my childhood was almost totally devoid of the arts, a major gap which Margaret has tried to encourage me to fill, a filling which happened in one gigantic, busking cello load in Riga, Latvia, in 2002.

The Grammar School was set within an ancient castled[22] market town with a long narrow main street, (now by-passed), that crosses the Ouse river. The town has a long and colourful history. Anne of Cleves[23] House was situated between the two Grammar Schools. Most notoriously, Lewes had a history of anti-Catholicism which could be traced back to the Counter Reformation, the Marian persecutions of 1555–1557, when seventeen Protestant martyrs were burned horrifically in barrels of oil. Their deaths were annually commemorated on Guy Fawkes Day. November 5 was always well celebrated and a vivid childhood memory. In the weeks prior to the day we would forgo money spent on gob stoppers and purchase as many fireworks as we could: Catherine wheels, rockets and of course crackers that we let off in cowpats to very great effect. Although the burden on mother's washing was not inconsiderable, she joined in the fun with everyone else. I suppose there were terrible accidents, but I never knew of any, despite the fact we had rockets in bottles all around the garden and Catherine wheels pinned to many of the trees.

---

22 The Battle of Lewes was fought on 14 May 1264 between Simon De Montfort and his brother barons and King Henry III and his son Edward. The barons' victory meant a humiliating defeat for the king. The signing of the Mise of Lewes, for a short time at least meant the powers and authority of the royal house were severely weakened. While the first version of the Magna Carta was passed into law in 1215, prior to the battle of Lewes, the fuller version became law in 1295 restricting for all time the absolute power of the monarch. The battle of Lewes is thus seen as one part of the struggle that led to the Magna Carta.

23 Anne of Cleves was the not much-loved German born fourth wife of Henry VIII. She was Queen of England for a few short months in 1540. The King confessed to Cromwell the honeymoon night was not a great success; in fact, the marriage was not consummated. 'I liked her before not well, but now I like her much worse'. The house in Lewes was one of many that constituted her divorce settlement; she probably never lived in it. While she at least kept her head, she did not enjoy a long life, dying probably of cancer in her 40s. While buried in Westminster she was a committed Lutheran.

The eight children.

As I became a teenager, the lure of fireworks in Lewes became too strong. Every year, November 5 was heralded for weeks prior with a banner across the high street proclaiming '*No Popery*'. The 'Cliffe' firework society was the strongest. Every year an effigy of the Pope rather than Guy Fawkes was burned on the pyre. Large barrels of burning oil were tossed into the river, symbolic of the burning of the martyrs. It was dramatic. My first slightly frightening experience of the long arm of the law occurred as I stood in a doorway watching the procession. A blue coated arm came through the smoke and semi darkness to grab the person next to me. What he had done that I had not done, to this day I have no idea. My other childhood experience of the law was riding home one evening on my bike from Glynde station. I had taken the train to a rugby game in London. For some reason, my bike had lost its lights. A police car pulled me over. I was confronted with a man in blue carrying a pad and pencil. After the inevitable lecture I was given my ticket and told not to ride the bike any further. Of course, when the lights of the car were out of sight, I hopped back on. It did not occur to me that they would turn around for the sole purpose of catching me again. This time I stayed off until I arrived home. I did not turn up at the court for the hearing, but I did pay the fine.

Until I went to the Grammar School, I had no sense that there was any denomination other than Anglican, everyone in the village was connected by right of residence to the parish Church. Because of Lewes' history, I became very aware that I was an Anglican (not Protestant) and that we were the custodians of all that was true, right and appropriate, at least in England! Initially, appreciating denominational difference was to understand that 'others' had erred. In particular, Roman Catholics were definitely not brothers and sisters. Father held a strong prejudice against 'Catholicism'. It was anathema to think that a member of the family might marry a Roman Catholic.

I am not sure where father's prejudice originated. His children now embrace a great cross section of Christian identity and practice. His mother, Marie Louise Blomfield, was a descendant of the *Blomfields of Dedham and Colchester.*[24] Despite this strong nonconformist heritage, she was the most Anglo catholic of all members of the family. In later years I have understood that all Christians are brothers and sisters of one another because of our common fellowship in Christ.

My years at the Grammar School were marked in my mind by sport, the cadets, and a constant struggle to see relevance in the academic subjects. I lived for the rugby season and captained my age team each year until the under 16's, when I left my formal education behind. My favourite position was breakaway, which really enabled me to be in the thick of both the forwards, and the more exciting movement of the backs. I played representatively for East Sussex, which Aunt Joan very faithfully would come and watch, much to my great joy.

We had of course grown up to be proud of Aunt Joan (mother's only sibling), and her sporting achievements. As a family we had watched her captain the All English Hockey team at Wembley stadium. We always

---

24 *The Blomfields of Dedham and Colchester* is a 47 page monograph written in 1924 by Mr LC Sier. It records the history of Non-Conformist piety in Essex that dates back to the reign of Elizabeth I. A copy can be found in the file of family history.

looked forward to her return from overseas tours, especially from South Africa and Rhodesia (Zimbabwe), for she would return with exotic presents and colourful stories. My childhood stamp collection was largely influenced by the stamps that came on cards and letters from her many journeys. No one was more influential in our extended family than Aunt Joan; she always had time for each one of us and was invariably present for birthdays, Christmas, and other celebrations.

She took David and me to the pantomime, to treats in restaurants, and would visit us at school. She was never able to embrace faith and towards the end of her life felt that going to Church with the rest of us was hypocritical. Greatly loved and highly respected, I found her lack of faith deserving of honour and respect. Her values and principles I greatly admired. A good example was her insistence that in coming to Australia (which she did soon after us), we should take out Australian citizenship. Mother and Father never did. I am sure that AJ was right. As a principle everyone should be committed to the people, place, and citizenship of the country they have chosen as their permanent home. When I stayed with her at her Maroubra unit we sometimes spoke of faith as an aspect of life that she had not done without, so much as never discovered. I have continued to find it challenging that she knocked on a door, which for her at least, refused to open.

Father's parents, Granny and Grandpa, were also influential. Clearly both strong personalities, they separated in the 1950s when I was at Ardingly. At the time, differing Christian traditions were yet to make themselves known to me. Had I been aware, I might have asked Granny where her Anglo Catholic faith came from, given she came from a long line of East Anglian Puritans!

After her separation, she often stayed for some weeks at a time in the farm cottage, sometimes with her friend, the 'motorbike lady'. One of the greatest impacts she had on me occurred one summer afternoon when I was about nine. I had been raking hay and had come back, parked the tractor in its shed and then to my horror realised that I had left a wrench somewhere out in the field. I was terrified to tell Father. She found me skulking behind the garage, clearly a little distressed and asked why I was troubled. I explained the situation, her immediate response was 'no problem, let us pray that St Anthony will show us where you left the tools'. Following the prayer, we walked straight to the tools! Just a pity she was not around the day I brought the tractor back to its shed stood up from my seat to disengage the clutch and then sat down again without moving the gear stick. The sudden lurch forward caused the protruding front crank handle to push through the brick wall that separated the tractor shed from the dairy. Bricks cascading into the Guernsey feeding trough in full sight of father was arguably the most dramatic moment of my childhood, from many points of view!

Grandpa's influence was exercised not so much in his visits to us, but in our visits to him. From him I learned to play rudimentary chess, etiquette at meals, including how to set the table, and croquet. He had a well-established croquet lawn. Learning the art of this most English of pursuits was always a pleasure. He drove a large black Vanguard; the lovely leathery smell that old cars used to have stays with me. Although Grandpa (Albert Quintus Browning)[25] was very 'proper' he was also a load of fun, if not slightly naughty. I remember him

---

25 Albert Quintus was the fifth child of John Thomas Browning. John Thomas's father was also John Thomas. His father and grandfather were both Robert. It is now clear that the Brownings originated from Devon in the 18th century. John Thomas junior, (AQ's father), was born in 1849 and was a manager of a gas works in Colchester. His first wife died, he then married my great grandmother Annie Dibley, the daughter of a school headmaster from Reading. AQ was born in 1882. When Annie was pregnant with her fourth child John Thomas disappeared. It appears he told her he was going to Australia for when the child was born he was named Sydney John. John Thomas did in fact migrate to Australia, leaving England on 18 April 1885 and marrying an Irish lady he met on the boat. He had five daughters in Australia although only one went on to have her own children and as far as we know there are no children from this marriage living in Australia. One, Di Parker, is living back in the UK. John Thomas lived at one time in Muswellbrook. It appears he was before the Sydney courts for bigamy. He died in 1911 after falling into the stoke hole of a ferry. He is buried in the Gore Hill cemetery, North Sydney.

whistling as the girls came out at the pantomime and did the 'can-can'. I am doing my best to model my grandparental responsibilities on him! Grandpa was also a person of faith, but I cannot remember ever discussing it with him. The last few years of his life were dogged by cancer. Inevitably it won, but he stayed in his Ovingdean home until the very end, barking instructions from his upstairs bedroom. He is buried in the graveyard of the Parish Church.

Grandpa's croquet lawn was kept to a reasonably high standard. At Sheeplands we had a full-size lawn tennis court, fitting between the macrocarpa hedge, a line of elms, and the driveway. It provided many happy afternoons of casual play and competition. It was always the focus of attention when entertaining visitors. While Grandpa kept his lawn with a motorised mower complete with a large rear roller, ours was kept by a hand mower which required two of us to operate, one in front pulling and the other in the rear pushing.

School cadets provided an engaging and challenging weekly activity. Each had their own rifle to clean and use for target practice in the WW2 bomb shelter. It was with considerable anticipation that I joined David at the annual cadet camp at the famous army base of Catterick in Yorkshire. It was a challenging week in many respects. The overnight march sticks in the mind. For several hours we conducted night exercises and, worn out, were about to board the trucks back to the compound when they were driven off. Clearly this was fully planned. We faced a march of several hours more before finally arriving at the camp. A couple of hours rest was rudely broken by the sergeant major who suggested, none too subtly, that we should rise and face the challenges of the new day. I for one thought we had already explored most of its possibilities!

I also enjoyed the simulated parachute jumping tower, about the only training I did prior to two jumps later taken in Australia. When we left the camp, the truck became thoroughly lost in the Yorkshire countryside. An hour later we found ourselves driving past the Catterick gate for the second time. This misadventure meant we missed trains and arrived at the Lewes railway station an hour late. Father had arranged to pick us up in the Land Rover. He got himself so cross, he did not bother to return later. We had therefore to find our way to the bus station, catch a bus to Ripe Lane and then walk the one- and one-half miles home with all our kit. All a jolly good learning experience!

That I was struggling to find relevance in my academic study was obvious to all. Mr Bradshaw, the revered headmaster, generously suggested 'I would do well in later life'. My homework was virtually nonexistent. I would sit in father's office looking vaguely out of the window, or better still I would get out of the window, finding an excuse to drive the tractor or do something with the cows. It was therefore no surprise when I was solemnly asked to join father and mother in the lounge room one evening in late spring 1958. It was explained that finances were tight. David was doing well with his studies and would go to University to study medicine. Clearly, I was not going to do that. A decision had been made not to waste any further investment in my education. I would sit the GCE O Level standard a year early and come to work on the farm.

I was overjoyed! The only problem was that I would not journey on to play for the Grammar School firsts and instead joined the Lewes open Rugby Club at age 16. I sat the exams and passed maths, English and the French oral but failed everything else.

In July 1958, two months before my sixteenth birthday, I commenced paid employment and proceeded to 'keep myself' in the paid workforce, a journey which would continue for the following 51 years.

Surprisingly, father and I got on well for the two years we worked together. Perhaps it was that I had a natural inclination for the land and indeed seemed to pick up many things that he had missed. I was always careful to inform him so that he could be seen to be the one that took the action. It could also have been that I enjoy working hard; the necessity of working to the clock, worrying about starting and finishing times has never occurred to me. It could also be that face to face I could cope; being on the farm Father did not need to write any more letters to me!

For many years I had been a beater on cross farm pheasant shoots, but in these years father, to my absolute joy, insisted that I join him as one of the shooters with my four-ten shotgun. I would leave early in the morning to skip around the back of some of Lord Gage's Estate, trying to drive some of the game on to our farm so that when the shooters came through there was something to shoot! Chaka was father's gun dog. When he became too old to be useful, we walked him slowly to the back field. Father carried the gun. I carried the spade and dug the hole. I was then encouraged to choose my own dog in his place. I chose a beautiful black Labrador cross called Bruka. Bruka and I were inseparable. He went shooting with me on a very regular basis and would be so excited every time the 4.10 was taken out of the gun rack I had made at school.

Annual holidays were not a feature of our life. There is only one that I can remember as a child. It would have been soon after we came to the farm. We went to Bognor Regis and stayed in a waterfront hotel. I can remember the beach, the bucket and spade and most particularly the family bicycle which mother and father pedalled while David, Rosemary, baby Nick and I sat huddled under the shade of the canopy. As a holiday it was one that father would care to forget. A message came through that our hay-stack, the stored winter fodder for the cows, had caught fire, presumably the hay was gathered too green, it had combusted.

When I left school in 1958 David and I enjoyed two hiking holidays together in successive years. The first was to North Wales. We stayed in youth hostels in Betws-y-coed, Bangor and Snowdon and of course hiked up Snowdon. Not one for research, I was quite shocked to be confronted with a train terminal and tourist centre at the top, both were hidden from our view until we breasted the peak! The second year (August 1960) we journeyed to Switzerland and hiked from Lucerne to Interlaken. Looking at, but not climbing the north face of the Eiger was still awesome, not least because a fallen hiker was still hanging from his rope waiting for the retrieval team to cut him down. In the youth hostel at Grindelwald David and I completely fluffed our first major encounter with young females. We arrived at the hostel to find it had no places in the male dormitory. We were informed we could stay in the female dormitory. As astonishing as it must now sound, we walked on to the next hostel!

When 1959 dawned, I could tell father no longer had his heart in the farm. Perhaps it was the finances, perhaps itchy feet, perhaps concern for the future of the children. The obvious point was made that the farm would not feed me as well as mother and father. I was encouraged to go to night school at Brighton Tech which I did half-heartedly, never passing the O levels I had previously failed. There was vague talk that I should try to get a place at Newton Abbot, the Agricultural College in Devon. At that stage I had no inkling that our forebears had come from Devon, otherwise I might have been more interested.

Eventually we were informed the farm was to be sold. Father had yet to make up his mind whether he would take a cattle lease north of Inverness in Scotland or purchase an apple orchard in Australia. Transference to a rather bleak, and even to this day, under-populated part of Scotland would not have been a very smart idea. Much to mother's chagrin we journeyed to Australia House in London, with serious intent. Father explained he would like to purchase an apple orchard, but he would also like a place with good educational facilities for the family, the majority of whom still needed to pursue their primary and secondary education. The obvious place seemed to be Armidale, NSW.

The farm went on the market, the asking price now sounds ridiculous at £10,000. It did not sell easily, but eventually a couple decided to purchase. At the last minute, another couple arrived. Father paid them scant attention, and, convinced of the sale he had made, asked me to show them around. This I did; as a result, they agreed to increase the purchase price by £250. I am sure it was because of this that to my joy and great surprise father offered to pay for the transporting of Bruka to Australia. He went on his own cargo ship for £70 while the children sailed free; mother, father and I were ten-pound Poms.

The auction of stock and equipment on Friday 16 September 1960, was not an easy day for me. The cows were as personal friends and I recall a mixture of sadness and anger as the hammer fell progressively on each one. The catalogue of sale refers to *23 excellent dairy cows, 5 promising in-calf heifers and three weaner heifers.* I was also particularly sad that the bees were sold, they did not produce much honey in the short English season, but I was fascinated by them. Stock together with machinery and equipment realised £2,344/3/6. The 1953 Land Rover at £170 was retained for the long trip to Australia and became for many years the Browning mode of transport at Uralla, NSW.

Chapter 2
Where you go I will go

Where you go, I will go: Where you lodge, I will lodge; your
people will be my people, and your God will be my God too.

Ruth 1: 16.

We embarked from Tilbury dock on board the *Strathnaver*, her final
antipodean journey, on Tuesday 11 October 1960. The previous four days
I had spent with Uncle Bobby and Auntie Grace at Aldershot. Derek
was at that time deciding between a career in the army or a path towards
ordination. In the end he chose the army, a relatively short career, for
following his marriage to Carol he became a partner in his in-laws' plant
nursery, eventually being ordained by the Bishop of Guildford as a local
priest many years later.

Farewells are not easy, although I must say it was not nearly as an
emotional moment for me as it must have been for mother who was leaving
so much behind. My emotion was mostly excitement for the journey ahead,
although handing Bruka over to the quarantine officers prior to his being
loaded on his cargo ship inside his especially designed kennel was not an
easy moment. Nor was it easy to visit him at the South Heads quarantine
station in Sydney after his arrival. I only went once. He was so excited to see
me, walking away felt as if I was abandoning him. It was not long however

until he was free to join us in Armidale and eventually, notwithstanding one blacksnake bite, happily saw out his days at Glenaire, Uralla.

I was also sorry to say goodbye to David, we had been and have remained good friends. Being in the midst of his studies at the University of London, then was not the time for him to migrate. David took his responsibilities as the oldest sibling very seriously, a responsibility I was not conscious of shouldering in Australia until his eventual arrival. I have only recently discovered that notwithstanding his romance and subsequent marriage to Daphne Green and the not unreasonable hopes the Green family would have cherished for continued proximity to their daughter and her new husband, father made it crystal clear that he expected David to put foot on Australian soil at the earliest opportunity.

Our home for the next six weeks was two crowded cabins on the lowest deck 'H', at the stern of the ship. Mother and the five girls were in the six-bunk cabin; father, Nick and I were in the three-bunk space. It was noisy, smelly, and rather claustrophobic, we did not need much encouragement to be out of the cabin. For most of the voyage we slept on deck, to be woken in the mornings with the touch of the deck stewards' brooms: 'wishy washy decks' was apparently their early morning duty!

By Thursday 13 October we entered the Bay of Biscay and I was to discover another piece of unwarranted good fortune, travel sickness was not to blight the pleasure for me of this or many other future journeys. Others were not so fortunate. The 'little ones' were amongst the first to succumb.

Friday 14 October, we passed the Straits of Gibraltar, that very odd British outpost which must constantly rub up against Spanish sensitivities. Sailing quite close, the colonies of monkeys were easy to spot.

Saturday 15 October, we docked for our two day stay in Marseilles. This was not a normal stop en route to Australia but was necessary because of industrial strife at Tilbury. The liner had been unable to properly unload its cargo from its previous return trip to Tilbury. Marseilles was therefore the most convenient spot to offload. In the 1960s dockside strikes were frequent and quite crippling to maritime nations dependent upon their ports for trade. Australia was not immune. Margaret Thatcher was the British Prime Minister to finally tackle strikes, both in the ports and in the mines. In Australia this was largely, and brutally, undertaken by the stevedoring group Patricks. Ports that refused to modernise in the false hope of safeguarding their rather bloated workforce placed an intolerable economic noose around the country. Modern ports made uneconomic ports in the UK or Australia seem like lumbering dinosaurs. Modernisation did occur, and with the benefit of hindsight we might wonder what the fuss was about. We now face a similar situation with the changes required in the face of climate change. Enormous energy is being mustered to delay or dilute a realistic response. And yet, what is required is within relatively easy assimilation for countries like Australia. For reasons of blatant self-interest those who resist change exaggerate the estimated cost and magnify potential disruption.

With other young men, I went to the local stadium to watch a game of Rugby between the All Blacks (New Zealand) and the Les Tricolores (France). I do not remember the score line; but having squeezed myself into Twickenham on many occasions in proximity to the game, I was not prepared for the wire fences that caged us in and separated us from the field. On the spare day, we took a tourist bus on a 25 kilometre hairpin ride along the east Mediterranean coast.

As we sailed from Marseilles we were well settled into life on board with regular routines. Every day a new schedule of events was printed comprising deck games, and various competitions, while the evenings provided a programme of concerts and films. A single-minded scout leader from Melbourne began a scout group and dragooned me into sharing the leadership. I kept in communication with 'Skip' for a few years after our arrival, I think he saw me as one of his protégés. On board were the Rev'd Norman Crutwell and his aged mother, missionaries returning to Papua New Guinea following their UK furlough. As well as being a priest missionary he was a keen botanist and had the honour of a PNG orchid named after him.

Travelling the Mediterranean is to pass places with familiar ancient biblical history. We passed close by Sardinia and Corsica and slipped between the Italian mainland and Sicily, in doing so passing under the electrical and telephone lines that connected the island with the mainland.

Saturday 22 October saw us begin to traverse the Suez Canal with docking at Port Said. It is a strange experience to be in a large ship travelling through a narrow channel with land close on both sides. In her diary Rosemary comments 'we observed camels, oxen for ploughing, turning water wheels, donkeys, water buffalo, mules, thin cattle, wild dogs, measly chicken, mucky ducks, geese, FLIES, hawks, maize, date palms, bananas, cotton fields, salt bush, sand dunes, filthy water, slow trains, speedy cars, women in black, and dirty children'. My memory of Port Said is disappointment that we were not allowed off. I understand it was because we were migrants and did not have the appropriate paperwork. Why it should have applied here and not at any other stop I do not know. However, we were greatly entertained by the sellers of trinkets and the 'Gully man' who came on board to entertain us with his tricks. Watches and jewellery disappeared from wrists and necks, however all seemed eventually to be returned! Passing through the canal had to be done in convoy; we had an eight hour wait for this to assemble.

Saturday 25 October, Nick's birthday, was to wake to a day of unexpected excitement. After lunch the cry, 'man overboard', rang out and everyone ran to the same side to see what had happened. There was indeed a man overboard, but not from the *Strathnaver*. He was in fact the second officer of the Egyptian steamer *El Gamil*, which had gone down some 12 hours before. He was the only survivor.

One of the more salutary experiences of life on board a liner for a few weeks is that people become ill and some die. On at least two occasions we stood silently by as a brief service was held for someone who had died. A piece of canvas hid our eyes from the coffin, we did not see it slide solemnly to its final resting place in the deep. These days all major liners are fitted with large refrigerated mortuaries, protecting fellow travelers from brutal exposure to life's fragilities.

On 26 October we docked at Aden, the first of many times I would set foot in a culture vastly different to my own. Nick and I wandered around together for a couple of hours. There were many poor on the streets, it felt oppressively hot. Visiting Aden today would be no less confronting given the unrelenting Yemini civil war. We were only allowed a couple of hours, for the liner sailed five hours after it docked. Clearly this was insufficient for two female shoppers, not wishing to miss a bargain: they missed departure time! Somewhat ignominiously they chased after us in a little motorboat and had to be helped up the side of the liner on a rope ladder!

Sunday 30 October saw us dock around midday in Bombay. We were keen to get a feel for the city. We walked through the streets, encountering poverty on a large scale for the first time. My young mind could not really grasp what we were experiencing through the smells, the crowding, and the human misery on the streets. Years later I was more able to absorb the significance of global inequity which sentences a third of the world's population to live below the poverty line. I am still struggling to deal with the ethics involved in purchasing cheap consumer goods that have been produced by hands which have not been properly compensated for their labour. Our experience was made even more confusing when we entered the Taj Mahal Hotel and experienced air-conditioned luxury, the like of which we had not seen in the United Kingdom. Even then my mind intuitively considered our experience in the hotel to be more obscene than the smells that affronted our nasal sensitivities on the streets.

Wednesday 2 November we docked early in Colombo. I put my name down for a trip with other migrants to Kandy in the centre of Sri Lanka. Following the confronting sights and smells of Bombay, this was a very pleasurable journey through lush countryside with sights to delight the eye. Elephants were being washed in the river while others were being worked moving logs. Metre long lizards lazily crossed the road, seemingly confident that they had right of way over any vehicular traffic. The city of Kandy with its University and well-kept gardens was clearly a proud legacy of British colonial investment. Then I knew nothing of Sri Lanka's complex ethnicity which would later erupt into a fully blown civil war and cause thousands of Tamils to flee as refuges to Australia.

Friday 4 November, we crossed the equator and were all provided with a certificate signed personally by Neptune himself. This was an occasion for celebration, for readjusting the compass, and undoing 18 years of conditioning that the sun at noon is in the southern sky. When the sun set, we were ceremoniously taken on deck to see the Southern Cross, but I have to say that on this first occasion I did not have a clue what I was supposed to be observing.

Thursday 10 November, we set foot on Australian soil for the first time. It was an exciting experience, but at this stage what life would be like in the country of our adoption was, as yet, a closed book. Our first day offered very few clues. We were met at Fremantle dock by friends and taken on a tour of the sights, primarily featuring Perth's glorious King's Park. Perhaps the only real clue to our future was the swatting of insects as we settled into what would be a lifetime of BBQs.

The journey through the Great Australian Bight was as difficult for those with a weak stomach as the Bay of Biscay. Having by now learned that eating in these circumstances posed no problem to me, my only disappointment was that the dining room was closed because the movement of the ship rendered the task of keeping crockery and cutlery on the tables impossible.

Tuesday 15 November, we docked in Melbourne. We were met again by friends, but I am afraid by now I was anxious to arrive in Sydney, which we did early in the morning on 17 November. I was extremely glad to have been woken early, to enjoy the unforgettable experience of passing though the heads and observing the iconic Sydney Harbour Bridge.

I arrived on these Antipodean shores, I am ashamed to say, in almost total ignorance of Australia's history, of the pain inflicted upon its indigenous people by those who had arrived before me, or of its evolving place in the 'new world'. I arrived to find what I knew; the locals spoke English! But not only that, I was immediately counted as one of its citizens. I voted in State and Federal elections and from the day of my arrival called myself an 'Australian'. It frankly did not occur to me that I needed to seek any further reassurance of citizenship. However, as the 1988 bi-centenary celebrations drew nearer, it dawned on me that I could not speak with integrity in this iconic year if there was doubt as to where my loyalties lay. Thus, on 22 January 1988, in Brisbane, I lined up with others (from all the nations upon earth) to receive official documentation, signed by Mick Young, Minister of State, with crest of kangaroo and emu, to tell me and the world my first loyalty was Australia. Not that I would ever lose my sense of pride and loyalty to the lion and unicorn and the place of my birth. I strongly believe that loyalty to the chosen place of residence is paramount. (I am a fierce and one-eyed supporter of Australia's cricket and rugby sides). I am very much in favour of Australia's multi-cultural identity, that we are all enriched by the demonstration of, and interaction with, differing ethnicity and outlook. However, I also believe that our chosen place of residence must have our loyalty and affection. Prejudices and burdens of history from places of origin must be left behind. Above all we need to wear the local 'guernsey'. Despite an unequivocal loyalty to Australia, I feel deeply privileged to carry two passports.

Newcomers to Australia have arrived, and continue to arrive, in all manner of ways and for a variety of reasons. It is thought that Australia's first inhabitants arrived 50,000+ years ago when there was still a land bridge connecting the continent to Asia.

Knowledge of Australia's first nation people by later immigrants is shamefully scant. Most, if they think about it at all, would consider 'Aboriginals' a suitable generic description, unaware that the 300+ nations that existed before colonization enjoyed distinctive language, and cultural identity. In addition, few appear to understand that the Torres Strait Islander people's ethnicity is Melanesian.

In the last 200 years people have arrived, as explorers, adventurers, free settlers, gold diggers, convicts, and in a post-Second World War flood, as assisted migrants. Initially the vast majority were from Europe, but increasing numbers now arrive from Asia, with many refugees being resettled from Africa. Those whose arrival was most painful, and for which an official apology has been recently elicited were British children of poor circumstance who came with or without consent from family, often being told they were orphans when in fact a parent was still living. These children were placed in Government and Church institutions, often on farms. Many were sponsored by the Barnardo charity.

Those who stepped off the *Strathnaver* on 17 November 1960 either went straight to their prearranged home, to the home of their sponsor, to a dormitory style hostel, or, as we did, to a comfortable suburban hostel. Our home (in my case for about five weeks) was a very pleasant large suburban home in Dulwich Hill, which had been turned into a first stop for migrant families.

I stayed longer than the rest of the family because I had secured a temporary position in an electrical goods retail outlet in Margaret Street, just down the road from Wynyard station in the Sydney CBD. In 1960 anyone who wanted to work could find work. We arrived on a Thursday. I commenced work in the shop the following Monday. It was a good introduction, if one is required, to the commercial side of Christmas. The shop sold electric frypans and electric beater mixes, etc. From the moment the shop opened in the morning until close in the evening we never stood still. A constant stream of customers ensured that Christmas 1960 would mean well mixed Christmas puddings and nicely browned roasted chooks.

After about three weeks father took the family to Armidale to the house he had bought in Mann Street. I followed on Friday 23 December, catching the Glen Innes Mail which left Sydney Central in the evening. It was a slow overnight trip in a set of dog boxes drawn by a steam engine. Although the middle of summer, I remember it being quite cold in the early hours of the morning. At Werris Creek new tins of hot coals were tossed into the carriage to warm our feet. Climbing up from Tamworth to the Tablelands, I remember thinking I could probably walk faster than we were travelling!

That first Christmas in Armidale is a bit of a blur. I recall mother did her best to create the same atmosphere we had always known in the UK, traditional fare, presents on chairs, nine instead of ten, Church in the morning at St Peter's Cathedral and full-blown Christmas lunch with all the trimmings.

The house was adequate, but I was keen not to be cooped in it too much. As Boxing Day dawned, I was up early enough to greet the milkman, Mr Lucas, delivering milk from his churn into the jugs mother had left at the door the night before. A brief conversation resulted in a job offer I was glad to accept. For the next four weeks I travelled out to the dairy to assist with the milking, feed the pigs and provide young legs for the milk run. It was fun. I particularly remember the smell of apricots ripening in the lush Armidale gardens, as I ran with the can ready to tip into the waiting jugs. I hope the residents weren't counting their fruit for a few went missing in the mouth of their very newly arrived English milkman. Looking back with the eyes of modern health and safety regulations it seems odd that milk straight from the udder could be presented in non-sealed containers at the door of the house.

Travelling the 6kms or so along Long Swamp Road to the farm, initially on a push bike then on a motorised scooter I would pass, morning and evening, the aboriginal reserve in East Armidale. The humpies, the dirt, the children, the discarded sherry flagons provided disconcerting images that then I found too hard to process. I had so much to learn. I did not then realise that when white people arrived, we had declared the land *Terra Nullius*. I did not realise that in 1960 Aboriginal and Torres Strait Islanders were still not counted as Australians in the census, that they had almost no status in a country where they had the right to be known as its First People. I did not know many had fought for Australia and the British Empire in two World Wars and yet on their return they did not qualify for the same pension and rights as other returned soldiers. I did not then know that there had been more than three hundred proud Aboriginal nations in Australia before white colonisation, each with their own language, culture, and customs. I did not then know that I was passing a 'reserve' like hundreds of others throughout the country where First Nations people lived on the edge of society, because that was the way white society demanded it. I did not then know how much had been stolen and how much pain was being borne, pain that has not yet been erased.

The Hilder family lived next door to our home in Mann Street. Jack was a research scientist with the CSIRO. While working for Mr Lucas was a nice stop gap, it was clearly not a career path. Jack Hilder arranged a position for me with the CSIRO as a technical assistant. I worked for a scientist who was researching sheep feeding habits and pasture growth. I can remember father saying that I now had a career for life! In fact, it was a noticeably short life, approximately five weeks! I would travel out to the offices at the New England University and then load onto a small truck for the field station 'Chiswick' near Uralla. There my job was to throw wooden frames of approximately one metre diameter randomly onto the ground and pick up everything within that circle into a bottle. On the off days we would then begin to process the content of the bottles. While my scientist boss was a most wonderful human being and extraordinarily kind to me, I hated the job. I hated the fact that it was regimented to short bursts of working hours between morning tea, lunch, and afternoon tea. I hated the attitude of fellow workers which was to do as little as possible. I disliked being rebuked by other workers for being 'too keen' especially when I tried to get through the backlog of bottles. It was my only venture into a 'public service' position and one which I was not keen to repeat.

While working for Mr Lucas I was aware of a larger property next door, the centre of which was contained within a tall hawthorn hedge. I made enquiry as to the possibility of a position on 'Palmerston' and was delighted to learn that Mr Peter Dangar was happy to employ me as a stud groom with his newly established Poll Hereford stud 'Baroona'. And so began two very happy years on Palmerston in a job I loved and with people who accorded me respect and trust. At the time of my appointment I would have been utterly disbelieving if I had been told that several years later, as Rector of Singleton, I would be laying Peter Dangar's ashes to rest in the Dangar mausoleum in the grounds of All Saints Church, the gift of his grandfather, Albert Augustus Dangar.

Henry Dangar was the first member of the family to emigrate from his native Cornwall to Australia in 1821. He became assistant government surveyor under John Oxley and for his work was granted land; the first near Singleton called Neotsfield after his Cornish village, St Neot. With brothers Richard and William, they established several successful businesses and their landholdings grew. To Neotsfield was added Baroona, also near Singleton, Myall Creek near Bingara, Gostwyck station at Uralla, Palmerston at Armidale and Yallaroi Station near Goondiwindi.

Myall Creek became infamous. On 10 June 1838 28 old men, women, and children of the Weraerai mob of the Gomeroi nation were massacred on Myall Creek Station by a group of blood thirsty whites, ostensibly in retaliation for the loss of some cattle. The leader of the group was never brought to justice, but seven men were eventually found guilty of murder and executed. The Myall Creek massacre is one of the most notorious of the Aboriginal and Torres Strait Islander massacres because of its brazen brutality (after being butchered the bodies were burned). It is also notorious because sections of society and media, including the *Sydney Morning Herald*, reacted with frightening racism, proclaiming the 'blacks' to be unworthy of sympathy or indeed the protection of the law.[26]

My time on Palmerston was extremely happy. While the property was owned by Mr Peter Dangar and his wife Anne (daughter of Vice Admiral Sir Richard Lane-Poole) I was largely responsible to Peter's son John. The stud,

---

26 *The whole gang of black animals are not worthy of the money the colonists will have to pay for printing the silly court documents on which we have already wasted so much time.* 5 Oct 1838 *SMH* Parliament of NSW Hansard June 8 2000.

its buildings and equipment were new. I am afraid it was all rather self-indulgent in the sense that while the surroundings were idyllic the stud's strategic management was very much a case of the blind leading the blind. The main sire, Milton Cardinal, was a fine animal, but many of his female offspring were somewhat stunted in growth, I fear there had been too much in-breeding. The young calves and bulls were accorded first class accommodation and feeding.

One of my first experiences was learning to ride. As a young migrant I was advised not to admit to any ability, for fear that I would be proved wrong. This was not difficult in relation to horse riding. I had never ridden. We rounded up the horses; I was invited to choose one. Not having any idea what I was looking for, I chose a grey. As it turned out it was a good choice. I was invited to bridle the horse, saddle it, and go for a bit of a canter. At that stage I did not know there were two straps that held the saddle to the horse, the girth strap, and the surcingle. The men watching me saddle the horse managed to conceal their mirth as I trotted off without the surcingle. Within a matter of seconds, I and the saddle were under the horse, posing a most unbecoming and somewhat hilarious spectacle. The laughter was eventually reined in sufficiently for the men to extract me from my embarrassment. This was followed by a lecture about saddling a horse, which by now gained my full and undivided attention. I probably left the horse involuntarily a further half a dozen times in the first fortnight but am glad to say that I have not been off, other than through my own choice, since.

One of the great experiences of my time at Palmerston was being sent to the Sydney Royal Show as a groom for the Anthony Hordern[27] owned Aberdeen Angus stud, Milton Park. We slept in the loft above the cattle and literally had ringside seats for the main events. Flying to and from Armidale

27 Anthony Horderns was for many years the largest department store in Australia. By the beginning of the 1960s the company fortune began to change and eventually the store was sold to Waltons and the Camden estate was sold to a large Texan based company. The Anthony Hordern motto was: *while I live I grow*. The motto was pinned to a large tree alongside the Hume Highway. Mysteriously when the store and the property declined the tree died.

in the trustworthy twin-engined Fokker was also exciting, the first time I had ever been in a plane.

I managed a most stunning calamity during my time on the property. It happened this way. Peter, Anne, and John had taken themselves off with a few cattle to the Brisbane Show: I was left in charge and slept in the big house[28] along with the bulldogs and their terrible snoring. The stud heifers were calving and each morning I took the Land Rover with bales of hay to feed the stock in the paddocks.

I parked the Land Rover close to the main buildings from where I observed one of the heifers was in the process of calving. I walked down the hill to check on her and noticed out of the corner of my eye that the Land Rover was coming down the hill to my right. My first reaction was to think, great, the gardener is coming down to give me a lift back. A closer look revealed to my horror that no one was in the driver's seat. I watched with galloping anxiety as the Land Rover gathered speed down a grassy but also rocky incline towards a line of fencing that I already calculated I could probably fix in the couple of days before the Dangars returned. Then to my horror the Land Rover, as if being driven to its garage home, turned several degrees to the left and headed straight for what was called the ram shed. The shed contained hay, but in its right-hand section housed a hammer mill used for turning lucerne hay into feed chaff. The Land Rover could have chosen the hay, but whatever unseen spirit was driving it that day, chose the hammer mill instead, entering though the wall as if it was an open door and coming to a stop when the Land Rover engine and the hammer mill were locked in a metallic embrace. This was not a good moment. The smashing, grinding noise attracted the attention of Mr Hind the gardener who came rushing down the hill. The sight was not pretty. His concern for my welfare was very touching. We pulled the Land Rover clear of the hammer mill with the tractor. I could not wait for Mr Dangar

---

28 The homestead was built in 1912, I was told, but have never been able to confirm, that it was built by the Dangars in time to host a visit from the then Prince of Wales.

to return from Brisbane to pass on the news! I have seldom made a call with more apprehension but finished it with more relief. I blurted out the story to the poor man who was probably relaxing with a scotch in his Brisbane hotel. To his absolute credit, he filled the silence that followed my blurted confession with a simple question: 'are you alright'? When I confirmed that I was, he simply said good, everything else can be fixed when I return. It was a great lesson in appropriate response making, a lesson I did my best to apply over the years when as a Bishop news that I did not want to hear from various parishes or institutions was conveyed to me.

Approximately 12 months after arriving in Australia, aged 19, my life was to take one of its two major turning points. Having been a church goer in the UK it seemed only natural to continue the same pattern in Australia, although at this stage it was more habitual and social rather than driven by belief. St Peter's Cathedral in those days was packed for all services, it was difficult to find a seat if your arrival was less than 15 minutes before the start of service. The Dean, Evan Wetherell, was ably assisted by his two curates, John Beer (Frothy) and David Bowden. Towards the end of 1961 the Dean organised a Parish Life Mission to which he invited the then Archdeacon of Melbourne, Bob Dann,[29] as leader. I accepted the prodding of John Beer and enrolled. So too had Margaret Joy Rowland. This pretty, capable, and very organised young lady became the focus of my attention. She was far more mature, articulate, and able than I. At that stage I was, well, awkward, having virtually no skills or ideas about how one might woo a young girl. Fortunately, the mission lasted a week, so I had plenty of opportunity to find myself in her company. I can truthfully say that Margaret was not the only life changing outcome the week wrought in this young man. The mission made me think seriously about the Christian faith for the very first time, and while it was not the only influence, it was the main catalyst to a life's commitment: but more of that later.

From the mission, Margaret and I began our relationship and the long journey of getting to know one another. I was painfully shy, and it was quite

---

29 Bob Dann was later to become Archbishop of Melbourne.

some time before we even managed to exchange our first kiss. I think this spine-tingling moment was several weeks later, at a YAF (Young Anglican Fellowship) party in the Emmaville Vicarage after John Beer's appointment as the Vicar.

The second year at Palmerston was more pleasurable because of the developing relationship with Margaret. She spoiled me by bringing goodies out to the shearing shed where by then I was sleeping and 'cooking'. Cooking hardly extended beyond the absolute basics of boiling potatoes and opening a few tins. She also joined me on a couple of occasions for a meal in the main homestead at Palmerston. One Friday evening I was to accompany Margaret to a social dance organised by the local Country Party younger set.[30] I wanted to be ready in good time and so hurried on with my stock feeding chores. One of the many machines I managed was a feed mixer which mixed chaff and grain together. It was a big drum with slow turning blades. Being a little impatient to extract the final mixture I put my hand into the drum. The result was frightening. My hand was slowly drawn into the drum by the blades. Fortunately, with my left hand I could just reach up and press the off button thus stopping the motor. By then two nails had come off and my right hand was not a pretty sight. I made it to the dance: it is fortunate that in those days one danced in the company of a partner and my heavily bandaged right hand spent the evening in a slightly higher position on Margaret's back than would otherwise have been the case!

When I eventually announced to the Dangar family that I was leaving to enter theological college they seemed really chuffed and generously threw me a party. While I have since been to many such affairs, this was my first experience of a large formal dining room table with rows of forks and spoons and an etiquette that had me totally out of my depth. When the formal meal came to an end, Anne Dangar disappeared into the kitchen

---

30 Given a growing commitment to social justice and a period spent in Queensland when the Premier was Sir Joh Bjelke-Petersen, association with the Country Party was relatively short lived.

to come back with a cake which was placed in front of me. She went on to apologise that she had had a bad day in the kitchen and the cake had not turned out the way she had intended. It certainly looked flat and a bit bumpy under the icing. Speeches were made with reference to the more hilarious and perhaps embarrassing moments that surrounded my two years on the property. I was then passed a fine knife and invited to cut the cake. I began in a seated position but try as I might, I could not make any headway. Flushed with embarrassment I got to my feet to give the knife a bit more weight. So intent was I on the task in hand that I did not meet the eye of any of the other guests around the table, had I done so I might have saved myself excruciating embarrassment. Eventually the knife did its thing. Rather than cut the cake, it is more truthful to say it cracked it open. When the rest of the table could contain their laughter no longer, I realised how badly I had been set up. John Dangar had been down to the bull-shed earlier in the day with a shovel to pick up one of cardinal's best. They had baked it dry, iced it and adorned it with its two candles. With perspiration seeping out of every pore I finally sat down and managed to laugh with them. Finally, a wonderful cake did emerge and my formal time at Palmerston sadly came to an end.

Chapter 3
I am not a prophet
nor a prophet's son

The best rules to form a young man are: to talk little, to hear
much, to reflect alone upon what has passed in company, to
distrust one's own opinions, and value others that deserve it.

Archbishop William Temple

Was Paul converted 'cold' on the road to Damascus, or did God soften him up with many previous encounters? Clearly one such encounter was the stoning of Stephen, when Saul found himself a willing, but passive accomplice (Acts 7: 54—8.1). This impressionable young man found that, rather than witnessing a routine stoning, he was having the Christian faith witnessed to him by Stephen. The role of witness was being reversed. Stephen became the first μάρτϋρ (martyr), witnessing the faith as he gave up his life. Presumably, Paul had to digest this testimony, a testimony which finally and completely confronted him on the road to Damascus (Acts 9. 1-19).

I really cannot say how I came to discover that being a priest was what I was born to do. My earliest epiphany, or was it a theophany, had been when I was only about 10 and is best understood in retrospect. I was bringing the cows in one early misty summer morning. The sun broke through the clouds to shine on the ground where I and the cows were making our slow walk to the dairy. My childhood imagination took me into the story of Jacob at Bethel.

In his dream Jacob saw a ladder connecting heaven and earth. Was I to understand that my life was to have something to do with the connection of heaven and earth? If so, how would this eventually play out?

Connecting heaven and earth can never be simply a personal ambition. It can only result from participating on a greater, more inclusive stage. Sharing this stage, it is important to have heroes or exemplars. If the faith is really about connections, Jesus connecting earth and heaven, time and eternity, humanity and divinity, then the connections made during our outward earthly journey are essential for the feeding of the inner journey. One of these connections was made at my confirmation, at St Andrew's Church, Alfriston, 'the Cathedral of the Downs' by George Bell, Bishop of Chichester (1929 -1958).

George Bell is, to me, a hero of the faith. He was honorary president of the World Council of Churches and a great ecumenist. During the World War 2 he incurred the wrath of Winston Churchill by his consistent speeches in the House of Lords railing against the bombing of German residential areas in retaliation for similar bombings in London and Coventry. This courage may have cost him the See of Canterbury, for following the untimely death of Archbishop William Temple in 1944 he was by-passed by Geoffrey Fisher, probably on Churchill's recommendation. His liberal Catholicism insisted upon an incarnational (rooted in the world) faith, connecting word and sacrament. These days being 'liberal' is derided as meaning not standing for much. In its original sense it meant all embracing, generously inclusive, drawing on many traditions. I would like to be known as a liberal. By way of contrast, there is not much that is 'liberal' about the modern-day Australian Liberal Party.

Bell's intimate relationship with Dietrich Bonhoeffer introduced me to another giant of 20th century Christianity, causing me to see more profoundly the linkage between belief and living.[31] Many of his letters

---

31 Dietrich Bonhoeffer was a German evangelical pastor, theologian, anti-Nazi dissident, and key founding member of the Confessing Church. His writings on Christianity's role in the secular world have become widely influential, and his book *The Cost of Discipleship* has been described as a modern classic. He had been part of the failed conspiracy to assassinate Hitler and was put to death in 1944.

and papers from prison were written to Bell. They had known each other through the ecumenical movement prior to 1939.

Undoubtedly members of my family were influential. The influence of my father (John Russel) remains extremely difficult to weigh. Did I follow this path despite him, or because of him? One day perhaps I will find the answer to that question. I have consciously set aside his dogmatic stance, and yet remain inspired by the strength of his faith. The subject of my Ph.D. was born out of his abiding passion in the sabbath which I considered misconceived. John was a member of the Sabbath Day Society, a tool of conservative, if not fundamentalist Christianity. He was right to place an emphasis on sabbath, but wrong to connect it legalistically to the seventh day. You may find this a strange statement. Christianity consciously abandoned sabbath practice during the period of the writing of the New Testament, instead celebrating Jesus as the one in whom sabbath is fulfilled. In my Ph.D. I argue that sabbath is not about one day in a sequence of seven, but is a commentary on how life, inclusive of all creation, is to be celebrated and lived.

John had an exaggerated sense of the judgement of God and tended to a 'conservative evangelical' view of belief and practice. He wrote to the Bishop opposing my ordination. He told me 'there are enough hopeless clergy without adding you to their number'! Unfortunately, we had so little in common theologically that we never had a serious conversation about the faith, or indeed anything else come to that. I regret now not challenging him. While at the time I simply did not want to engage in conflict, I can see now that I let him down by not engaging. While I preached later at his own ordination, we had a rather distant relationship until his death. A few months before he died, and to my great surprise, he asked me if 'everything was under control'. I asked what the 'everything' was and learnt that he meant arrangements for his funeral. It had never occurred to me that he would want me to take the service let alone arrange it.

In the fortnight before he died, I went to the hospital to read morning and evening prayer for him. A few days before he died, he was clearly very distressed. I asked what the problem was. He just shrugged his shoulders and said, 'I simply do not know anymore'. There have been a few moments in my life when I have listened to words coming out of my mouth without being conscious that I was responsible for forming them! This was one of those occasions. I said: 'John Russel Browning all of your life you have said it is grace not works, grace not works. I have to tell you that you are not fleet enough of foot to avoid the grace of God'. He gave me a hug, the first time I can ever recall this happening.

Barbara's influence is much clearer, not so much through any formal teaching, but through the values that undergirded her living. Such loveliness in living is sufficient to feed any soul. Undoubtedly Barbara had a strong faith, lived in the practicalities of life. She would have had many reasons to resent her husband's control of her, his inability to recognise that she also had the right to choices, but such resentment never once showed itself, quite the contrary. She would also have reason to resent her husband's farming choices which seldom resulted in greater provision for the family: again, not a word of it. Her acceptance of others is remarkable. Valerie's marriage to Ismael, an Afar Muslim, could have reasonably caused her some misgivings: not at all. She told Val that she was truly fortunate to be married to such a fine man. An orphan from the age of three, Barbara May refused ever to see herself as the victim, but the recipient of much grace and joy in living. She put little store on material things. She could boast a very modest wardrobe. She saw her wealth in her family, the garden, and in life's celebration. Having so many children and grandchildren, praying for them all filled a large slab of the day! The *Barbara May Foundation*[32] is a fitting and lasting tribute to her, as is the *Barbara May Maternity Hospital*[33] at Mille in the Afar region of Ethiopia.

Undoubtedly the land has played its part in revealing the nature of God. The psalmists testify to the truth that the natural world reflects

---

32 https://barbaramayfoundation.com

33 https://barbaramayfoundation.com/projects/barbara-may-maternity-hospital

the hand of its creator.[34] Who can deny this? When confronted by ugliness in human activity, escaping to the forest, or beach; field or desert, refreshes and re-enlivens the soul. Growing up at Sheeplands farm has proved a deep well from which to draw strength throughout my life.

Towards the end of 1961 and into early 1962 sitting in St Peter's Cathedral twice a Sunday, it began to feel as if the sermons were being preached directly toward me. Evan Wetherell[35], the Dean of the Cathedral, was a fine teacher. The Parish Life Mission was undoubtedly a strong catalyst, for which I was glad to thank Archbishop Robert Dann later in his life. When these early stirrings were beginning to sufficiently disturb my simple equilibrium I remember kneeling down beside my bed one night and saying to God that if he really wanted me, he would have to do two things, both of which I thought at the time were most unlikely. First, God would have to do something about my confidence and capacity to speak in public, and secondly, provide me with a helpmate for I was certain the task on my own would be beyond me. I did not realise then, but have come to realise since, you should be very careful what you pray for, you may find yourself on life's travellator before you have really thought it through! Very soon after that prayer I found myself at the Parish Life Mission, confronted with outcomes to both petitions, the rest as they say is history!

When sufficiently disturbed by this sense of call I felt the need to ask counsel from a trusted mentor. Father John Beer was now vicar of Emmaville, north of Glen Innes, so I made an appointment and journeyed up the New England Highway on my Heinkel. Bachelor John had insufficient bedding, so we called at the Emmaville pub for sheets and blankets. I was still sufficiently unexposed to the ways of the world to have been shocked

---

34 Psalm 19:1 The heavens are telling the glory of God, and the firmament proclaims his handiwork.

35 Dean Wetherell had previously been rector of the evangelical St Andrew's South Brisbane.

when the publican said to Father Beer, with a twinkle in her eye: we can provide your young guest with a far more friendly way of keeping warm!

John was aware of my lack of education and said he thought I should contact ABM for possible training as a missionary, but in any case I should make an appointment with the elderly, stately and somewhat daunting Bishop of Armidale, his Lordship John Stoward Moyes. The Bishop was receptive, kind and to the point. He suggested that for the rest of the year (1962) I should undertake some study at the local technical college. It has had such an impact upon me that to this day I have no clear recollection of what I did, if anything at all! Towards the end of that year I kept my return appointment with the Bishop. To my astonishment he announced that he had booked me into St John's Theological College at Morpeth (Newcastle) NSW and stated that I should prepare to be present for the commencement of term 1, toward the end of February 1963.

The theological college had begun its life in Armidale, but quickly became too much for a single rural Diocese to fund and staff. In 1926, under the leadership of Ernest Burgmann, the College was moved to Morpeth and became jointly the property of the Dioceses of Newcastle, Goulburn, Bathurst, Armidale, Grafton and Riverina. It is sad that Armidale's connection with St John's came abruptly to an end in the mid 1960s when Bishop Moyes was replaced by Bishop Clive Kerle, a committed evangelical who sent all his students to Moore College, Sydney. It was the stated aim of the joint Dioceses to establish at Morpeth the first regional University College in the Country. Ironically, this was achieved in Armidale with the creation of the University of New England. It possessed no theological faculty, despite Bishop Moyes being its driving force.

I have pondered since, what could have been in the mind of the Bishop when he made this decision? What was it that he saw in me that made the risk of such an investment even remotely worthwhile? I will never know the answer to this question, but it was one of many unwarranted investments that others made in me. In the process I have been helped to understand that investing in others' lives is about the most significant thing that any of us can do in our lifetime. How fortunate we are when we are recipients of such grace. How poor we are when no such investment is made. This investing mimics the activity of God, who invests in the whole created order. If there is a phrase which might sum up my own ministry and its driving ideal, it is 'find out what God is doing and do that'. God's constant investment in us is extraordinary, the primary investment of life, the investment of freedom and choice, the investment of forgiveness and the opportunity to start each day afresh. This was the first of two reasons why I have much to thank God for John Stoward Moyes.[36]

At the ripe old age of 20 I travelled from Armidale by train and walked the 8kms with my modest luggage from the East Maitland railway station to St John's, arriving to commence my training for ordained ministry in the Church of England in Australia and Tasmania.[37] While young, I was not the youngest, Brian Farran, later to become Bishop of Newcastle, and Brian Norris, later to become Registrar of the Diocese of Canberra and Goulburn and then Gippsland were younger. Those were the days when students were male, young, and single. (Ron Tuckwell and John Walters from SA were exceptions).

---

36 John Stoward Moyes was Bishop of Armidale from 1929–1964. He was a significant member of the Australian bench, capable of becoming Archbishop of Sydney, but even in those days, probably too open and perhaps too controversial. He backed unionists and workers during and after the great depression. He was instrumental in founding the University of New England. He sought a balance in his Diocese between 'catholics' and 'evangelicals'. He was almost too successful for following his retirement the synod was deadlocked in its choice between Archdeacon Bob Dann of Melbourne and Sydney's coadjutor, Bishop Clive Kerle. It is said the deadlock was broken when a farmer from Narrabri could stay no longer and went home to harvest his wheat, thus enabling a majority for Clive Kerle and the transition of the Diocese of Armidale into Sydney's country cousin. I was the last student from Armidale to be trained at Morpeth.

37 The Church officially changed its name to the Anglican Church of Australia on 24 August 1981.

It was not long before the culture changed, Bishops then thought it best to send young men away 'to gain experience in the world' before training. Many never came back. Today it is incredibly sad that few students commence training in their 30s let alone their 20s, and the Church is much the poorer. Students who commence training in middle age unsurprisingly perpetuate the church which molded them. If our capacity to influence others is restricted to people ten years either side of our own age, without young leaders, the Church has little chance of influencing a young generation of believers.

My first term was to be somewhat disrupted with a bout of cellulitis. The diagnosis was as vague as the treatment. The initial infection took some time to retreat while duty doctors alternated in their advice from total bed rest to exercise. I spent one week in the Maitland hospital. As a result of it all, I gained an undiagnosed thrombosis in my left calf. While this is minor encumbrance, it has meant managing a leg that swells, necessitating the wearing of a pressure stocking for the rest of my life.

When I entered College, I was ready to learn and be moulded. I was fortunate to find myself in the company of fellow students and staff who opened the doors of my heart and mind; doors I have endeavoured to keep open these past 50+ years; and to encourage similar openness in others. We are born with a capacity for imagination, how wonderfully we see this capacity played out in children. And yet in adulthood this capacity is so easily abandoned as we seek security in what we mistakenly believe to be certainty. We like to use the language of certainty, whether it be certainty of ethnic superiority, certainty of religious dogmatism, certainty of economic structure, certainty in social reconstruction *(no child will live in poverty)*[38] or certainty in the natural order—turning the rivers inland, we will *drought proof Australia.*[39] Extreme forms of religion use their particular brand of certainty

---

38 Prime Minister Bob Hawke on 16 June 2007 promises that by 1990 no Australian child will live in poverty.

39 The promise of many conservative politicians during the long drought 2000–2010.

to entice believers and to distinguish between their members who are saved and outsiders who are infidel or lost. I find trade in such certainty offensive. I have complete confidence that the nature of God and the true nature of humanity is revealed in Jesus and that heaven and earth meet in him, but I also know that I see through a glass darkly. I am increasingly convinced that truth is seldom if ever a single verity, but is found in the taxing capacity to hold together seemingly irreconcilable opposites. But much more of this later.

In my first year I slept in a dormitory and shared a study. Ron Tuckwell, an Adelaide student in his 30s shared my study, while Ron, Peter Mumford (Newcastle), David Pullen (Tasmania) and I shared a dormitory. These were halcyon days for the Church, many ordinands, large numbers at worship; the place of the Church in the wider community was strong and respected. Unfortunately, only a relatively small proportion of those who commenced their training in 1963 would see out their ministry until retirement. Peter Mumford and I were the only two to achieve this milestone from the dormitory of four. I suspect the overall numbers were less than half.

Life at Morpeth had two significant foci; the lecture room and the chapel. The latter saw us on our knees four times a day. Each morning commenced with Morning Prayer, meditation, and the Eucharist. Lunch was preceded by the Midday Office; tea was preceded by Evening Prayer, and Compline ensured we headed for bed in a prayerful manner. It is easy to be critical of what appears to be a form of monastic regimentation. However, centuries of practice have shown that a discipline that becomes part of the rhythm of life has the capacity to carry one though the inevitability of arid times. One of the enormous advantages of this rhythm is the familiarisation it offers to substantial slabs of scripture. Staying for the daily Eucharist was not compulsory, although we were encouraged to be present three times a week, inclusive of the compulsory College Eucharist.

During my college days I began to understand that there are as many varieties of spirituality as there are personalities. Some seemed to find contemplation and solitude a genuine source of strength and inspiration.

Sadly, I have never found such wells places from which I could easily drink. Nor did I find Father Peter Joliffe, the anglo catholic college spiritual director and chaplain, a helpful mentor. I think I was viewed by the dominant Anglo Catholic wing with some suspicion. On the other hand, I found the assertiveness of evangelicalism claustrophobic. This has meant a lifetime on the periphery of the two major camps within Australian Anglicanism. I have never wanted to waste my time and energy on the turf wars in which both love to engage.

From both camps I, and others like me, have suffered from the pejorative label 'liberal', by which they mean wishy washy, by implication neither one nor the other. Today both Evangelicals and Anglo Catholics would consider themselves conservative. Conservative verses liberal has become today's ecclesiastical fault-line. In the process, 'conservative' and 'liberal' have had their meaning changed, mostly out of an obsession with false certainty. I would consider myself a conservative in the sense of wishing to conserve the essence of things. Those who call themselves conservatives, through their words and actions, appear more akin to literalists or fundamentalists intent on preserving form rather than substance. I also consider myself a true liberal in the sense of wishing to embrace the best of traditions.

The most surprising element of my time in college is that the classroom became a place of freedom, liberation. While all previous attempts at study had floundered, here, for the first time, I was in my element. I should have felt daunted by the fact that all other students had finished their secondary schooling, and many held a university degree. In the first year we were required to undertake introductory subjects to both Old and New Testament, Theology and Greek. There is a tendency these days to think the ubiquitous Bachelor of Theology is somehow more rigorous than the Licentiate in Theology we sat. I am not so sure, not least because we did three years of Greek, while the vast majority of BTh students do little more than a single semester. I particularly loved Theology and the Biblical subjects. While the Greek lecturer, Dr Colebourne was a reputable scholar, most staff were non-academic, ministerial practitioners of some experience. My first principal was Bishop Robert Davies, soon to be elected Bishop of Tasmania and replaced by Canon John May. The Vice Principal was the Rev'd Gordon Griffith, soon replaced by Canon, later Bishop Geoffrey Parker. Seven years later when I returned as Vice Principal, I found myself in the same category, a non-academic practitioner, and worse, with ignominiously limited ministerial experience!

The College year was based upon the old fashioned three term cycle. Each holiday I sought a salaried position to earn sufficient income to carry me through the ensuing College term. The Diocese of Armidale paid all academic and boarding fees, but I was responsible for all incidentals. It was not hard to find work. The three long vacations were spent, filling petrol drums in a Tamworth oil depot, looking after a pastoral property near Uralla and pulling marijuana from along the Hunter River for the water board. Smaller vacations included driving a Mr Whippy van in Sydney, working in a corner store in Armidale, and cleaning cotton drums at the Bradford cotton mill on the outskirts of Maitland.

Pulling marijuana was an eye-opening introduction, albeit at a distance, with the drug trade. Later I was to have the sad duty of ministering to many families dealing with a family member's struggle with addiction. Apparently, an enterprising farmer had cultivated a crop in the river's upper reaches, only to have it destroyed by one of the many floods that frequented the valley in the 1950s and 60s. The seeds spread across the alluvial flood plain. A team of us, working in the formation of beaters at a shoot, spread out across the flood plain on either side of the river from Branxton to Raymond Terrace.

Our extended family includes an attractive and able young man who developed schizophrenia in his late teenage years. Prior to this onset he had been a marijuana smoker. While the correlation of cause and effect cannot be definitive, there is sufficient corroborative evidence for the link to be made. Drug use as we all know, is endemic in our society. I must own up to drinking alcohol for pleasure, but fortunately I can never recall having done so to excess nor have I tried any other drug.

Life knowledge and sagacity are gained through experience and take a long time to absorb. As has been frequently reflected, it is a pity the energy of youth and wisdom of years cannot be better coordinated! For youngsters in a hurry, drugs are a convenient short-circuit. There is no short-circuit. But life needs to be experienced in the raw with all its moments of sublime delight as well as moments of darkness and despair.

I understand pain, physical, mental, or emotional, can sometimes be too intense to be tolerated and needs to be blotted out. Beginning a habit in these circumstances is unwise, but it might be a choice hard to avoid. Taking a drug to simply heighten hedonistic extravagance is another matter altogether.

One of the few regrets that Margaret will own up to in her life is her claim that I encouraged her to destroy all the letters I wrote to her during my college days. I agree, they would have been a revealing account of those student years. I wrote at least twice per week. No doubt the letters told of personal interaction with other students. Friendship with Ray (Dr.) Williamson has endured for nearly 50 years. They would have revealed insights into the daily routine, of chapel, classes, meals, and the compulsory physical work roster. Having driven a tractor since my primary school days, care of the open acreage areas was my responsibility and saved me from toilet cleaning and other less desirable chores.

Whether in my letters I admitted the occasional, but thoroughly innocent visit to the Maitland Hospital nurses home is perhaps doubtful. I certainly would have recounted the pranks in all their detail, for I was involved in most of them. Re-establishing a student's study far from its appointed place was a common temptation. Kidnapping a student, tying them up in the back of a utility and driving them through the main street of Maitland to eventually leave them simply in their underpants some kilometres away on the banks of the river was less frequent. A student who could be relied upon to reveal the names of the culprits of the prank to the principal went on later to become a Bishop! Those of us who journeyed together for those short years met mixed fortunes in later life. Several died early including an incredibly sad suicide. A number left after a short ministry for a variety of reasons. Some, I am extremely saddened to say, were in later life convicted of paedophilia.

I have recounted the fact that the only examination I experienced prior to entry into college was two short conversations with the Bishop. He had been in episcopal orders for more than 30 years and perhaps thought he could quickly sum up character. I suspect little more preceded the enrolment of my fellow students. In my time as bishop I quickly realised some more objective and scientifically verifiable examination was required. Even so, this was never foolproof, students were accepted who should not have been and I suspect some were rejected who should have been included.

In my youthful naivety it never occurred to me that many of my fellow students were gay. This is probably just as well, for like most of my generation I was culturally formed to be homophobic. Because some of these students were later convicted of paedophilia, an erroneous link has been made between sexual orientation and abuse. Sexual orientation, either homosexual or heterosexual, is not an indicator of potential abusive behaviour.

In an ideal world Church leadership should reflect a true cross-section of civil society, inclusive of ethnicity, gender, and sexual orientation. It is a matter of shameful record that women, gay people, and people of ethnic diversity are under-represented in leadership, and worse, many have suffered humiliating discrimination.

The 2018 Royal Commission into institutional child abuse gave particular focus to the College at Morpeth. In my view wrongly. Students were selected by their sending dioceses, not by the college. The college only selected 'independent' students. I am unaware of any independent students being subsequently accused of paedophilia. In my view the Royal Commission should have focused on the Diocese of Newcastle with the question, 'what was it about the culture of the Diocese that disproportionately attracted paedophiles'? In my view the nub of the problem was a theology that allowed these men to believe in the superiority of priests over ordinary people and thus gave them a sense of power from which abusive behaviour emerged. This was not a theology taught at the college, indeed, staff in my time found such theology abhorrent.

While many signs of student growth are looked for in progression through college life, the only one on record is academic. However, I strongly believe the academic record should be far more nuanced. I look for a student with an open mind, one who has the capacity for theological reflection. Without this gift and ability, preaching will be less than inspiring, while pastoral counselling could be quite damaging. Developing this skill from a solid academic achievement is undoubtedly an advantage. As my first year in the college rolled into the second, it was becoming clear that my enjoyment of study was being translated into a personal academic record that defied reasonable expectations from my school days! My highest marks were in Greek, Old Testament and Theology. While the former has not been kept to the standard I achieved in those days, it remains a working tool, while Old Testament and Theology have developed into a life-time of fascination and further exploration. As the second year drew to an end I was advised that in my final year I should accept the extra discipline of first class honours study, which involved two extra units in addition to an average across all subjects in excess of 75%.

News of my progress was undoubtedly being conveyed to Bishop Moyes. Halfway through 1964 I made an appointment to see him. I had previously been warned that if you did not announce your business soon after the commencement of the interview, you would find yourself back on the road before you had raised it. I knocked on the door and received a 'Come in' from behind the desk. Without any movement or gesture in my direction, the Episcopal bottom remained fixed to its chair. 'Yes George', he said while continuing to write. 'I have come to ask your permission to be married in my third year at St John's', I blurted. The pen was placed in its holder and the Episcopal eyes searchingly engaged with mine. I did my absolute best not to look away. 'Humph! A bit young aren't you' he responded. 'I don't know about that' I rather weakly retorted. 'I am too busy to think about it now', he went on. 'Come back in a month, goodbye'. The interview was at a close, Margaret, very keen to hear the result, had to be persuaded that the possibility was still alive!

The month passed agonisingly slowly before I found myself again standing outside that Episcopal door with hand raised ready to knock. 'Come in', he said, for the second time. 'Yes George', followed on cue. This time he came out from behind the desk and shook my hand, it was a promising start! 'You asked me to come back in a month Bishop', I responded, searching for his response without having to re-put the question. The Bishop was not going to let me off that easily. 'Did I', he said, 'Why did I do that'? 'I asked for your permission to be married in my final year at college', I repeated. 'Oh yes, so you did', the bishop responded with a glimmer of a twinkle. 'I have not had time to think about it yet, ring me back at lunch time, goodbye': and so concluded my final face to face interview with the bishop before his retirement.

Young as I was, I was aware the question I was asking him did not come with a cost-free affirmative answer. It was not simply a matter of my age, 22 was young, it was then common for people to marry at that age or younger. It involved a substantial increase in fees for me at the College for I would now require a married quarter. It would also mean more thought required in any appointment he or his successor might want to make in my years as a curate. Single men were easy to place. They were generally housed in the spare back room of a redoubtable parish matron. Houses for curates were as scarce as hen's teeth and a very considerable burden upon Parish expenses. I do not think, these days, clergy think enough about the sacrifices that parishioners make to house and keep them. It is not infrequently the case that clergy are housed and kept in a far more comfortable lifestyle than the average parishioner.

Our reliable guess is that between the interview and lunch the Bishop rang his Vicar General, Archdeacon Cliff Rothero, for advice. This was fortunately game set and match because Margaret was one of Cliff Rothero's most favourite young people from her days as a child growing up in Glen Innes. In any case when I rang back at lunch time the Bishop said: 'Yes that will be alright, don't let it affect your study, goodbye'. This then is the second occasion for which I am most grateful for the risk the Bishop took by investing in me and my future, risk that I hope I have repaid.

A less formidable hurdle had to be negotiated, although I was not completely aware of it at the time. My father wrote to Canon John May asking him to dissuade me from marriage. I am not sure if he disapproved of Margaret or disapproved of my marrying at this stage. As already noted, he had earlier tried to dissuade me from the vocational path. Neither Canon May nor the Bishop were persuaded by the letters, perhaps their young candidate had shown a small glimmer of possibility that their investment in him would not fall on stony ground.

Margaret and I made plans to be married at St Peter's Cathedral Armidale on 30 January 1965, we had known each other for a little over three years. Armidale was Margaret's hometown on her mother's side of the family. Jack Savage, Margaret's grandfather, was the descendant of White Russian Jewish immigrants who had escaped persecution in Lithuania, towards the end of the 19th Century. They had come to Armidale via the UK. A tailor by craft, our Lithuania immigrant had set up shop at Hillgrove, a Gold Mining town outside Armidale. As this settlement declined, the business relocated to Armidale, and although no longer in family hands, the shop still exists under the same name today.

When Poppa Savage died, I had the privilege of conducting his funeral from the Cathedral. He no longer identified as a Jew and could hardly have been deemed a committed Anglican either. His funeral, a significant civic occasion, was not an appropriate moment for subtleties of Christian doctrine. It is helpful to be reminded that: 'The Spirit and the Bride say "come". And let everyone who hears say "come". Let anyone who wishes take the water of life as a gift' Rev. 22:17).' It is undeniable that anyone can say 'no' to God, but Poppa was not one of those people.

My marriage to Margaret was like any other, but in one major dimension it was quite different to most. My bedside prayer was now taking on real flesh and blood. It was no longer I who was called to serve alone, but from the very outset whatever modest achievement I have been able to attain has been attributable to the partnership and devotion we have shared, a partnership which has more often than not called for more sacrifice from her than it has from me. We would be destined for more than 40 years to serve wherever the Church decided, (I never once applied for a position) and often to live in houses which we saw for the first time when the furniture truck arrived with our possessions.

Margaret's sister Robyn and my eldest sister Rosemary were bridesmaids, Ron Tuckwell was best man. Robyn's fiancé, the Reverend John Croyle, conducted the marriage, while the Dean proposed the toast. We left for a honeymoon on the Gold Coast. The most memorable photograph from this week or so away is one of Margaret on the shoulders of another man enjoying an exciting ride behind a speed boat. I had unfortunately cut my feet on an oyster bed and could not water ski!

We took up residence in half the house that John Walters had built on Morpeth Rd. Margaret says it was the hardest year of our marriage. I am sure my attitude was more than half the reason for this. She worked in a solicitor's office in Maitland while I was absorbed with the routine of study and College life which at that stage saw wives and families as an awkward appendage rather than an integral part of College life. Wives could join the worship in the chapel but were expected to sit in the gallery. With our limited means we had bought a new bedroom suite and a dining room suite, both have long since gone where redundant and damaged furniture go. From a secondhand shop in Maitland we picked up a lounge suite for £5, a suite that has now survived an additional 50 years and going strong.

Each year I played with the college Rugby league team. In our first year we boasted an ex All Black in Michael Barbara, a Canberra and Goulburn student. In my final year I captained the team. We played our home games on the oval near the Conference Centre. It was extremely difficult to train the Victorian students to carry the ball any distance without it hitting the ground! My clearest memory is of an 'away' game played against a team from the Morpeth pub. It was a somewhat bruising encounter played on an oval at the back of the village. What the pub could not muster in skill or fitness they more than compensated for in cunning. It appears they distracted the referee long enough to have me hoisted in a ruck, and then speared into the turf. The game continued as I limped off on my way to the medical centre to have my right shoulder put back in its joint. I was somewhat gratified to hear later in the day a collection had been taken around the bar to cover my modest medical expenses. Age 22 it was sadly the last game of rugby I was to play.

Rugby team, St John's Morpeth, 1963.

By 1965 the liturgical revolution was well under way and Canon May, our principal, was keen to lead the charge. From the outset he was under pressure from the Anglo Catholics, the dominant faction in the Diocese of Newcastle, who were determined to retain outward form, regardless of its meaning or relevance. All my ministry I have struggled to help Anglicans understand that our liturgical practice unfolds the drama of Jesus' death and resurrection. It is not tied to immutable rubrics, essential hand movements or liturgical garments, in the right context they serve this higher purpose.

Anglo Catholicism,[40] at its worst, appears wedded to the protection of an outward form without any obvious understanding of the Gospel it has evolved to reveal. At its best, as the SMH correspondent Elizabeth Farrelly will say, it lifts the worshipper, through all his/her senses to the very throne of grace. When I rejoined John May as his Vice Principal seven years later, it was clear that a Church, struggling to retain its vigour, orthodoxy, and capacity to engage an increasingly secular society with the Gospel, would rather scapegoat the Principal than tackle with him the issues he was manfully struggling to address in a rapidly changing cultural environment. Ordained in 1966, it is important to be reminded that my first few years of ministry were faithfully fulfilled through the 1662 Prayer Book (in its 1928 form). One of the residual jewels of this experience is being able to remember by rote many of the wonderful collects that were its crowning jewel.

I was hopeful, but not confident of first class honours. To achieve it, I had to surpass the achievement of my peers for the previous decade. The results finally came in the mail in January 1966. Margaret opened the envelope before I returned from my day in the sun pulling marijuana.

---

40 Anglo Catholicism in its modern form owes its origins to the 19th century Oxford Movement and figures such as John Keble and Edward Pusey who defended the Church of England as a divine institution with origins in apostolic times. They also defended the Book of Common Prayer as a worthy depository of orthodox faith. The Oxford Movement emanated in much missionary work in the 19th and 20th centuries. Sadly, it is now a very pale shadow of its former self.

The result was a source of great joy. In fact, David Crain had also achieved first class honours at a marginally higher average than me. No other St John's graduate was to achieve the same result for the next 20 or more years.

We moved to Inverell in late January 1966 just prior to my ordination on 2 February, the Feast of Purification. The little weatherboard cottage, our new home had served the previous year as an extension space for Sunday School and showed some of the scars. We were told we could paint it, a task we undertook with relish and pride as the little cottage was gradually transformed. Interestingly, Margaret chose a light shade of green for our retirement home at Long Beach, clearly the less subtle green we slopped on the walls of the Inverell curacy has remained in her subconscious as the colour of homemaking! The bathroom was three steps lower than the rest of the house, flood water found its rather muddy way through during periods of heavy rain. A chip-heater warmed the water, lighting it a task that had to be remembered in advance.

The ordination was a proud moment, shared with Professor John Bishop, Rod Turner and Tony Michael. We were Bishop Clive Kerle's first ordinands and the last to come from Morpeth.[41] Bishop Kerle was kind, generous and pastorally motivated. However, he did not share John Moyes' vision for a Diocese which embraced both an evangelical and catholic stream, nor from his metropolitan background did he have a great understanding of rural life. Sadly, from the outset of his ministry, the battle lines were drawn between the two traditions of the Diocese. Diocesan occasions, including ordinations, became moments for point scoring. Unfortunately, the senior clergy of the Diocese felt increasingly let down and their contributions either not understood or not valued. This feeling was exasperatingly felt by Archdeacon Cliff Rothero of Glen Innes, Canon Gerry Baker of Tamworth, Archdeacon John Stockdale of Tamworth, and Canon Bob Marshall of Narrabri. I know this frustration

---

41 St John's began its life in 1898 in Armidale under the leadership of Bishop Arthur Green. Its vision was to serve the needs of the church in rural NSW.

Ordination Day February 2 1966.

Ordained to the priesthood February 1967.

and deep disappointment was also felt by the Cathedral Dean, Evan Wetherell. He had been brought to the Diocese by Bishop Moyes as a broad Evangelical, but evangelicalism formed at Moore College, in the Diocese of Sydney was another breed all together. How is it so different? An answer that has made a lot of sense resulted from a recent conversation with Professor James Haire.[42] 'Sydney, he explained, is not a Protestant Diocese but a Puritan Diocese'. I said: 'I like your definition sufficiently to repeat it, but explain what this means'! 'Well' he said, 'Protestantism is commitment to reform within a context, Puritanism is commitment to an ideology regardless of context'. That seems to approach a truth many intuitively feel but are unable to articulate.

The Diocese of Armidale that I knew was committed to serving the whole community in Christ's name and to embracing the whole community in its membership. The Diocese that has emerged is a 'membership' diocese, where 'Christians' become defined as those who have had made commitment to a formula of belief through a conversion experience. Such a definition leaves me on the outside. I do not have a single experience of conversion, but a journey through which stories and people, places and events, have contrived to make me assert with some confidence that 'Jesus is the Christ the Son of the Living God and that in him I have life'.

A good example of the Church I inherited can be illustrated by my first visit to the Inverell District Hospital for their weekly Holy Communion. Our pastoral visit, the previous day, had ascertained which patients would like to receive Communion. I nervously took the reserved sacrament from the Church to the hospital to administer the sacrament to these people, shadowed by the Vicar, Father Ralph Evans. Commencing in the men's public ward, (more than a dozen beds) I began to pull a curtain around the beds of those who were to participate. Ralph roared, 'Pull those curtains back. The grace of God is not to be restricted. You will stand in the middle of the ward and with a loud voice you will pray for and with all members of the ward. Don't forget the whole host of heaven has come to be with those in their hospital beds today!' Suitably rebuked and with head in the book

---

42 Professor James Haire was the Dean of the Brisbane College of Theology when I was its President. He became National President of the Uniting Church in Australia and then the Executive Director of the Australian Centre for Christianity and Culture in Canberra.

I began to lead the prayers. 'Louder', he said: 'and keep your head out of the book'. When we came to give Communion, the numbers receiving were more than double those who had indicated their intention the day before. I took Ralph's point and throughout all my subsequent years as a parish priest followed the same pattern, encouraging my curates to do the same. Those early years of ministry were to see packed Churches, large confirmations, and vibrant membership of children and youth groups. There are a variety of cultural reasons why more than 40 years later it is a vastly different era. However, it is my contention that the church has made a profoundly serious mistake by increasingly identifying its membership with those who are drawn out from the world rather than identifying with those who are immersed in the world.

February 2, 1966, the day of my ordination, was a Friday. On the Saturday Ralph insisted I complete the Parish pew sheet. Fortunately, I taught myself to type in the three months following the end of the academic year. Using Margaret's portable typewriter, I began to cut the two stencils required. Copious red corrector fluid was necessary. Remembering which side was reversed was tricky; eventually I had the stencils cut. The next task is one that I do not care to remember. Running off copies on the Gestetner was the dirtiest of jobs: it was less than edifying to be using a machine which was used to bad language being expressed in its direction! By about 9.00pm I had the 300 or so copies run off and took them across to Ralph. He had a quick look through and stated the obvious, they were a mess. I started again and finished in the early hours of Sunday morning. The first celebration was at 7.00.am, at which I had been asked to preach. As folk departed, they were polite; but I am sure my first sermon was less than convincing. As we processed into St Augustine's for the main celebration at 9.30.am, Ralph leaned forward and said: 'We did agree you would preach at this service didn't we?' There had been no such agreement but preach I did. As I did at Gilgai for their harvest festival later in the morning, at Elsmore for their service in the afternoon and back at St Augustine's for the well-attended evensong that night. I had been told that under Ralph you either went under or you thrived. Margaret has always maintained that Ralph was the makings of me. From that first day, I learned a style which has enabled me to respond no matter what the circumstance and to fit in no matter what the reason for the gathering. I agree with Margaret, I have a lot of reasons to be grateful to Ralph, for the opportunities he gave me and for the excellence in performance that he demanded of me.

Ralph's strong personality and somewhat eccentric style polarised the congregation. Many absolutely idealised him and an almost equal number were infuriated by him. However, this did not seem to affect Church attendance, the main services were always packed. In my second year I confronted his strongest critic and asked why he still bothered to attend? He replied that he would not like to be down the street on Monday and hear about some eccentricity or extravagance and not have firsthand knowledge of it! It was relatively easy for a curate to be a focus of discontent. Young as I was, somehow, I intuitively understood this, I did my best to be loyal throughout my two years in the Parish. This loyalty was not hard because I genuinely loved him, however there were many who had reason, some quite justified, for being aggrieved. The experience was an early lesson in the importance of loyalty. It is tempting to gain cheap credibility in the eyes of some by taking sides, but such action seldom if ever brings glory to the gospel. Loyalty in Christian ministry is essential, loyalty both to those who have authority as well as loyalty to those for whom one is responsible. When loyalty dies ministry is at best ineffective and at worst collapses. Loyalty needs also to extend to those who have served before and to those who will follow. Half my years in active ministry have been spent as a Bishop. I support the maxim that you give 100% support to all whom you have appointed, unless or until their ministry is terminated. This loyalty does not extend to supporting or indeed accepting unacceptable behaviour. I will come back to this later.

Ralph Evans was an activist in ministry, experimental with technology, flamboyant in liturgical style. He could flare up very quickly, but with equal speed the emotion ebbed away. (At a Parish Council meeting, a verbal dual between Ralph and one of his main adversaries overtook both the business and dynamic of the meeting. To resolve the situation, he invited the person concerned to step outside so that they could settle their differences)!

He used the Roman Missal, but never quite found his place! His sermons were colourful and entertaining. The great occasions, Christmas, Easter Pentecost, Patronal Festival, etc. were celebrated with energy and passion. After an extremely complicated liturgy for the blessing of the Baptismal waters on Easter Saturday, ready for the reaffirmations on Easter Day, I retreated to the cottage for a rest. There was an earnest knock on the door. Mrs Burtenshaw, the cleaner, looked very distressed. Margaret and I insisted she come in sit down and have a cup of tea. I asked what was wrong. She replied that she had done a terribly wicked thing. I was not convinced that even in her most wild moments Mrs Burtenshaw was capable of a mildly naughty thing let alone a wicked thing, so I pressed her as to what this wicked thing might be. She said: 'I was cleaning around the font and without thinking I have pulled the plug, all the blessed water has gone'. She looked quite ashen. I did my best to reassure her. She was even more shocked when I insisted that she finish her cup of tea while I slipped over to the Church and refilled the font. Ralph never knew and I am certain that the renewal of all our vows that year were particularly blessed because of the faithfulness of that dear lady.

In one important area of pastoral ministry Ralph's confidence seemed to leave him—pastoral care *in extremis*. Consequently, I found myself involved with situations which were really beyond me in the early months of ministry. All I had to fall back on was the clinical pastoral education I had received as part of my training in the cancer ward of the Austin hospital in Melbourne.

The first critical incident followed a horrific road accident in which the young adult daughter of the owners of Inverell Station, was critically injured. I rushed to the accident and emergency ward to find a team of doctors working desperately on this poor woman. She laid naked and unconscious on the stretcher with obvious signs of her injuries. I felt terrified and woefully inadequate. One of the medics signaled me forward. I had brought the oil of unction from the church and stumbled through the words of anointing. I felt embarrassed by my own inadequacy and terrified by the thought that I was here as a representative of the God who heals and restores and yet this beautiful young lady was clearly going to die. The image of her death has remained with me. Other images of dying have also stayed, either because of the tortuous and terrified journey of the dying, or its opposite, the serenity and peace of the departure. In this case I am remembering my own fear and total ineptitude. It took years of experience to learn to trust God in these moments and the ability to enable a space in which the journey of the spirit takes precedence over the last desperate clinical and technical endeavours of the medical team.

If I am ever to be in that position, I would like someone to walk into the room and exude the quiet confidence of the presence of God. What is said and done is of far less importance than the quality of presence that is imbued. However, in bringing that confidence, talk to me in Jesus' name: I will be listening, even though unconscious.

The second critical incident was even more tragic. Barbara and Brian Tester were members of the congregation along with their lovely five-year-old daughter, Kirsty. Kirsty contracted measles and became quite ill. She was taken to the District Hospital suffering dehydration, her condition rapidly deteriorated. She died before I arrived. I had known the Testers sufficiently to understand why Kirsty was special. There had been a long series of miscarriages. The possibility of another child was extremely remote, enquiries had already commenced which eventually led to an adoption. There was so little to say that made any sense. We stayed around Kirsty's bed, as the tears freely flowed. Eventually Barbara began to hum 'Jesus loves me this I know for the Bible tells me so'. It felt right and better than a thousand words. It is easy to be dismissive of such simplicity.

Morris West[43] in his final book, *A View from the Ridge*[44], says that when he was young he was certain of all manner of things, now in his old age he says he is certain of very little, except this one thing: *Jesus loves me, this I know for the Bible tells me so.*

Around 7.00.am the following morning the phone rang, Barbara asked if I could come around as something had happened that she wanted to talk through. When I arrived, Brian had already left for work, keeping the vestiges of normality going is often the best way of coping. I had no idea what to expect. It is hard to describe the Barbara I met that morning. Tears were still clearly visible and yet there was also a sense of peace that I was not expecting. We sat at the kitchen table as she explained her experience. She said: 'I slept a little but awoke early. I had been awake for some time when I was conscious of a light'. She went on to explain that it was not the bedroom light that had suddenly come on, but more the light of someone's presence. She said she then heard Kirsty's voice say: 'please do not be sad mummy, I am OK and we will meet again'.

Barbara asked me to confirm she was not mad and to explain what I thought had happened. It would be quite easy, if not somewhat patronising, to talk of profound stress, the activity of the mind that is half asleep and half awake, which mixes reality with projected hopes. While at that time I had no personal experience of such a phenomenon, I was aware of many who had, including folk I talked with regularly in the Hospital and Nursing Home. Subsequently I did have a similar experience as I have recorded on page 93. It was exactly what I needed to hear at the time and the effect was

43 Morris West is perhaps Australia's best religious author as a reading of *The Devil's Advocate* or the *Shoes of the Fisherman* will quickly confirm. In his early years he entered a seminary to train for the priesthood, but he is better known for his books which enhance faith while challenging ecclesiastical certitude. I was very blessed that he accepted an invitation, along with Mick Dodson and Peter Hollingworth to speak at a forum of ideas which helped launch the Australian Centre for Christianity and Culture in 1995.

44 Published in 1999.

transformational. Barbara's experience did not take away her enormous sense of loss, but it did give her an assurance which was transformational, and which gifted her in a surprising manner, she found a gift of poetry.

Both critical moments changed me. I studied my formal theology, a theology of the mind, at St John's and achieved creditably well. But I really learned a theology of the heart in my first curacy and am forever grateful. I learned through these experiences, and subsequently hundreds of others, that God is not responsible for the painful and tragic circumstances of life. God suffers with us. However, God does work an extraordinary act of redemption through them, if we are open to it. It is not that they happen in order that God can be redemptive, but rather they become a rich soil for transformation, a depth that is seldom replicated in the passing moments of success, or even triumph, with which life occasionally seduces us.

The summary of life is not to be weighed through the things that happen to us but weighed through the changes that are wrought in us through these activities, both good and bad. We are familiar with the trials and tribulations of Job and the wrestling he had with the three comforters, with Elihu, and finally, with God out of the whirlwind. The book, and these struggles, come to an extraordinary climax when Job blurts out *'I had heard of you by the hearing of the ear, but now my eye sees you'* (Job 42:5). Through the hearing of the ear Barbara encountered words, but her experience was bathed in light as an inner understanding of the presence of God dawned upon her.

In 1967 Ralph invited Father Gordon Coad and Father Bill Childs, priests of the Newcastle Diocese, to conduct a week's mission. Some years later Bill invited me to conduct a Mission for him in the Parish of Hamilton, Newcastle. It was probably the most challenging week of my ministry, then or since. Bill was a priest of extraordinary energy and zeal. Every day commenced at 7.00. am with prayer and meditation followed by a Eucharist. We were expected to have thoroughly read one national newspaper before the prayers began, for, as Bill stated, how do you know what to pray for unless you know what is going on in God's world. Since that time, I have been as committed to reading a paper of substance as I have to daily Bible readings. Bill was convinced that if you did not find God in the world you would not find him anywhere. While there was an expectation that folk would be in Church every evening, to the best of the missioners' ability they had already been encountered in the community first. In the days before the mission officially began all the pubs were visited, Bill would simply bang on the bar, tell the publican he wished to speak with the men and then launch into his spiel. Shops and sporting clubs were also visited, as were all the schools. Each evening the Church was full. Both missioners were competent musicians and led the congregation with as much energy through the music as the preaching. On the final evening commitment cards were handed out which needed to be returned at the Sunday Eucharist. This commitment included an altar call. My memory is that these returned cards provided Ralph and me with follow up which took many weeks to complete.

Missions like this have long since disappeared from the ecclesiastical landscape. These days what passes for a mission is a challenge to those who are already members of the Christian community. Recent involvement in the parishes of Yetminster, Diocese of Salisbury, and Moruya, Diocese of Canberra and Goulburn, has reignited my appetite for imaginative, creative engagement with the wider community. It remains my conviction that most folk have an experience of God which leaves them with a desire for that experience to be named and validated. Unfortunately, the formal language of church is not a conduit which connects with the vast majority.

From the outset we have lived an 'open house'. A couple with their child were the first of many to shelter under our roof and to experience Margaret's generosity of kitchen and heart. I am probably guilty most of the time for issuing the invitation without giving adequate thought to the consequences. Margaret was always the most generous and willing of providers. It later turned out that the couple were not strictly in need and we had been taken advantage of. The trouble is, how can you take the risk of refusing when the need may be desperate? Over the years many have been fed from our door and a few have stayed.

One who stayed regularly was Frank, a traveler who made his home with us in Singleton on roughly an annual basis. When he arrived, the boys would walk behind him with an air-freshener until he reached the downstairs shower and his clothes had been dropped into the washing machine. When he had eaten, he would sit down and regale us with gossip about the life of the Church from Victoria to Queensland! He would generally stay for a week to ten days, doing odd jobs. If others knocked on the door seeking a handout when Frank was with us, he would see them off! He had no time for folk who wanted a handout without doing something in return. One evening we left him in charge of the boys. He made Tim take off his shirt and wash out the tomato sauce before he would let him go to band practice! Were we foolish in those days to trust a 'traveler' with the care of the children, or has society lost the level of trust that enabled this reciprocity to be possible?

Prior to the building of the Copeton Dam the little village of Copeton was one of my pastoral responsibilities. Amongst many others I used to visit a couple who loved one another, but for whom alcohol fueled violence was a major issue. One afternoon I was called to the Inverell police station because the woman had asked for me. I rushed down and asked for a briefing before I saw the woman. I was informed the man had come home drunk as he had a thousand times before and then beaten her. It was the last straw. When he fell asleep on the verandah rocking chair, she took the 22 rifle from its place on the wall and shot him in the forehead at point blank range. The extraordinary thing was that he was still alive. She had been charged with attempted murder. I went into the 'lock-up' and did my best to comfort her, assuring her that he was indeed still alive. Initially this information was absolutely no comfort as she bewailed her own incompetence, even in this.

As we now know domestic violence is one of our nation's most serious pandemics with one in three women suffering physical abuse sometime during their lifetime and one in five sexual abuse. This is a far more serious reality than home grown terrorism. Its origins lie in an accepted gender inequality from which the Church is far from guiltless. I am personally aware of many occasions when a priest has counselled a woman to go back to an abusive man on the basis that he is the 'head of the house'. 'Headship' may have its place, but in as much as it gives rise to inequity between genders it has no place in Christian teaching. In marriage both men and women are subject to their marriage vows and serve each other through them.

I left the police station and hurried to the hospital to see the man. What I was about to encounter remains as astonishing today as it was then. The 22 bullet that hit his forehead split in two, one piece superficially entering his skull and exiting right with the other piece grazing his skull and ricocheting out though his left ear lobe. He was groggy but conscious. He asked after his wife without rancour or anger. The rest is a long story, but for the remainder of our time in Inverell they came to Church Sunday by Sunday, holding hands, dropping a dozen eggs into our cottage on the way!

In 1968 we moved back to Armidale and again were well taught, this time by Dean Evan Wetherell. He was himself a fine preacher and an exceptionally good pastoral administrator. The Cathedral was pretty much full three times every Sunday.

From the Dean I learned punctuality. He had a clock in every room of the Deanery. Before each service we stood in the vestry, after prayers, looking at the second hand on the vestry clock. We processed into the cathedral precisely at the advertised time: an important lesson which sadly is not these days to be relied upon. In addition, I was expected to be in the vestry half an hour before the service began robed and quietly ready. I have done my best to follow this pattern ever since. Only once have I been late, or more truthfully forgot altogether. I was settling down one evening in Brisbane to watch the news when I received a phone call from Phillip Freier (later Archbishop of Melbourne and Primate) the rector of St Oswald's Banyo. 'Are you enjoying the evening' he enquired. 'Yes' I responded. 'Good' he said, 'we are also having good evening, the Church is full, and 15 candidates are ready for their confirmation'. While most of the blood receded from my head there was sufficient left to apologise and say I would be there in 20 minutes.

'Don't rush' said Philip 'we will sing a few hymns and cover some of the non-bishop bits!' Fortunately, that evening I did not encounter any of Brisbane's radar police.

From Evan Wetherell I also learned to manage a busy schedule. He would say, 'Do not worry if you are over booked in the evenings. What you should do is go to the first function, move around, shake everyone's hand, quietly slip out the back and go to the next, repeating the same strategy. If necessary, go to another. Slip home, put your feet up and then return to each function doing the same thing. Folk will think you have been there all night!' From both curacies I learnt to expect that work does not discriminate between morning, afternoon, and evening. I have been concerned in recent times that clergy are conscious of the clock and certainly do not expect to be on constant call, or indeed to work more than eight hours a day.

Another important lesson I learned from the Dean was the need, when presiding, to pray the service, not read it. Collects had to be learned by heart as was the rest of the service. I have practiced this art over the years, putting to memory seasonal greetings, blessings, prayers, etc. It makes a huge difference to the way the service is perceived by the congregation.

I also learned that you cannot always expect to remember names, but you can learn tricks. At the cathedral door, the Dean would keep his eye on at least three behind the person in front of him. If he was unsure of the name, he would either ask the person in his immediate vicinity to glance that way and help, or he would have a person standing nearby with the express task of prompting, (this needs skilled discretion), or if things were desperate, when the unknown or forgotten person came alongside, he would apologise and ask the person for their name. When thy replied 'Bill' he would say 'Yes Bill I know, it is your surname I have forgotten'!

While in Armidale we were connected through our television to one of the most memorable events in human history. It is still almost incomprehensible that it occurred so long ago. We had purchased our first black and white set while in Inverell. It was a very heavy square box with numerous valves. These valves constantly 'blew' and I found myself frequently at the electrical retail shop purchasing new ones. On this day it was important that nothing go wrong, it didn't. We sat absolutely glued to the set as we heard Neil Armstrong say: 'One small step for man, one giant leap for mankind'. The moon, the lesser light to rule the night, long the fascination of humanity, sometimes the focus of superstition and evil, for millennia the 'clock' setting seasonal rhythms, including Passover and Easter, had finally met humanity face to face.

Part 2
Giving Account

What does the Lord require of you but to do justice, and to love kindness, and to walk humbly with your God.

Micah 6: 8

Chapter 4
So that is what it is about
Speaking to the Grandchildren

*Earth's crammed with heaven and every common bush afire
with God: but only he who sees takes off his shoes.*[45]

Marriage, family, and ministerial vocation have been intertwined. It is difficult to extract one from the other. It was perhaps inevitable that as formal ministry came to an end in 2007, this ending should be reflected through family. What follows is my presidential address to the synod of the Diocese of Canberra and Goulburn; a reflection not on ministerial activity, but on the pains and joys of living a faithful life. It is in fact a grandfather giving an account of his faith and life to his grandchildren.

Diocese of Canberra and Goulburn
7–9 September 2007 Goulburn NSW

It is a great delight to welcome you to the third session of the 42nd Synod of the Diocese. If anyone is counting you will know that this is my fifteenth session of Synod in the Diocese of Canberra and Goulburn, and my last as your Diocesan Bishop.

It has been an immense pleasure and privilege to have been your Bishop. I will miss it very much—up to a point. I will not miss, even for a second,

45 Elizabeth Barrett Browning. *Aurora Leigh.*

the daily grind of sorting out problems, dealing with issues and the stresses that go with it. I will not miss the struggles and trials that go with running a large institution. But I will miss trailing along with God in your company, doing my best to keep up. This has been a privilege beyond words; there has never been a moment in the last 15 years when I have not felt this is the only place I have wanted to be. I can say, through the grace of God, there has never been a day when I have not sought to give the best I could. I am sorry for those occasions when that best was not good enough.

For a fleeting moment I thought of trying to give an account of my stewardship over the last 15 years, but that was never a serious option, the Synod itself, up to a point, is going to do that.

You will know that Margaret and I have recently become grandparents to twins, Jessica and Benjamin. I have crafted this synod charge as a letter to them and through them to all the grand children, and I would be glad if you would listen in.

My Dear Jessica and Benjamin, Samuel, Zachery Matthew, Anna, Noah, Tommy, and Bella

Welcome! Welcome to a world of wonder and delight, welcome to a world of meaning and purpose, of grace and destiny, of fulfilment and mystery—welcome to God's world. Welcome to a world that is at once inexplicable, unjust, manipulative, distorted by the misuse of power at every level, a world of pain and alienation, of injustice and greed, a world in which the righteous are not always rewarded or the evil punished; but, at the same time, welcome to a world deeply and profoundly loved by its creator, a world in which you will discover heaven and earth kiss one another, time and eternity embrace, a world in which meaning and destiny is revealed, empowered and renewed in the dying and rising of Jesus—keep your eyes on Him, this is the secret. Welcome also to a world in which the way you play your part is profoundly significant for you, for every life you touch, and for destiny itself; a world in which the company you keep matters, for you will become that company.

I wonder what you are going to make of it all. I wonder what you will make of my life, the life of your grandfather, of the contribution

I have made, and the opportunities I have wasted. I am sure you will wonder why I have spent so much time and energy on some things and not on others, why I did not see things more clearly, why I have been so slow to respond, why I have not thought more about your world and the impact my life has had upon it.

But more, I wonder what contribution you will make, what values you will hold, what beliefs you will make your own, with what stories you will identify and be prepared to pass on; what hopes you will cherish. I wonder how the knowledge that you are profoundly loved will make an indelible impact upon your life, or whether you will refuse any meaning to life, see it as a hotchpotch of circumstances without any meaning or purpose.

I want to tell you that we live in, and by, Hope. It undergirds everything we are. I hope for a world in which God's Kingdom comes on earth as it is in Heaven, a sustainable and just world, a world in which the Servant, the Lamb, reigns.

I need to say that for me the fundamentals of belief have been reduced in size as I have got older, but they are like stars of certainty in my spirit. I know and believe God is. I know and believe God has come in Jesus, and all I need to know about God and about myself, is revealed in Him. I know and believe the Spirit of God, the Spirit of Jesus, is the wind that should constantly fill my sails. With all my heart I can say I do want to be where God is, to find out what God is doing, and do that. To sum it up, I know that life is on offer, I want to say 'yes' to life, I know that when I say 'yes' to Jesus, I say 'yes' to life.

Jessica and Benjamin, I have no desire to limit your growth in spirit except to say, live and search within those fundamentals. While you have breath, life is to be lived, and your searching will not be over. You will need to give your life to God in Jesus every day, otherwise, it will be as if you never gave your life in the first place. Be very wary of people who present you with too much certainty, it is most probable that they have long since stopped their personal journey of exploration.

I believe in God because I cannot make any sense of this world without God. I believe in God because God, God in Jesus, is personally real to me. I believe in God as Trinity because if God is the source of everything, you should be able to see the hand of God in the created order and in human experience. I see the Trinitarian God everywhere. Everything belongs to everything else just like the members of the Trinity belong to each other. Nothing can exist on its own; we human beings live in communities just as God, in Trinity, is community. I believe the ultimate truth is relationship, just as God is relationship. I hope this does not sound over the top, but I find thinking about God as exciting as thinking about the Wallabies winning the World Cup—perhaps a tad more certain! I believe in the God of Jesus because pitching my tent fully in the person God has made me, in the time that God has given to me, with the people God has surrounded me, is my human vocation, just as God has pitched his tent in Jesus amongst, and with us all.

When you are a little older, you will begin to hear and understand the stories of our faith, the stories of Jesus. The Gospel story tells us that it is all about life. Jesus came that we might have life. We are invited to choose life. It is said that when Jesus began his ministry, he came proclaiming the Kingdom of God. It has taken me a long time to nut out what this Kingdom of God is. I have come to understand it to be where the Life of God is celebrated. Of course, where Jesus is, God's life is perfectly celebrated. Where love reigns, the Kingdom of God is present, it is also present where forgiveness is offered, and received, where folk are freed from living as victims, enabling the present to be experienced, without being overshadowed by the past. The Kingdom is also present where an act of generosity buries a culture of meanness, and hospitality overcomes alienation. The Kingdom of God is therefore not restricted to the Church, this is a rather humbling thing for me to say, having been a leader in the Church all my adult life; however, it is the distinct calling of the Church to herald or proclaim the kingdom and to be humble in spirit in the knowledge that daily living in the Church does not always point to it. The Roman Catholic Church, in some of its recent pronouncements, has tended to say that it, and the Kingdom of God, are the same. This is rather sad for them, for in believing the Kingdom can be institutionalised, let alone restricted by the pronouncements of some old men, they are less likely to be able to be surprised by its coming, or to recognise it when it is present.

I naturally hope you will become committed members of the Church, Anglican of course, but you and the Spirit will need to constantly reshape that Church, so that it might continue to be a worthy vehicle of God's mission, as well as the home in which you are most comfortable to hang your boots.

I am particularly interested in the new emerging forms of Church. In our Diocese, I am fascinated by the development of Basement Ministries and Open Sanctuary, as well as our newest geographically based church at Lanyon and the fact it has coffee half-way through the service! Having just returned from Africa I feel deeply drawn to the culture, music, and colour of our two Sudanese congregations. I will die an Anglican, not simply because I was born one, but because I love it dearly. It has been a rich and fulfilling home to me. I love its history and tradition, (do not let anyone tell you it is a Protestant Church), I love both its Catholicity and its Reformed nature, I love its incarnational leanings, its desire always to be immersed in the world of which it is a part; I love its capacity to embrace all people and to wrestle with the nuances of faith, while at the same time being rock solid on the fundamentals. I love its universality and its refusal to allow any single congregation, or Diocese for that matter, to be fully the Church without the rest, but I also love the freedom and independence it gives to the local community. I love its capacity to take the shape it needs for the sake of God's mission, wherever it finds itself, if folk have the courage to accept that freedom and be accountable with it. I love its heroes of the past and its diverse communities in the present; I love its courage to stand up for the voiceless and to be a voice for justice in the world. I do worry about its seeming lack of relevance to any generation other than my own, but because of its deep and abiding treasures, I have no doubt you and God will sort that out. Benjamin, I worry that females are more demonstrative with their faith than males, and yet I see commitment to faith, living out its values and disciplines, as about the manliest thing you can do.

It is trendy to criticise the Church for being an outdated institution. The reality is that any aspect of life that is worth preserving beyond a generation, has some institutional elements. The Church is no different; the trick is to distinguish that which is essential, from that which is peripheral.

As you know members of your family back as far as your great grandfather and great grandmother have been, in their own ways, leaders within the Church.[46] I hope you will consider this as a possible vocation for yourselves, and that you will ask yourselves why you shouldn't, as much as why you should.

Now, I would like to take you by the hand to places and people where I have found God's life, before inviting you to take my hand that we might together explore the stories yet to be told, and to visit the places so far unseen.

First come with me to the world of story:

All that has ever happened in the past has become a story; all that is happening now is becoming a story, while the future waits to become known in story. I would like to share with you the story of my birth during the Second World War, of my growing up on the land, of the influence of a large family, of the adventure of migration, of the movement from stud groom/jackeroo to theological student and falling in love with your grandmother. When I tell you the story it is the meaning you and I give to it, the life direction it provides for us, and the capacity it has to give us life, that will be more important than the detail itself. So, it is with the way in which God has become known to us. The details of the story are far less important than the life directions we gain from it, the influence it has in our lives, and the capacity it has to make sense of our own little life story, connecting it to the great story of God, and God's purpose for all. (It never ceases to sadden me that so many folks stop only with the details, the literal telling, and miss the values, the truth the story has to tell. While you are children you will not fall into that trap, your enquiring, imaginative minds won't let you. I hope the company you keep will prevent you from doing it when you become adults).

I do not know who the first human beings were, or where they lived, or how long ago they lived, but I do know that like them, you and I are made in the image of God, like them, you and I live between the waters that are above the earth that bring blessing, and the waters below the earth which constantly threaten darkness chaos and destruction, I open

---

46 Appendix 3: Ordained members of the Family.

my spirit in longing for the first, while constantly putting my big foot in the second. You and I are Adam/dust, you and I are his descendant Noah. Like them we must be prepared to die (empty ourselves) to live: the ones who were saved in the great flood were the ones who entered the coffin –the ark. Like the men and women who built the Tower of Babel, the puffed-up towers you and I build are an affront to God and a source of confusion for those around us.

Jessica and Benjamin, I long for you to know and be immersed in the great sacred stories. However, I would rather you never heard the stories in the first place than that you heard them with the ears of a fundamentalist. You can be no greater gift to the world of your generation than to live with a heart of faith; you can be no greater danger to the world of your generation than to be a person of closed mind, of arrogant certainty, one who puts themself in a place of greater worth, truth or value, than others. Islamist fundamentalists are well known for their danger to the world; their evil acts are done in the name of their God. Jewish fundamentalists, Zionists, are not so universally seen as a great threat, but their very attitude to ownership of others' land, is a contributing reason for the rise of Islamist fundamentalism. Christian fundamentalism has contributed to an imperialist and arrogant intrusion into the lives of others, exemplified most shamefully by the influence of the religious and political right in events post September 11. (It does not take one long travelling in the poorer countries of the world to discover that the powerful countries of the world, countries which are generally understood to be Christian, are despised for the way in which they are perceived to interfere in the lives of others, and to manipulate politics, and trade, in their favour).

At this stage of the 21st Century, sadly, I could not say whether religion generally, and the Abrahamic religions in particular, are going to contribute to a world of respect, human dignity, openness and justice, or whether these religions between them are going to contribute to some of the most intractable, bitter and alienating struggles the world has seen. God may have to do some bypassing of the very institutions that claim his patronage. Benjamin and Jessica, I pray that you will always be on the side of openness, of respect, of listening and courageous justice.

This is the side Jesus is always on. If this leaves you in the minority, if you end up worshiping in a Church without great numbers, (for certainty of any kind will always draw a crowd), do not be anxious, for Jesus himself predicted that the gate is narrow that leads to eternal life. Do not be cowed by those who want to tell you that faith is about spiritual matters alone, not matters of this world; on the contrary, journey with the One who took human flesh, this is the only way that can lead to the Kingdom of Heaven where the angels of God welcome the faithful from every tribe and nation.

Story then is all about your inner transformation. The greatest story of all is the story of Jesus, his coming amongst us, his dying for and with us, and his resurrection; sealing victory over death. What belongs to Him belongs to us because we belong to him. A new day has indeed dawned.

Let me now take you from story into the lives of those the Bible tells us God loves the most—the poor.

On the 15 June this year, in the company of 15 young people from the Diocese, I arrived in the black township of Guguletu, Capetown. Like hundreds of other townships throughout South Africa, Guguletu is the legacy of apartheid, a legacy of continuing separation and generational poverty that is unlikely to change any time soon. We arrived at 2.30am and under police escort we were taken to our billets. The township seldom, if ever, sees the face of a white South African. While we were there the water worked sometimes, but not always, the same with the electricity and the sewerage. Many of the people are unemployed. The official figure for HIV/AIDS in South Africa is 25% of the population, but it is known to be much higher in the townships. On the edge of all the townships are countless numbers of shanties where people eke out a living in circumstances which most of us in Australia cannot imagine. (Mind you, South Africa is a beacon of prosperity compared with Zimbabwe.) And yet in the township we experienced a sense of community which is rare anywhere in Australia. We experienced a sense of joy and expansiveness of time which is almost absent from many of our lives, and in the faith community we experienced a commitment and exuberant faith which most of us have never known. Sunday worship at St Mary Magdalene's lasted

4.15 hours. It was full of singing and dancing (Africans worship with their whole being) and it was driven by the spontaneous exuberance of the laity; Anglo Catholic in its worship style and Evangelistic in its message; it was led by the charismatically gifted priest Father Mxolisi Mpanbani. St Mary Magdalene's on Sunday morning had something of the exuberant loving generosity of its patron. Father Mxolisi said that when Africans sing, they forget their pain.

Jessica and Benjamin, I do not want to romanticise poverty, poverty is painful and at times humiliating, poor people are not saints either; we saw some shameful acts of terror against others, and we observed the need, even in poverty, for the human ego to flourish. However, to be present amongst such people is to be open to the cleansing of the soul like no other experience. I want to tell you that being in the company of the poor has been one of the most enriching experiences of my life. Yes, I want to do something about their poverty, to speak for them, to bring about some justice for them; but to be with them, to live, even for a little while, where they live, to eat from their most generous table, to sleep in their most humble circumstance, is a gift. I do hope you will go out of your way to understand and listen to the poor of the world by being present with them, if only for a little while.

Presence is another way of understanding the Kingdom of God. God in Jesus has become present with us. God has taken our flesh, has taken our human condition. If in the future either of you aspires to a position of leadership then you should consider it essential to be present to the poorest or most marginalised of those for whom you have responsibility. Many of the worst traits of human nature arise out of a refusal to be truly present. You could say the world is divided between those who will always want to be present in the place they find themselves and with the people who share their company, and the cynics. Cynics are those who choose always to be disconnected observers, separating themselves from the people and events around them. Many years ago, your grandmother and I visited a refugee camp on the border of Thailand and Burma. We were fed with the rice ration of the refugees. It was an experience that changed our lives. Since then I have never been seduced by the tables of the rich and powerful. Come with me therefore into the lives of those who are different to our own, lest you fall into the trap of judging that which you do not know, or presuming that which should not have been taken for granted. I hope neither of you will ever be materially poor, however, I would rather you were materially poor, than spiritually poor. To be spiritually poor means there will be no resources to draw upon for your inner transformation.

The final leg of the recent Youth Pilgrimage took us to the Holy Land and contact with the Christian community there. Yes, we did visit many of the Sacred Sites, most of them left us feeling cold, but what we will not forget is our meeting with the Christian community, the Palestinian Christian community, the remaining 2% or less of the population who follow the man from Nazareth. Their plea was 'Do not forget us. Do not let the world forget us. Remind the world that we are displaced people. Remind the world we are people who wish to live at peace. Remind the world we are the indigenous people, named amongst those present on the Day of Pentecost. Remind the world that they should not come and visit the Holy Stones of the Holy Land, without visiting the Living Stones, the faith communities.' I hope you will both visit the Holy Land and that in visiting you will not be put off by the fear that engulfs folk on all sides. I hope you will spend time with those who find it so difficult to be heard, with those whose pain should not be borne alone. Jessica and Benjamin, put yourself about amongst the poor and needy and be transformed by them, in the transformation you will find Christ has transformed you.

Wilderness/Difficulty is the place where God is intensely present:

I now want to take a risk and lead you to difficulty, or wilderness, as a place in which I have found God to be intensely present and to encourage you not to be afraid of difficulty. It will occur in your life often enough. In the tradition of our faith, wilderness is sought as a place where God can be intensely found. Sometimes wilderness comes upon us without being sought. I want to tell you of a difficulty I have experienced, and how it has been a gift to me.

In 1984, before I became a Bishop, on one occasion I did something I should not have done and for which I have always felt ashamed.

The other person, while freely participating, had every right to be cross with me, your grandmother even more so. I accept full responsibility. In 1999 this matter took on a life of its own through the processes of the Church. While officially advised it was not a matter about which I should resign, nevertheless, I felt I should. I will be forever profoundly grateful to the senior staff of the Diocese who were unwavering in their support, and fearless in their counsel. I cannot thank your father and your two uncles enough; they rang literally hundreds of people who deserved to hear from us, before they heard indirectly through the media. Your grandmother and I were humbled by the folk, who with extraordinary generosity, assisted us financially; similarly, we are much in the debt of the Bishop who offered me his largest Parish and that Parish for keeping the offer open until the Diocese of Canberra and Goulburn had an opportunity to express its will. I will always be immensely grateful to Mr Graham Downie, the Canberra Times reporter, who came to see me in my home, to whom I told the story, even though he was half listening through a transistor radio to a very important AFL game at the time! I did not like seeing what he wrote, but it was fair. Subsequently, I and your grandmother had to read, or hear of numerous other media accounts, which wrote as fact what simply was untrue. As you can imagine it was a time of very great difficulty.

In the intensity of these few weeks, I experienced three moments which I cannot fully explain but would like to recount and you can make of them what you will.

The first was on the day I decided, with advice, to resign, knowing that the press would otherwise relentlessly pursue the story, create conflict, spread opinions not based on fact, and cause even more hurt and embarrassment. I sat for many hours on a rock at the base of Mount Ainslie. After a few hours Bishop Stephen Pickard arrived with bread and wine accompanied by members of my senior staff. Without engaging me in conversation he then commenced to celebrate Holy Communion around me and the rock I was sitting on. It was an extraordinary experience and will be for me, the most intense experience of communion.

The second[47] was a few weeks later, early in the morning. I was awake and clearly feeling sorry for myself. In the silence and breaking light of a new day I heard a voice say: 'George read psalm 43'. This was not just a thought in my head it came to me as an audible voice. I cannot explain how I heard it. If you look it up, you will find that with psalm 42 it has a refrain: 'Why are you so downcast O my soul and why so disquieted within me? Hope in God, for I shall again praise him, my help and my God'.

The third occasion was the day of the synod which asked me to withdraw my resignation. Margaret and I had retreated to Elm Grove the retreat house of the Little Followers of St Francis in the hills outside Tumut. Stress prevented me from being able to move my back, I could stand or lie down but not sit. I took myself off to the riverbank with my bible to think and pray. I decide to do what I advise people not to do, open the bible and take a passage as a revelation for that moment. The bible fell open at the commencement of deutero-Isaiah: 'Comfort O comfort my people says your God. Speak tenderly to Jerusalem and cry to her that she has served her term, that her penalty is paid, she has received from the Lord's hand double for all her sins'.

This was no longer a pain to endure but a gift to cherish.

I do not think we should go searching for difficulty as a source of grace and life, however, I have not previously, or since, known so much personal growth and transformation. I am sure this is why in the tradition of our faith the wilderness is such an important place. The Children of Israel found themselves in the wilderness; Jesus sought the wilderness, as have many godly men and women down the centuries. First, despite intense pain, the sense of the presence of God grew stronger, and not weaker. I do not think your grandmother, or I, for one moment doubted we were carved in the hand of God. Reading the Psalms was an especial source of strength and comfort to us. I should state the obvious, you have the most remarkable grandmother, who through this difficulty suffered at least as much, if not more, than me, and yet never ceased even for one day to be supportive, confident and encouraging that whatever

---

47 Already referenced on page 52.

happened all would be well. In the darkest times, it was she, rather than I, who believed God still had a future for us. We received more than 1,000 letters and cards, messages of goodwill. People will never know what source of encouragement and strength they were, especially the ones from children and from non-Church people whom we barely knew. It was a deep experience of the reality, that light continues to shine, when others care.

Most particularly I want all the members of the Diocese of Canberra and Goulburn, who are looking over my shoulder to read this letter to you both, to know how deeply humbled I have been by their grace, trust, goodwill and acceptance. This has been a gift beyond price which I have never taken for granted. I have felt the loyalty, generosity, and trust of the Diocese to me as Bishop, has been more than I could have ever expected.

And so, Jessica and Benjamin, I now look back on the events of 1999 as a gift. It is part of my story and I am glad, not because of what led to it, but because the big story that God turns all that is dark and painful into life, is true in my experience. May God give you and me grace to feel it as intensely when 'the shades lengthen, the busy world is hushed, the fever of life is over, and our work is done'.

I want also to say that when difficulty strikes, do not drag your feet in it. It will pass; it will have within it the seeds of making you a far better person, and equally the seeds of your own self destruction. Remember, God does God's best creative work through redemption. Re–membering, putting back together takes time and reflection, but that is the role of the prophet in God's name. The lawgivers tell the story, the prophets reinterpret it and call us back to it. In this process, I honestly believe my whole story, including the bad bits, have been redeemed, and through it, creativity has blossomed.

The Future—The Olive Agenda:

Now, Samuel, Zachery, Matthew, Anna, Noah, Tommy, Bella, Benjamin and Jessica, I would like you to take me by the hand into your future, not that it will be disconnected from the reality I have known, but there are various reasons why you will understand your world more thoroughly than I have ever understood mine. May I humbly suggest that a major clue to the understanding of your future is the olive tree.

Yes! The real live tree that spans more generations than we can imagine, producing beautiful oil from the same tree for grandfathers and grandchildren alike; its branch that has become a symbol of peace; and its most famous ground, the Mount of Olives, where Jesus prayed in the Garden of Gethsemane. In addition, I will do my best to explain why I am in the debt of the South African Professor of Theology, Stephen De Gruchy and the novelist Wendell Berry, for developing the olive as a metaphor.

At this moment I am writing on a computer, in a few moments I will warm a drink in the microwave, later today I will send an sms to your mother—all products of the industrial and other technological revolutions, all products of the big economy which drives our world.

However, there is another reality of equal importance to us all, the space in which we live. The word we use for this space is the environment. It is incredibly beautiful; robust but vulnerable; made up of a complex web of individual and independent forms; yet all strangely dependent upon one another. You are now part of this environment. You are both unique, independent and with rights of your own, but you are also utterly dependent and the decisions you make, good or bad, will have an effect upon the balance of every other part of the environment. Another word for the environment is ecology.

I like to understand the whole universe as a single house, created by God, providing for beauty and chaos, beginnings and endings, individuals and families, the simple and the complex, the mundane and the inspirational. In this house we know that, in the image of God, we humans have a unique destiny. Working out what that destiny is to be, that is, the theology of anthropology, is arguably the greatest challenge you will face. It is a more acute challenge for you than it ever was for me, because of the severe global challenges with which your generation will have to grapple. I hope I will be around long enough to catch in the wind a few words of your conversations about these challenges.

I have no doubt you will find this house has two pillars:

Ek nomos or economy—the rules of the house; and

Ek logos or ecology—the wisdom of the house.

I am deeply sorry that my generation has lived as if there was only one pillar supporting this house—the economy. Now, the benefits of the economy are clear. I have already pointed out that you would not be here, an unthinkable possibility, without the economy; but meaning, why you are here, and how you are to live while you are here, has much more to do with the wisdom of the house, the ecology. What your generation must do is find a balance between the two, and perhaps in the short term, place more emphasis on ecology to bring them back as equal partners.

This is where the Olive as a metaphor comes in. Let me explain.

Earlier in this letter I have spoken of the poor of the world and of my challenge not simply to seek to redress their inequities and injustices, but to be willing to be in their company, allowing our lives to be transformed by them. This challenge is to allow the 'law' of the house, the 'Ek nomos' to be applied to all human beings: 'Make Poverty History' is the slogan that goes with it. This is sometimes referred to as the 'brown movement', the world's call to address global economic inequities.

Alongside this legitimate priority is the call for environmental justice. It is painfully clear that economic advantage is too often achieved at very great environmental cost; not to put too fine a point on it, at the cost both of stealing your future, and also of upsetting the diverse balance which ensures life on earth, as we have known it, remains possible.

Now, if you put green and brown together you produce olive. It is unthinkable that the environmental movement, of which I am proud to be a strong advocate, should seek the implementation of policies which diminish the lives, culturally or materially, of the most marginal people on earth. On the other hand, it is unthinkable that in seeking to relieve the pain and disadvantage of the poorest on earth one would seek a temporary solution that undermines long-term ecological sustainability. Not only are those options morally unsustainable, but they are also theologically contradictory. The faith tradition of the people of God, is that the health of the created order flows over into the health of the people of God and the health of the people of God flows over into the health of the created order.

Jessica and Benjamin, I challenge you to be at the forefront of the Olive movement, the moral and theological challenge of confronting the inequities of economic reality, for the peoples of the world, while at the same time undergirding a sustainable, healthy, and life giving environment for you, your children and your children's children. I feel profoundly sorry that my selfish lifestyle, coupled with the ignorance of my generation and the inept, selfish and cowardly leadership of the politicians of my time, has made the task you have inherited far more challenging than it need have been.

I would like to say a little more about olive as a metaphor, but first let me put into your mind Wendell Berry's immensely helpful distinction between the 'big' economy and the 'great' economy. Each evening, at the end of the news, you will observe your Dad listening to a diagnosis of how the 'big' economy, in which we are all immersed, has fared in the previous 24 hours. The stock market, inflation, mortgage rates, house prices, the cost of bananas, are all part of the 'big' economy, an entity which politicians tell us is the only thing that matters. However, they neglect to recognise, let alone understand, the 'great' economy from which everything derives, namely the whole created order. Everything we make, everything we consume, everything we throw away, has come from the 'great' economy which none of us owns, but for which all of us are stewards for a period. It is one of the great lies of the modern era that you are to be understood through what you consume. What we own is at best transitory. As you struggle with the theology of anthropology I hope one of the matters you will discuss is the destiny of humans to steward the 'great' economy, not allowing the 'big' economy to put the balance of the whole created order at risk for the sake of appalling, acquisitive, greediness and fear. What a huge responsibility has fallen on your noticeably young shoulders!

I have mentioned earlier that olive is a metaphor for many ideas: oil; health; food; inter-generational accountability; peace; suffering as a shared burden through prayer, in contrast to suffering as a result of violence inflicted upon another; contemporary struggles for peace and justice; the balance of brown and green. The olive movement then, in the broadest possible way, is the movement that brings together all that is necessary for health and well-being.

Many activities threaten health and well-being. As I write to you, one matter is threatening to fracture, perhaps even mortally wound, our beloved Anglican Church—the debate on homosexuality.

If either of you in your adolescence or early adulthood discovers you are gay, I am sure there would be an initial flurry of readjustment (to say the very least) in the hearts and minds of the family who love you. On the other hand, I have no doubt that should this happen, that love for you would not diminish one jot. Also, having made the discovery, as your grandfather, I would be hoping that you would discover meaningful intimacy. I would be mortified if your life were lived outside secure boundaries of intimacy, which I am sure is God's will for all his children. The current debate on homosexuality in the Anglican Church is an indulgence we cannot afford because it distracts us from so many other vital matters. I know it is essentially a debate about the Bible, but why pick on this topic?

Why not pick on the abuse of women? There are far too many examples of this abuse in culturally conservative communities, abuse which happens without comment and therefore with the tacit approval of the Church. Abuse of women, and the dignity that should be afforded women, was one of the most distinctive counter cultural focuses of Jesus' teaching and ministry. Or, why not pick on usury—the practice of making money from exorbitant rates of interest—or at least the love of money? Money should be seen for what it is, a means of trading a haircut for a kilo of pork chops. In our culture most of the wealthy become wealthier because their wealth is reinvested at high interest rates. Folk even borrow money from their mortgage at a low rate and invest what they have borrowed at a higher rate. Some even make a living out of buying and selling money! The value of one human being's work, no matter how skilled or responsible, cannot be worth more than a few times that of an honest labourer.

The Bible has much more to say about usury, and the love of money, than it does about homosexuality. It is astonishing that homosexuality should be allowed to so dominate, and potentially fracture, the Church, let alone be the defining issue at the forthcoming Lambeth Conference. Those on the one hand who aggressively pursue a gay agenda without reference to the rest of the Church, or on the other, those who use this disagreement for their own self-indulgent ends, have absolutely no right to derail the Church from more important agendas of the Kingdom of God. Please look up your history books to see what happened at the 2008 Lambeth Conference! Was it the beginning of the end for the Anglican Communion, or was it a moment of profound humility in the presence of God? Did those who threatened not to attend, stop to think that they eventually may be sitting at the heavenly banquet with someone God clearly loves, but whom they had thought was a bit dodgy? Are they then going to leave the table?

Jessica and Benjamin, God and you have lots to talk about and many journeys to travel together. Be confident that there is nothing in this world, or the next, that can separate you from the love of God. Be confident too that love bears all things, believes all things hopes all things; endures all things. Be confident that love never fails.

Travel well

With deep love and affection, your grandfather,

+ Penge

Margaret and I will hand back to the Diocese our symbols of office and its shared burdens of oversight in St Saviour's Cathedral Goulburn, on Saturday 2 February 2008, the feast of the Presentation and my anniversary of ordination. I do hope it will be possible for you to be present. I am hoping the night before, Friday 1 February, in Canberra, there will be an opportunity for us to say farewell to the wider community in which we have been privileged to contribute. My official resignation from the Diocese will be effective on 7 August 2008 at the conclusion of my Long Service Leave, soon after which I am sure the Vicar-General will summon an election synod. It is probably a good thing for there to be a six-month transition to allow some memories to fade and new expectations to build. As you know we have built a house at Long Beach, Batemans Bay, and we are very much looking forward to taking up residence there. However, initially this will be for a short time, for soon after Easter 2008 we will be heading for the UK where I will take up a Parish in the Diocese of Salisbury. I have also been asked to take some wider roles. We look forward to continuing interests such as the environment and advocacy for the Church in some of the developing countries.

Thank you so much for all you are and have been to us. If I had my life over again, I would ask for none of it to be changed, not even the hard bits.

May God's love and grace in Christ continue to go before us and further us with His continual help that in all our work, begun, continued, and ended, we may glorify his holy name and finally in his great mercy be inheritors of his eternal kingdom through Jesus Christ our Lord. Amen

The Right Reverend George Browning

Bishop of Canberra & Goulburn

8 September 2007

Part 3
What God and I have talked about

Silence in the face of evil is itself evil: God will not hold us guiltless. Not to speak is to speak. Not to act is to act.'
Dietrich Bonhoeffer.

God loves nothing so much as the person who lives with wisdom.
Wisdom of Solomon 7:28.

Chapter 5
Truth is Seldom Singular
The Defects of Individualism

I am what I am because of who we all are[48]

When in Brisbane In the late 1980s I was invited onto a panel for one session of *Hypotheticals*, at that time a popular ABC TV series, the brainchild of barrister, Geoffrey Robertson.

The theme he wanted to explore in this session called 'All in the family'[49] was child abuse. Interestingly, on this occasion he focussed on abuse in the home rather than institutional abuse.

> *'Behind respectable brick veneers lie alarming statistics of child sexual abuse, dilemmas created by the need to uncover this social evil are debated by lawyers, doctors, social workers, etc., while at the same time respecting the rights of possibly-innocent parents. When should the State intervene to remove a child from parents, on mere suspicion of sexual abuse?'*

The imaginary setting for this exploration was the fictional Queensland outback town of 'Melanoma'. My role was parish priest of this fictional town. The Premier of Queensland was the mayor, and the Victorian Commissioner of Police, the town policeman. (The Queensland Commissioner of Police

---

48 Definition of Ubuntu. Archbishop Desmond Tutu.

49 https://www.abccommercial.com/librarysales/program/geoffrey-robertsons-hypotheticals.

could not fulfil the role, being himself in gaol at that time). In preparation, we were gathered around a smorgasbord dinner for an hour or so prior to the filming, while Geoffrey Robertson paced up and down, outlining his approach and appraising us of our various roles. He explained that the success of the programme depended on the participants' capacity to play act the hypothetical situations he created and spontaneously respond to the prompts he would randomly give us.

Geoffrey Robertson and the Hypothetical *panel.*

In his research he had discovered that as well as three sons, Margaret and I have two foster daughters. At one point in the programme he asked the Commissioner of Police, aka Melanoma's bobby, to come knocking on my door, because there was a rumour the girls had been taking valuables from the local jewellery shop. He acted out an entry to my home at which point Geoffrey intervened in my direction with 'you have just noticed a piece of jewellery on your coffee table you have not seen before, what are you going to do about it'. I responded: 'I think I am just about to drop a napkin over it'! He then asked if he could inspect the girls' bedroom. I responded: 'certainly not'. He asked, 'why not'? I responded: 'Because I would never enter their room without their permission, and I am jolly sure you are not going to'.

Teenagers notoriously explore their independence while still being uncertain of the societal relationships in which they might safely invest their trust. Dealing with teenage misdemeanours is always a tricky mixture of enabling creative space in which trust can grow, and yet imposing discipline. All trust and no discipline and boundaries are never learned or respected; all discipline and no trust and young people are impeded from growing into healthy, interdependent and responsible adults. Trust is the universal and indispensable lubricant of life. It is a necessary prerequisite for the renewal, or redemption, upon which all human lives depend. Public response to juvenile crime in today's world tends to be all about discipline (almost always punitive) with almost no energy directed to the building or rebuilding of trust, the necessary precursor of rehabilitation in a healthy and life-giving community.

When the programme went to air this exchange was shown in full, along with many others. The interesting feature of the final programme was that the Premier, Sir Joh Bjelke-Petersen, hardly featured at all, despite being the most high-profile person on the panel. This was because he could not put himself in a hypothetical situation, he was the Premier of Queensland not the mayor of Melanoma! The premier was not able to make connections or understand the potentially negative implications that flowed from his prosecution of development and profit at all costs. It was this inability which led to the development, on his watch, of a culture of corruption, a culture which enveloped some of his most senior colleagues. I do not believe he was personally corrupt; however, he was culpable by allowing individual wilfulness for personal advantage at the expense of the good of the State of Queensland. Under Joh's watch individuals ran roughshod over the good of society.

The genius of the Geoffrey Robertson devised programme was its use of the particular to illustrate the universal. Using a hypothetical situation, which was time and place specific, the listener was invited to transport themselves into almost any other comparable situation in real life. The Bible uses this technique in various ways. 'Go to the ant thou sluggard, consider her ways and be wise' (Prov.6:6), is a good example from Wisdom literature. Through this programme Robertson invited us to grapple with the emergence of personal identity which needs be nurtured through wholesome relationships.

Having been a lifelong Anglican, I have had plenty of time to consider what the distinctive elements of Anglicanism might be. *Via Media* is one way of describing a core value or characteristic of our expression of Christianity, but it is erroneously misunderstood to mean 'the middle way' if middle way means, for example, midway between Roman Catholicism on the one hand and Protestantism on the other. Who wants to be stuck between, being wishy washy, neither one thing nor the other? Over more than half a century in ministry I have grown into a richer and more purposeful understanding of Anglicanism. It is commitment to the road less travelled, the more difficult path of understanding and embracing truth as both this and that; often valuing and holding in tension what appear to be irreconcilable opposites, for 'this' without 'that' is half-truth. This is far from the middle point between apparent alternatives and is in stark contrast with the binary world in which we now live.

In politics, standing for something is currently achieved through opposing something or someone else. Political parties have become locked into a culture of opposition, even when in government. An oppositional binary mindset prevents the enactment of policy reform which, by its very nature requires bi-partisan support. Political parties have come to define themselves through what they oppose rather than what they propose. They especially oppose good policy if it has emerged from the other side. Worse, parties will even oppose propositions that would normally be proposed by their own side, if in the first instance the proposition comes from the other side of the chamber. Politics has degenerated into binary propositions, rather than the art of negotiating good policy. Party supremacy has become a priority, or worse primacy of a faction within a party rather than the good of the community or country.

Shamefully, and at great cost to the country, appropriate climate policy in Australia is being held to ransom not by cross-party division, but by factionalism within the governing conservative party. Australia has languished without an energy policy. To achieve supremacy, politics are marketed, promoted, and branded, through three-word slogans. 'Good money managers' markets the right of politics, while 'protecting the poor and vulnerable', markets the left. Marketing has everything to do with brand distinctiveness rather than good policy. The right brands the left as socialists. The left brands the right as friends of the wealthy. In the binary world of Donald Trump, brand is about winning, but of equal importance, it is about triumph over someone else's loss.

While Donald Trump has not invented 'fake news', he has done more than most to weaponize it. In his world, anyone who does not fawn over him is trying to take him down; therefore, he claims to be justified in spreading a narrative that demonizes and demeans, however devoid of truth. The same technique is used against those who inconveniently stand in the way of imperialistic ambition, be that ambition economic, environmental, or social. In populist media, particularly *News Limited* or *Fox,* a terrorist is a person in the way of US foreign policy, no matter the person thus described might be doing no more than attempting to protect their family and home, freedom, and livelihood. This is particularly the case in relation to Palestinians.

In 2018 the Australian Department of Home Affairs refused the visa of Bassem Tamimi, the West Bank Palestinian who has been labelled a terrorist for trying to save his home from demolition in the village of Nabi Salih and who refuses to accept Israel's unlawful annexation. He is not a terrorist. He is doing exactly what any human being would seek to do—protect his home and family. For this action Australia summarily and without any justification condemns him as a threat to our society. In Australian foreign policy it appears that if we accept Israel as our 'best friend' then necessarily Palestinians who resist Israel's aggressive and illegal colonisation must be our enemy.

In contrast with a binary world, Anglicanism is commitment to the paradox of truth; the realisation that it mysteriously resides in the space between two opposites. Anglicans have long had a constructive and supportive conversation with both the Jewish community as brothers and sisters, and the Palestinian community, equally as sisters and brothers.

God is both singular and plural as the Christian doctrine of the Trinity wonderfully conveys. Jesus is not just a bridge between heaven and earth, but in him the fullness of heaven and earth completely dwell. I am an individual, but my individuality has been formed through all the lives and experiences that have intersected with me. In Anglicanism, Word is unintelligible outside the mystery of sacrament, and sacrament is mere superstition unless founded in Word. Indeed, I have concluded there are few truths worth embracing that are not the product of antinomy.

The problem with traveling this 'road less travelled' is that paradox is unattractive, indeed unhelpful, in a world where certainty is prized. Certainty, however illusionary, is offered through binary choices. The left and right offer their own versions of certainty; the further a politician moves to one or other polarity the more their version of certainty becomes a falsehood. A champion of polarising falsehood on the far right in recent past has been former Senator Bronwyn Bishop.

I have attended many dinner parties in my time, the vast majority I have greatly enjoyed, a few less so. In the early 2000s I attended a dinner party to celebrate the work and achievements of Anglicare. The party was held in a hotel on the outskirts of Canberra. The chief political guest was Bronwyn Bishop, then Minster for Aged Care. One of the burdens and joys of office is being placed on a head table with interesting people and sometimes with people less so. For the duration of the dinner I sat with Bronwyn on my left. Conversation was easy to my right, but far less so to my left. Ms Bishop did not privilege me with glimpses into the wisdom she had accrued after a lifetime in public office, but for the whole evening harangued me with her ideology of singularity, her belief that there is no such thing as society, there are only individuals. In this proposition any argument that furthers the Common Good is labelled socialism, the supposedly ever-present evil that lurks in hidden crevices ready to destroy the lives of ordinary freedom loving people. While she may have been channelling Margaret Thatcher, she certainly had well and truly made this song her own. She is self-evidently wrong. Individuals live within a society, indeed produce a society, no individual can live alone. I have become increasingly anxious that the exaggerated focus on the individual by neoliberal capitalism is destroying civil society.

In the 1920s Anglican leadership unapologetically badged Christianity with a socialist vision, with the ideal of serving good that is common. Now, because of the assumed affinity between communism and socialism, this connection is no longer considered appropriate, either in a political or religious context. The right (Christian and political) has successfully badged the left as the enemy of the individual, while the left has been cowed into a narrative that fails to adequately argue that economic capital should serve social capital—indeed that it should have no other purpose. What is claimed to be the political centre has moved dangerously to the right and contemporary attempts to serve 'common good' are labelled 'left leaning'. This is particularly so of policy to address global warming.

Unfortunately, those who win office become committed (out of the need to be re-elected) to short term economic goals within a political cycle, rather than long term sustainable objectives that inevitably reside well beyond that immediate cycle.

I want to affirm the appropriateness of badging Christianity with good that is common. In doing so I wish to address the relationship between 'particular' and 'universal', a relationship that lies at the heart of human interaction, and unsurprisingly at the heart of biblical theology. Every individual, like an instrument in an orchestra, or the colour of a rainbow, is distinct, but distinctiveness can only be known and appreciated from within its appropriate place in the symphony of sound or colour. The creation narrative informs us that God perceives the creation in its entirety as 'very good'.

The well-being of an individual is meaningless outside the health and well-being of the whole. Western civilisation has become obsessed with the individual. We are being led down a dangerous path. A correction is necessary. COVID19 may prove to be a catalyst for the correction, for in combating the pandemic it has been necessary to make economic priorities subservient to social or health priorities. Time will tell whether lessons learned through the pandemic will last. If they do not last, civilisation as we have known it, may well be dangling on a dangerously short rope.

In the early 20th century, followers of Karl Marx developed a political system that emphasised the state as the custodian of the individual's good. This ideal became corrupt almost from the start. Communism quickly came to serve the state's political elite, totally neglecting the respect, dignity, and prosperity of the individual. Indeed, within the communist system there was no incentive for an individual to excel. The system became grotesque and collapsed. With no rival, capitalism has been marching to a different beat and in the opposite direction. With all attention now accorded the individual, to speak of the good of community, or society, is said to be socialistic, or communistic.

Rampant individualism has become a form of madness, running counter to human need, as social beings. Political masters eschew levers that might save the world from this madness. Unreformed capitalism could well be every bit as grotesque and catastrophic in the 21st century as communism became to the 20th century. Worse, communism inflicted its suffering on the other side of the iron curtain. Unreformed, neoliberal, capitalism, is now ubiquitously present throughout the globe; therefore, the damage it can inflict is potentially far more universal. We desperately need a reformed political narrative that will defend both the individual and the society of which every individual is part.

Caring for the individual and caring for society, be it local, national, or global should not be the alternatives they have become in western democracies. To invest in one must be to invest in the other.

Let me illustrate the importance of embracing opposites from a different perspective.

Failure to understand that the' particular' and 'universal' need always to be held in healthy tension leads to tyrannies. Communism catastrophically neglected the rights and needs of the individual while neoliberal capitalism dangerously neglects universal responsibility.

The *particular* and the *universal* are in life-giving tension throughout the pages of scripture, but they come into stark focus in the bible's opening saga—the creation narrative. The first narrative (Gen. 1: 1–2: 3) describes creation in its universal dimension, while the second narrative (Gen. 2: 4–3: 22) deals with human particularity. Taken literally the two narratives are irreconcilable. However, understood through the lens of the universal and the particular, they are a priceless insight into truth in its paradox. The one must be understood through its opposite in the other.

In the first narrative life-giving space is created through the separation of light and darkness, earth and sky, water of blessing (above) and primeval water of chaos (below). Limits are placed on each primary element through its opposite. Through the imposition of limits, distinctiveness becomes possible. The supreme paradox of human freedom is that its discovery is only fully known when limits that flow from relationship, with God, the world and others is fully understood. Our lives are healthy when opposites are held in healthy tension. No meaningful freedom exists in autonomous isolation.

In this first creation narrative, humanity is given the universal and gender nonspecific name of Adam—of the earth—*adamah*. All humans are Adam and become who they are destined to be through shared life within the whole of creation. We are sentient beings with the capacity to understand that personal fulfilment is a by-product of selflessness, an essential prerequisite of harmony and sustainability. As the narrative of scripture unfolds, we learn we are also to think intergenerationally, we are to live with the blessing of seven future generations in mind. That we do not do this and capriciously think only of the present is, perhaps, the greatest tragedy of contemporary humanity.

In the first creation narrative, humanity's designated role is set beside the role of sun and moon. If you like, there are three players with a governing role within creation, the sun, the moon, and humanity. The sun, described as the greater light ruling the day, is responsible for the energy which enables life to exist. The moon, described as the lesser light, ruling the night, is responsible for the tides and seasons, the rhythms which make for diversity, continuity, and sustainability. Humanity is responsible for the nurturing or stewarding of the natural order.

Human population and evolved technical capacities have so exploded that we affect every corner of the planet. Scientists tell us that this ubiquitous capacity is altering the rhythms of the natural order upon which we rely, and have taken for granted. Thus, we are impinging upon the symbolic 'governing' capacity of sun and moon. Fundamentalist Christians rail against this notion, but they have not understood the creation narrative, climaxing in the Noah narrative, which suggests human selfishness and arrogance has the capacity to reverse the *order* implicit in creation.

Humanity has exceeded our allotted place. We have failed to nurture nonhuman creation, exploiting natural resources in service of human usefulness alone. While we have learned to safely, economically, and successfully, capture contemporary solar energy, we continue to rely on historically stored solar energy in fossil fuels. The planet is now asked to re-absorb carbon that had been stored for millennia. Carbon in the form of carbon dioxide is not a pollutant, it is a source of life to the world's fauna, but in the atmosphere, it acts as a greenhouse gas, trapping heat that would otherwise escape; thus warming the planet.

The first creation saga climaxes with sabbath, a festival of rest and release that almost certainly had its origins in lunar cycles. Sabbath describes how the whole creation is to be celebrated in generosity, reciprocity, respect, forgiveness, and connectedness. Its rhythm should permeate and sustain the whole of life. Living its rhythm produces shalom—harmony, well-being, wholeness To ignore the rhythm is to court alienation and corruption, indeed the possibility of reversing the order of creation, for the rhythms at the heart of the natural order can be ignored, but they cannot be abrogated.

Sabbath is the biblical principle that best gives a theological framework to the emphases of modern science that all is connected and that over exploitation at one point can affect balances and rhythms upon which all life depends at every point. This reality makes it more shocking that Christians of the political right treat environmental responsibility at best as a niche issue, and at worst in cavalier fashion.

In the second creation narrative (Gen. 2: 4–3:24), the narrative of Adam and Eve and the Garden, the focus changes from the universal to the particular—the individual. In this narrative, humanity becomes gender specific. While, as we read the narrative, Adam and Eve are symbolically the 'first' humans, in fact their story is the story of all humans. In the symbolism of the Garden of Eden we read of the paradox humans face in every generation. We desire to live without limits, but limits are the source of our prosperity and freedom. Tragically we read of our propensity for failure. COVID19 and the lockdown brought this paradox into stark reality.

The problem facing every individual is that our desire for autonomy and individuality is both curse and blessing. We cannot live without the limits necessary to companionship. While companionship with animals is possible, it is not enough, we need the companionship of other human beings and specifically of another human being. We are not created as autonomous beings. We are social beings who have lived most of our history tribally. How each tribe (more recently each nation) lives alongside other tribes or nations, is the complex and violent history of humanity.

A concomitant reality is that the created order has limitations structured within it, limitations that can be ignored but never abrogated. Indeed, the paradox of life is that freedoms are found in respecting limitations. Freedom is an illusion unless understood within the context of the limitations which make freedom possible. Acting with a singular or self-focus is always damaging, all actions have consequences, even with boomerang effect. What gifts others with blessing is blessing to us, actions that are detrimental to others are ultimately detrimental to us. Our lives are inescapably intertwined with all others. Taking from the 'Tree of the Knowledge of Good and Evil' is forbidden, because choosing good for oneself rather than good that is common, is destructive of life. Good must be common, or it is not good. This reality is intuitively known by most indigenous people the world over, but strangely unknown in the so-called developed world. The paradox of contemporary western society is that we should know better. The values upon which our civilisation have been built are rooted in the Judaeo/Christian tradition—upon this creation narrative.

Choosing good for oneself rather than good that is common is to imply self is the centre of the universe. This falsehood, tested in the innocence of childhood as boundaries are explored, should have been disavowed as adolescence gives way to adulthood. This is the crux of the matter. Whilst every human being is desirous of autonomous living, the more we strive for exclusivity and specialness, the more we miss the point that our specialness lies across the relationships and experiences we share with others. The more we set ourselves apart from or against others, the more we are diminished, notwithstanding the material spoils we may have accumulated. This second creation narrative dramatically ends with human expulsion from the garden. What is inferred here is that concentration on the individual (individualism) outside the context of the universal, is to exchange the harmony and peace of a garden for a diminished world of conflict, competition, and suffering. This reality is underlined in the narrative that follows, the account of Cain and Abel (Gen.4: 1–16).

Like Adam and Eve, the reader is to perceive in Cain and Abel truth about herself/himself. Both are potentially alive and well in each of us. *Cain* in Hebrew has the same linguistic derivation as *Canaan* whose god is a god of 'owning' or 'controlling'. *Abel* has the same linguistic derivation as wind, or spirit, life force. The spiritual struggle common to every human being is played out in the story of Cain and Abel. Triumph sought through controlling or owning is always won at great price. William Shakespeare conveys this through many of his plays.[50] Contemporary world dictators live it daily in the global news cycle, as do ultra-nationalistic leaders such as Donald Trump[51] and Benjamin Netanyahu.[52]

The most potent and destructive expression of individualism is unrestricted nationalism. I was born in 1942 when the result of the Second World War was still in the balance. The full horror of Nazi extremism against minorities it considered to be racially inferior, was yet to dawn. However, from the mid 1930s the nationalism of the third Reich was in its full threatening display. Hitler's grand ambition for a greater Germany included most of western and eastern Europe, with Berlin transformed into a new grand capital, Germania. It was to be modelled on the most triumphant images of the Roman Empire. German nationalism was to know no bounds.

Individualistic aggression on a single or national scale often begins from an aggrieved response to humiliation or defeat. Germany's nationalism had its genesis in the capitulation that ended the First World War and the humiliation it experienced in the Treaty of Versailles. Nationalism is individualism on a grand scale. It is belief that this nation, this leader, has the right, indeed the responsibility, to dominate. There are many contemporary examples. President Erdogan of Turkey has generated a nationalism that breeds intolerance towards any who dare to express a more liberal and inclusive society. Minorities are oppressed. Israeli President Netanyahu encourages a nationalism which permits an apartheid regime of oppression

---

50 *To thine own self be true, and it must follow, as the night the day, thou canst not then be false to any man. Hamlet*, Act I, Scene III.

51 *A little more moderation would be good. Of course, my life hasn't exactly been one of moderation.* Donald Trump.

52 *It doesn't matter if justice is on your side. You have to depict your position as just.* Benjamin Netanyahu.

against Palestinians. There is reason to fear nationalistic movements in many western countries that in the past have valued tolerance and inclusiveness.

Nationalism ignores global balances necessary for peace and harmony and is therefore dangerous. This was the case with Germany and Japan in the Second World War, it may be the case with an overly nationalistic China or US in the future.

Nationalism and patriotism are two different expression of identity. Patriotism is loyalty and pride in one's home and the willingness to serve it. Those who have fought in various wars on behalf of Australia were not nationalists, they were not seeking the dominance of Australia. They were patriots who expressed loyalty to universal values of freedom and democracy. When the young Australian men left for war in Europe in 1914, they were patriots serving with pride the honour and freedom of Empire and country. The tragedy is that 100 years later their patriotism is being turned into misplaced nationalism by politicians with an ulterior motive. Plans in Canberra for a massive extension to the War Memorial are an example of patriotism being used to shape a national identity through the glorification of war.

Nationalism has become rampant in the contemporary world. In Israel, Palestinians are trammelled both in the occupied territories and in Israel itself. In Turkey, freedom loving Turks have been trammelled for daring to believe in a more inclusive society, a more just society, a more liberal society, a more educated society. Nationalism's ugly face is present in the rise and rise of the right wing in Europe, Brexit, Trump's America and in Abbott's and Morrison's Australia. The right wing behaves as if individual nations can flourish, indeed have the right to flourish, without responsibility to other nations and the world. The catastrophic failure of the world to implement strategies to mitigate the effects of climate change is caused by a misplaced nationalism. Many of the powerful and developed countries of the world arrogantly assert their right to respond to a global problem based on internal and domestic economic factors. Taken to its terrifying conclusion, nationalism could bring about the end of civilisation as we know it, if it continues to reign over the priority of global responsibility.

As previously noted, the 1920 Lambeth Conference, called in the devastating aftermath of the First World War, declared national self-interest to be the most insidious evil on the planet, out-ranking individual self-interest in its capacity for serious disruption and suffering. It is a matter of considerable concern that nations behaving this way are not just mavericks, like North Korea, but nations that like to think of themselves as pillars of a free and democratic world, countries like the US, Britain and Australia.

Emphasis on the 'particular' has also bedevilled religious expression from the beginning of time and has been the cause of prejudice and oppression. I do not accept that religion has been the primary cause of global violence over the centuries, but it certainly has allowed itself to be the flag-bearer. Almost all violence has inequity and poverty as its primary cause, but religious fervour is used to rally the masses.

Once a year the Roman Catholic and Anglican bishops of NSW meet to discuss common issues. The meetings are never easy because conservative members of both sides have more in common with one another than with liberal fellows in their own denomination. Likewise, those of a more liberal perspective seek solace with like-minded colleagues across the denominational divide.

Those who like to be known as conservatives are faced with a double bind. While they share what might be called social conservatism in relation to gender and sexuality, their exclusivist doctrinal positions exclude one another. The Sydney Roman Catholic and Anglican Archbishops are gentlemanly and supportive of each other, but the fundamentals at the heart of their conservatism exclude the other. The Anglican Diocese of Sydney is notoriously conservative within the worldwide Anglican Communion, resisting the ordination of women and insisting on the theory of penal substitution in relation to the atonement as the only acceptable (biblical) means of explaining mystery at the heart of faith. The confessional nature of Sydney Anglicanism is exclusive—and intentionally so. On the other hand, Roman Catholicism as expressed through conservative leadership entrenched in the papacies of John Paul II and Benedict XVI, is equally exclusive. To believe that catholic clerical priesthood, guaranteed through apostolic succession, is the only conduit of God's grace and salvation is arrogant triumphalism, unsupported by scripture and excludes all Christians who do not accept catholic doctrine.

At one of these joint meetings, presided over by Archbishops Jensen and Pell, I found the unspoken presumptions of both to be patronising and somewhat demeaning. Being unable to contain myself I said to Archbishop Pell: 'It sounds as if you believe the Kingdom of God and Roman Catholicism to be synonymous'. Most of the bishops, Roman and Anglican, did their best to pretend they were not present in the room! In the evasive response that followed an awkward silence, it was clear that this was exactly what the Archbishop believed!

Christian particularity, like all particularities is vital, without it we have nothing to offer, no identity to share. John has us believe that Jesus is *the way the truth and the life. No one comes to the Father except through me* (John 14:6). On face value the text looks thoroughly imperialistic and exclusive. There appears to be no latitude for grace or salvation other than through faith in him. But what does faith in him mean? Does it mean a specific doctrinal confession: pass it and you are in, fail and you are out—eternally?

No, I do not believe this is what it means. Jesus is the human face of the invisible God; in him the fullness of God is pleased to dwell. To be united with him is to be united to life. On the other-hand he is also the new Adam, the universal human, the one through whom all humans have the right to stand in the presence of God. So, to accept Jesus as the Way, Truth and Life is to reject separation and exclusivity, it is to recognise the commonality of humanity under the sovereignty of God. It is to accept that service is our true modus operandi. It is to enter conversation with others whose journey to God has had a different starting point. It is to be corrected by those whose insights challenge one's own faithfulness, but it is equally, and respectfully, to reject false certainties. Any form of exclusivity is anathema to faith in Jesus.

In the present era, closer dialogue between Islam and Christianity must be a priority, with the starting point not being the differences between us, which are obvious, but shared commonalities. Unless Christianity and Islam are on the same page in the 21st century, singing from the same song sheet, in service of a sustainable and harmonious world, we will both contribute to global tensions, not global peace. Past-history and present realities make meaningful dialogue difficult. Aggressive colonising behaviour from the West, has been interpreted as Christian aggression. The opposite is also true. In 2019 I visited two Palestinian priests serving Arab communities in Israel. I was quite shocked by their sense of belittlement in the face of growing aggressiveness from Muslim Arabs. I suggested that this aggressiveness might have its genesis in their own alienation and suffering as a result of Israeli occupation. While they agreed this reality contributes an explanation, it is far from the whole story. They claimed a certain aggressiveness to be entrenched within Islamic faith and culture.

Perhaps the mirror opposite to an exclusivist Christian claim that a narrow doctrinal acceptance of Jesus as Lord is the only way, is an Islamic claim that all humans must be Muslim because there is but one God, Allah, and therefore any who do not follow Islam are necessarily apostate. Claims to universality without reference to particularity and diversity are as dangerous as assertions of particularity that refuse to acknowledge universal obligations.

No individual, no species, no locality, no time, can be properly understood, or valued, outside its place within a much greater whole. At the same time wisdom literature makes it clear that universal time and meaning can only be understood through the prism of the smallest part.

Chapter 6
The Loss of Wisdom
The Triumph of Capitalism

I hate him for he is a Christian; but more for that in low
simplicity
He lends out money gratis, and brings down the rate of usance
here with us in Venice.[53]

In the early 2000s I attended a formal reception for Australia Day at Government House in Canberra. The crowd was such that movement within the main reception area was difficult. At one point of the evening I found myself in one corner of the room and noted that Alexander Downer, then Foreign Minister, was in the opposite corner. Our eyes met and like Moses faced with the obstacle of the Red Sea, he cut a path for himself through the crowd, until he arrived a few inches from me and spluttered without any small talk 'and can't the rich be saved'? To this day I have absolutely no idea what was hidden in the recesses of his mind to provoke the outburst. I put out my hand and said: 'Good evening Mr Downer, George Browning'. He ignored the hand and responded: 'I know exactly who you are' and stormed off, presumably to confront someone else.

The simple answer to Mr Downer's question is of course—Yes—all are, or can be, recipients of undeserved grace. There is no problem with

---

53 William Shakespeare *The Merchant of Venice,* Act 1, Scene 3.

being wealthy, if there is a problem, it resides either in the way wealth has been accrued or in the way it is distributed. Jesus made it clear that wealth was not to be privately cocooned but used to benefit the goodness and well-being of life in general. Neoliberal capitalism and biblical faith cannot be reconciled. The bible insists that wealth serves good that is common, neoliberal capitalism asserts wealth to be individually owned. Neoliberal capitalism assumes the right of the individual to do whatever she or he desires with their wealth. Biblical faith assumes that, little or much, humans are custodians or stewards of wealth, for the benefit of greater good.

Of course, there are wealthy people in Australia who do not assume their wealth to be their private property and accept the biblical mandate of stewardship. Let me tell you of one. When the Australian Centre for Christianity and Culture was in its most embryonic form, we needed seed money both for an architectural competition and for the inevitable expenses associated with commencing an ambitious venture. I sought advice from an old friend, Everald Compton, about how I might raise a reasonably substantial amount of money. First, he said that unless I was committed enough to believe this was the venture for which I was born, the venture for which I was brought into the world, I would not pull it off. Such, he said, was the scale of the task. Second, he said I needed to go to someone who would be sympathetic, indeed enthusiastic with the idea of a spiritual home in the nation's capital hosted by the Christian community, but open to all. Someone who believed that a national capital without a spiritual soul was not a capital worthy of the name; someone strong enough in their own spiritual identity that they are not threatened to reach beyond traditional boundaries. Third he said that when I had identified such a person, I needed to go without any accompanying papers, but sell the vision out of my own commitment and energy.

The advice was sound, but its implementation more than a little daunting. The person we identified was the wonderful Dame Elizabeth

Murdoch. An appointment was made, and I took myself off to Melbourne. In the morning of the appointment I met Ethiopian migrant friends of my sister Val. As I left, they asked where I was going. When I told them I was heading for the Mornington Peninsula they insisted I take their car. Protesting sounded ungrateful, so I headed to Crudens Farm with a car blowing smoke and with doors that refused to shut properly. Cruising up Crudens Farm driveway, I was graciously greeted by Dame Elizabeth who did not blink an eyelid about my mode of transport. We immediately toured the garden in her electric go mobile. Our chat over lunch included light-hearted banter about the source of my transport that morning! She clearly approved of the Ethiopian contact and said she had read about my sister. We then retired to the lounge room and its open fire to speak of the reason for my visit. 'Now Bishop', she said, 'What matter of mutual interest have you come to bring to my attention'?

Her openness, indeed, excitement in hearing of another venture into which she could inject energy was extraordinary. She lived to make a difference, to be a person determined to ensure the world was a better place.

I spelt out a vision of the centre, sketching what I hoped would be its contribution to the national capital, and, by implication, to the nation. Dame Elizabeth was a fellow Anglican and a regular worshipper. I explained the site for this venture was the site set aside in the 1920s for a national Anglican cathedral, but that I felt this was a venture now past its use by date. What was now required, I suggested, was a site inclusive of all faiths and of none, a site of reconciliation and peace, however a site unapologetically Christian in its values and hospitality. Without hesitation she agreed to the seed funding and the rest as they say is history. Dame Elizabeth remains, in my mind, a living testimony to what can happen through the stewardship of wealth. The catalogue of projects she has resourced is endless: science, the arts, projects relating to the vulnerable and needy such as women in gaol, and many, many others.

No, Mr Downer, there is nothing inherently wrong with being wealthy, but the accumulation of wealth imposes a choice. Either the wealth remains cocooned in the service of the individual, or it becomes charitably available in the service of common good. Wealth imposes a vocation. Whether this vocation is accepted, or even acknowledged, is a test of genuine humanity, a test of whom or what the person has become. All rivers flow into the ocean or into aquifers, water that is unable to flow ultimately becomes stagnant.

While Dame Elizabeth is far from the only wealthy person to generously serve humanity, the reality is that her example is not the norm.

Wealth can be worn lightly, or as a badge of honour. When I grew up in a little English village a rather scruffy and delightfully eccentric squire figure gave me a valuable insight into human life. He said: 'George, if you are nobody and want to be someone, you need to drive a Bentley, if you are someone you can happily drive a Morris Minor'! In the early 2000s I attended a garden party at Government House which is always a good opportunity to network. Wandering around the garden I encountered a previous head of the Australian Public Service who now controlled a major piece of infrastructure that had been in public hands but, through changed government legislation, had become a very lucrative private enterprise. Being an enterprise without any real competition he benefited from considerable and continuing political influence. We greeted one another as old friends. I asked after his well-being to which he replied: 'extraordinarily wealthy'! Somewhat taken aback I asked if he was extraordinarily happy. His ignoring of the retort confirms what we know, wealth and human happiness have no necessary correlation. Hugh Mackay, the social commentator, has made this observation in many commentaries on contemporary society. So why the obsession with wealth? Why is economic growth the major, if not only, measure of national success and well-being? The question is, in part, answered through the correlation of wealth and the exercise of power.

Soon after I arrived in Canberra in 1993, I became aware that a significant legacy had been left to St Mark's National Theological Centre in Barton. The legacy included a treasured car number plate in single figures which was highly sought after as a status symbol. The owner of such a plate could pride themselves in being Canberran royalty, one whose roots went back to the foundation of the city. Sir Lennox Hewitt, another previous head of the public service, was somewhat irate that this symbol had been lost to his family and demanded its return. There was little that could be done because before I arrived it had already been sold at auction. Sir Lennox, not wanting to let the matter rest, wrote a series of letters to various figures that included the Anglican Primate of Australia, the Archbishop of Canterbury, and various political figures he assumed could ensure the item concerned was returned. All the letters ended up on my desk with a little hand-written note from the various receivers saying this was not a matter they wished to be involved with, but if there was something I could do to resolve the matter with charity, they would be glad.

I decided the best thing to do would be to invite Sir Lennox around for afternoon tea at our home in the suburb of Campbell. I invited the Diocesan Chancellor, Professor Lindsay Curtis, who had previously been in his employ, to be present. The first half an hour or so went extremely well as we exchanged pleasantries, talked about the cricket, etc. I noted however that Lindsay was far from at ease, being awed by someone who had clearly exercised dominating power over him in the past.

We eventually came to the matter at hand. Sir Lennox set out his case. I responded that the Diocese, before my arrival, had followed the intention of the benefactor and while I understood his view, that really was the end of the matter. At this point Sir Lennox became very agitated and began to treat me as if I were one of his lower caste staff, with the expectation I would do as I was told. The problem was that it had the reverse effect, the more he demanded, the more I unexpectedly found myself with a fit of the giggles. I did my utmost to be respectful to the elderly gentleman, but I found it very funny that he considered wealth, title and position gave him the right to speak and act in this way. The rest of the afternoon had a certain awkwardness to it, Margaret was grateful she had remained in the kitchen.

It is sad that very wealthy and powerful people, perhaps because of their wealth and power, are so often oblivious of the transformative power of generosity. In 1969 I became Vicar of Warialda on the north west slopes of NSW. The Parish and its people taught me a very great deal. In the Parish there were two elderly single women, sisters, who shared the same very modest home a couple of doors from the Church. I was stunned to discover they were amongst the Parish's most generous contributors each placing a $5 note on the plate each Sunday. An analogous figure today, fifty years later, would be a very considerable sum. Similarly, in Singleton, a few years later, a single woman who acted as a live-in companion/maid was always the first to contribute when the call went out for a worthy cause. Often there were two gifts, one from her and one from the cat! Perhaps it is no coincidence that when Jesus had cause to draw attention to true generosity, he focussed on a widow and her mite.

In 1999 I faced a crisis documented in Chapter 4. It was a very dark time. It could have been, would have been, quite calamitous were it not for extraordinary generosity. One bishop flew down from Brisbane to check that we were ok and to offer whatever support we might need. Another bishop placed a significant cheque in the mail, not from a Church source, but from himself. Another bishop made a significant position available in his diocese, should I require it. These were extraordinary acts. But equally so were acts from people in the Diocese of Canberra and Goulburn. A couple, together with a senior lay person in the Diocese ensured that any expenses we might have incurred were covered. I would love to place our very deep gratitude to them on public record but realise this is not possible. By no means least was the generosity of the whole Diocese who, by a very substantial majority, insisted I withdraw my resignation and return as their bishop. In addition, the 1000+ messages of support (now in the Diocesan archives) were extraordinarily life giving. Suffice it to say, the last 20 years or so of what I hope has been productive living is entirely due to the generosity of people who thought it worthwhile to ensure that the self -inflicted crisis in which I found myself was redeemed.

Generosity in all its manifestations is the only power which should be coveted. Generosity is transformative for both giver and receiver. Generosity builds the only capital that matters, social capital.

Economic capital must never be allowed to assume pre-eminence, it exists to serve social capital.[54] Social capital is expressed through relatedness, equity, well-being. It needs to be remembered that economic activity is not an end, it exists to serve well-being. Economy which is insufficiently rooted in service of social capital fails to comprehend the mutual interdependence of life. Equilibrium, balance, harmony is lost when dominance is not kept in check. To be wise is to know one's place, to be part of a sustainable stream of living that existed before my arrival in this moment of time and will exist long after I have gone. Because social cohesion is not included within economic calculations, many are left with insecure employment and those in caring industries are remunerated at a fraction of the rate enjoyed by those in industries such as banking.

Economic gain is too often about advantage garnered in the present, without any necessary connection to long term sustainability. Fiscal activity, generated through the harvesting of natural resources, is calculated without adequate consideration of concomitant depletion of those resources. Future wealth inevitably declines as the availability of resources shrinks, as has been devastatingly the case for many past civilisations. The presumption that human activity can flourish while ignoring environmental sustainability is a serious misunderstanding and threatens generational sustainability. This dangerous delusion is spread by those who have self-interested investment in the continuing exploitation of primary resources, regardless of the consequences.

---

54 Appendix 4: Tony Blair and Speech to Australian Parliament, 15 April 2006.

Jurgen Moltmann reminds us that sin is not so much human weakness and failure, but physical, social, and spiritual disconnectedness that allows, even nurtures, weakness and failure. Life is connectedness, separation is death. Keeping people disconnected has many advantages to those in power, in these circumstances control is easier to exercise. Truth becomes arbitrary. In the absence of truth, disconnection is also fertile soil in which to nurture fear. Fear has become the weapon of choice for those wishing to gain political advantage. In a world of disconnection, we are far more vulnerable to economic offerings which sound attractive and feed our need for 'security',[55] but which turn out to be a house of cards. In recent times many, perhaps most, elections have been won by leaders who have been able to instil an existential threat in the mind of electors. Few elections are won because voters vote for a better world, they are won out of fear that the other side will make it worse.[56] Ambassador Arthur Sinodinos summed up politics for me as 'the game in which the [apparently] least ugly wins'.[57]

This Chapter addresses this situation and the urgent need for critical analysis of what is now known as neoliberal economics, the economic ideology of the right, so much in favour by political leadership since the Reagan/Thatcher era.

Neoliberal economics can be understood by way of contrast with Keynesian economics which held sway from the Great Depression until about the 1970s. In this theory supply and demand can and should be regulated through government intervention and the implementation of both monetary and fiscal policy. Keynesian theory assumes the role of government is to intervene on behalf of societal good. Keynesian economics enjoyed a resurgence in Australia following the financial crisis of 2008 when treasurer Swan

---

55 Appendix 5: A noble vision reduces our Uncertainty, 6 March 2005.

56 Appendix 6: Let Love Triumph over Fear, 7 November 2004.

57 *Sydney Morning Herald*, 17 October 2019.

injected considerable government spending into the economy to save Australia from recession and Australians from unemployment. At the time he was named the world's best treasurer. Subsequently he has been roundly blamed by numerous right orientated megaphones for national debt and deficit budgets. But shouldn't the blame be sheeted home to the conservatives who, following the end of the mining boom, have refused to curtail overly generous and unaffordable tax arrangements made by fellow conservatives in boom years? Neoliberal economics assumes the right of individuals to flourish regardless of the impact this may have on the many. Deficit budgets need not have continued had these unaffordable concessions to the upper-middle class been reined in.

Neoliberal economics emphasises privatisation of public assets, reduction in government expenditure, especially in social services, deregulation, free markets, and minimal government intervention. This ideology has seen:

A massive spike in inequity, to the extent that a few people enjoy obscene wealth and power while an increasing number rely on charitable food provision.

CEO salaries are struck on the assumption that companies will grow exponentially. Because bonuses relate to profit, they encourage less than ethical behaviour. It is estimated that the median income of a corporate CEO is 80 times the median income of the general workforce. Some salary levels appropriately described as obscene, have developed because of the perceived capacity of CEOs to make excessive profit for their company. Monumental salaries, together with large bonus incentives, encourage senior staff to embark on strategies on the very edge of ethical propriety. These strategies have often resulted in a burden being carried by those whose need or activity has been the source of the company's profit making. One of my predecessors as Bishop of Canberra and Goulburn, Bishop Ernest Burgmann, was of the view that no manager or CEO could or should receive a salary more than seven times that of the lowest paid in his or her company.[58] As part of necessary reform that capitalism must embrace within the next decade obscene salaries should not simply be reined in, but become culturally unacceptable. It is not acceptable for any human being to receive an eight-figure remuneration, least of all as payout following failure in the company.

Wealth accumulation has moved from wages to assets. Those with assets grow their wealth, those who rely on wages for income struggle to meet normal financial obligations.

In the wake of an asset boom, wages have stagnated.

Essential services have been placed in private, for profit, ownership, often but not always to the detriment of quality and availability of the service.

Multiple scandals have emanated from privatised institutions including correctional services facilities, vocational training centres, energy infrastructure, and asylum seeker provisions.

The ideal of 'Common Good' has become subservient to profit.

Neoliberal economics enables the wealthy to become wealthy at the expense of the poor. During the 2008 economic crisis and the 2020 COVID19 crisis the very wealthy greatly increased their assets. How does this happen?

The simple answer is the relationship between wealth and power. Wealth and power have always been bedfellows, but their manipulation in the current age by nations, individuals and corporations has become a source of local regional and global inequity that too often spills over into counter-productive and destructive human behaviour.

Those with money, those who control assets, have the power to control the lives of others both personally and globally. Cultures for which the

---

58 In comparative terms, CEOs now make 278 times the average worker. Top corporate executives have seen their pay grow by more than 1,000% over the past 40 years, nearly 100 times the rate of ordinary salaries. https://www.cnbc.com/2019/08/16/ceos-see-pay-grow-1000percent-and-now-make-278-times-the-average-worker.html.

making of money is the primary symbol of success, or even of identity, by default empower those with wealth and disempower those without.[59]

Critics of religion such as Christopher Hitchens and Richard Dawkins, like to argue that all world violence has a religious origin. It is true that some injustice relates to, or is perceived to relate to, religious identity. This was the case, for instance, in Northern Ireland. But in Northern Ireland Protestant or Catholic identity was secondary to deeply felt economic grievance. Human fracture almost always has economic inequality, if not injustice, at its roots.

As economic privation grows and inequality enflames the passions of the down-trodden, it is very convenient for grievances to be aired from behind a religious banner. Once that banner is raised others will rally to the cause who do not necessarily share firsthand experience of the grievance, or do not understand or care about the values and beliefs inherent in the banner under which they are now marching. Neoliberal economics bears no direct culpability for any specific act of global violence, any more than a single weather event, on its own, can be attributed to human induced climate change. However, it is culpable when the desire for profit overrides social obligations, when global or local societal issues are ignored or denied when they are perceived to stand in the way of company profit.

International examples of wealth and power exasperating inequity are not hard to find. In the West we purchase clothing and other consumables at ridiculously low prices. We can do this because workers in Bangladeshi factories are paid barely enough to purchase food for the evening meal, let alone send their children to school, or pay for necessary medical procedures. We should not be able to purchase a T-shirt for less than we pay for lunch, when those who have made the garment work for a month for that meagre sum. Our wealth is subsidised by their poverty. Fairtrade is a necessary and appropriate ambition. Perhaps this will become more universally accepted

---

59 Jeffrey D. Sachs. *Saving our planet, lifting people out of poverty* 'History is written by the rich, and so *the poor get blamed for everything.*'

and applied in the future, using technology which directly connects supplier with purchaser and therefore by-passes monopolies and large multi-national companies. While technology has many detrimental aspects, its capacity to transform trade back to a genuine and mutual exchange between producer and consumer is one of its brightest aspects. Neoliberal economics has not the slightest interest in economic justice, only in the accumulation of wealth.

In the past, European countries built their wealth and advantage through colonisation, enabling access to resources such as minerals and spices far from home, almost always without recompense to the indigenous population. Shamefully this colonisation also enabled the slave trade. Today powerful nations like the US and China do not exercise 19th and 20th century colonising practices, instead they covertly undermine foreign national interests, however democratic, if those interests are deemed to be at odds with their own strategic interests. The presumed subversive activity of China and Russia is the source of much current grievance in the West, but is it not reflecting the practice of the West, especially the US, over many decades?

There is legitimate concern over the global influence China is exercising through its investment in nation building infrastructure (Belt and Road), especially in the Pacific. This investment must be repaid. Small nations with limited resources are desperate for investment, but the long-term consequences might include their loss of autonomy or sovereignty through default on their repayments.

Australia is far from guiltless of international immoral behaviour as our treatment of East Timor following its establishment as a sovereign state in 2002 graphically and shamefully illustrates. Australia sought to steal Timor's legitimate share of natural wealth in the Timor Sea, using illegal surveillance to do so. To obtain justice, East Timor was forced to take Australia to the UN Court of Arbitration in The Hague in 2016. Australia was brought kicking and screaming to a more just outcome. The Australian government and the responsible minister should be on trial, not witness K and his legal counsel,

Bernard Collaery. That this is not the case and that transparency in their trial is denied illustrates how deeply entrenched the protection of power for economic advantage has become at a national political level.

But equally there are many examples of manipulation exercised by wealth and power domestically. It can be covertly illustrated by way of the protection given to the gambling industry.

Several attempts have been made by people such as World Vision's Tim Costello and the Tasmanian Independent MP, Andrew Wilkie, to curb the excesses of the gambling industry, especially the use of poker machines. These attempts have all failed because gambling revenue lines governmental pockets. Walking along the walls of poker machines in clubs and pubs, it is not hard to notice they are not being played by the wealthy, but by those less affluent, often pensioners. It can obviously be argued that no one is forced to play, that those who do, are doing so voluntarily. However, it is more complicated than that. The industry works to encourage those attracted to the machines, perhaps out of loneliness, to play longer than they should and at a rate they cannot afford. That this is the case is obvious when simple changes like requiring players to state in advance the limit of their intended play are fiercely resisted by clubs and pubs. Gambling reform in Australia has been an abject failure. What is the ethical concern? It is simply that the revenue creamed off from this industry, money outlaid almost exclusively by the poor is used to provide services across the breadth of society. In other words, the poor are subsidising everyone, including those more affluent. The lobbying of the gambling industry together with the prospect of lost revenue by State governments has denied any reasonable reform and continues the prospect of the poor making a higher contribution to public budgets than their fair share.

The combination of wealth and power is also notoriously obvious in the lobbying industry. It is scandalous that many politicians become lobbyists as soon as their term in office, voluntarily or more often involuntarily, comes to an end. Two examples from the mining industry will illustrate.

First the proposed Adani mine in the Galilee Basin. It is well known this company has a long record of corruption.[60] It is well known this company does all it can to avoid its financial obligations through royalties and taxation. It is well known this company flaunts environmental regulation. Yet both sides of politics continue to flirt with this company. For a variety of reasons this venture should be unthinkable, even if the company concerned had impeccable credentials.

The volume of water required by the mine will be a threat to water security from the artesian basin potentially affecting vast swathes of agriculture.

There is a threat to biodiversity and threatened species.

There is cultural loss by the local first nation people.

There is real threat to the Great Barrier Reef from the Abbott Point port and from ore carriers traversing the reef.

Above all there is threat to the total environment from the extraction of fossil fuel that should be left in the ground.

A green light to Adani opens the gate to other mining developments in the Galilee Basin.

The Barrier Reef supports more jobs than the mining industry ever can, this development is a real threat to the ongoing viability of this tourist industry.

Investment in renewables would produce at least as many if not more employment opportunities.

So why has this ill-conceived venture not been put to bed? Because the advertising capacity of big business influences results at the ballot box, as clearly demonstrated by Clive Palmer in the 2019 federal election. At this election, 25% of the Coalition's financial support came from the mining industry.

A second example is the failed attempt at a mining tax. In 2010 Twiggy Forrest and Gina Reinhart launched a huge advertising campaign to crush the government's proposed mining tax. We live in a world in which those with

---

60 https://adanifiles.com.au

money blow the loudest and least avoidable trumpet. Those with money have strong vested (invested) interests in retaining the status quo. These wealthy miners were able to garner support from the public to do what was not in the public's best interest, namely to lobby against a mining tax.

Planet Earth is packed with innumerable resources useful to humankind—but they are finite. They are harvested to serve human need. The harvesting adds value; ore is smelted, timber is milled, water is channelled, animals are butchered, etc. Currency, which acts as a means of exchange, enables contribution, or value garnered in one arena, to be exchanged for value or items of need, or desire, in another. At one level or another all human beings are part of this process, this economy. Those fortunate enough to live in so called developed societies usually accrue enough money to exchange items or experiences that exceed basic requirements; whereas those who live in underdeveloped areas are too often unable to accrue funds necessary for the basics of daily living. As some garner more than their fair share, others need to borrow from them, and debt becomes a major factor in the entrenching of inequity.

For centuries usury was forbidden in Christian countries. In the Middle Ages Jewish migrants from Europe to England became money lenders on the basis that while forbidden to lend to fellow Jews for profit, they could lend to Gentiles for profit.[61] An injunction against usury is understood and accepted by all three Abrahamic religions. The reason, supported by scripture, is that human beings should not be financially enslaved to one another. In practice Christianity has abandoned this injunction. Indeed, some popular, and fast-growing Christian communities openly promote a prosperity gospel, through which wealth is judged to be a sign of divine blessing. Pastors, especially in the US, have flaunted wealth as a sign that their ministry is blessed with divine approval.

---

61 Jewish migration into England almost certainly occurred following the Norman invasion of 1066. The edict of expulsion in 1290 saw their forced removal for 400 years until return under Oliver Cromwell in 1657.

Within Islam, usury is forbidden by the Quran, therefore lending money on interest is haram (sinful and prohibited). Instead of lending money in the conventional manner, the lender, in this case the Islamic bank, takes an equity in the property or item at the heart of the loan for the duration of the loan.

Inevitably those who lend money exorbitantly are loathed, for those who are owed money have power over those who owe the money. This was an underlying factor behind the violent assault on Indians in Uganda under Idi Amin, and the attack on Tutsi in Rwanda. It also became a slur against Jewish people and one of the reasons why anti-Semitism became such an evil reality in Europe.

Over a lifetime most people avoid backbreaking indebtedness, together with the emotional strain that attends it. For most, careful management and flexibility enables purchases to be delayed until they can be afforded. But for those who are poor, this is not possible. Survival often necessitates indebtedness. It is in these cases that excessive usury becomes reprehensible. When inflation is running at less than 3% annually, interest rates at more than twice that figure should not be acceptable. Similarly, small businesses, the backbone of most national economies, frequently need an immediate injection of funds to survive because of circumstances like natural disasters, or changes to government policy, beyond their control. A financial institution whose primary goal is to make money is not sympathetic to their needs. Post COVID19, debt will be a major factor in the lives of many, but especially the younger generation. There will need to be a radical overhaul of the financial system to address this issue and ensure that lives are not generationally enslaved.

In the future, financial indebtedness will become a primary source of coercive influence by nations and individuals over those less fortunate. The jubilee project in the year 2000 released some of the poorest countries from debt burdens which made repayment a higher priority than meeting the basic services needed by their people. It is crucial that the burden of debt not become the dominating priority in the lives of individuals or nations.

Why is the population at large so susceptible to the beat of the economic drum at the expense of the symphonic harmony of a healthy society and ecology? At every election, perceptions relating to the management of the economy dominate in the mind of the electorate. There are many reasons, but an overriding factor is psychological. All human beings long for security. We have been culturally conditioned to believe that this longed-for security is rooted in economic strategies. But this is almost always a deception, for what is offered is most often short-term gain at the expense of long-term sustainability.

It is said that the first obligation of government is the security of its people. If this were true, then governments the world over would concentrate on two issues and ensure that economic policy serves them. First, commitment to strategies that will reverse the threat of uncontrolled global warming and secondly commitment to nuclear disarmament. These are the most severe existential threats facing global citizenry, indeed either on its own could shorten the time span of civilisation as we have come to know it. There is little evidence that the most powerful nations on earth are committed to reducing existential threat associated with either reality, and therefore not meeting their obligation to protect their people. On the contrary, President Trump has increased nuclear capacity and has taken the US out of any agreement which might reduce its carbon emissions. Those who least exacerbate the problem, the poorer nations of the world, are most in danger of being impacted by the wilfulness of the wealthy. The latter protect their short-term financial interests, as if this is their primary responsibility, even if these strategies endanger the long-term security of their people.

In the West undue influence is exercised on the political system by those with wealth. It is a matter of urgency that funding of political parties be banned and that election campaigns be funded from the public purse. Until this happens it is a fact that well-funded self-interest will dominate the formulation of national policy. Worldwide, the production of armaments is one of the wealthiest industries and its capacity to influence policy is monumental.

As is well known, a mere handful of individuals now control a level of wealth equivalent to the combined wealth of half the global population.

Neoliberal economics has a singular focus upon financial capital with seemingly no regard or interest in social capital. Neoliberal politics has moved the political pendulum so far to the right that caring for social capital is called 'left wing' or 'socialism'. Commitment to social capital and economic well-being should not be alternatives between which choice has to be made. To be in the political centre should mean having equal commitment to both. The binary world so beloved of the political elite has to be resisted and defeated. Social capital cannot be supported without economic resources while the production of wealth is meaningless unless it contributes to common good.

Paul in his letter to Timothy is often quoted and misquoted: 'the love of money is the root of all evil' (1 Tim. 6: 10). Unless 21st century capitalist practice is weighed by the good it achieves rather than the profit it makes, capitalism will become a rapacious pariah, gradually consuming the very resources upon which stable and sustainable civilisation depends. For good to be good it must be common.

Chapter 7
I set before You this Day
a Choice

Science or Opinionated Ignorance

Life would be infinitely happier if we could only be born at the
age of eighty and gradually approach eighteen.

Mark Twain

In 1996 Canon Graeme Garrett, the Canberra and Goulburn Diocesan theologian, and I were flown to the NSW south coast by the timber industry because they were concerned that the voice of the Church was demonising their industry. They wanted us to understand the timber industry is responsible, that harvesting hardwood native forests is sustainable and does not threaten endangered fauna. We came away less than convinced. While some trees were left standing clearly this did not leave a habitat in which vulnerable species could survive. More importantly the timber was not being harvested for construction but was being chipped for paper production. It was clear that much of the timber was simply waste.[62]

The most useful part of our visit was a conversation that ensued over dinner in the local pub. Graeme had impressed the timber workers with his grace and intellect. After an hour or so of conversation a timber manager

---

62 Appendix 7: Christianity, the forests, and the environment.

turned to him and said, 'You are obviously a very able and intelligent man, why have you wasted your life in the Church?' His response was stunning. 'I have spent my life trying to nut out how things work. I have concluded that love is the energy that makes all things possible. Like everyone else, I have so much more to know and understand, but even with the doubts I have, I would rather put all my effort into trusting what I have come to know of God and of the world mirrored in God's likeness, than stand outside because of that which I am yet to understand'

It is unlikely that humankind has ever before so starkly faced the need to live with the future in mind, or face the possibility of catastrophe, and yet stumbles at the first hurdle out of misplaced self-interest.

It is often difficult to pin down the moment when awareness of certain truths begins to dawn. Truth or insight tends to creep up on you. Having grown up on a farm and being in tune with the seasons of the year, the importance of balancing harvest with the replenishment of the soil, I was intuitively aware that fertility and fecundity are fragile, nature has a habit of balancing itself out, but not always in the time frame of human need.

By the mid 70s I was aware of what has come to be known as climate science: the study of factors which contribute to or disrupt the fine balance which has enabled human flourishing over the period of human development known as the Holocene. This scientific study has thrown the spotlight on the consequences of a rapidly expanding human population and its rapacious appetite for finite resources. It is now clear that our combined footprint has become large enough to affect the life-giving natural balances upon which human life and species diversity have depended for at least 200,000 years. This science has demonstrated beyond reasonable doubt that energy stored as fossil fuel has contributed to the stability of the Holocene, while its release challenges that stability. The gradual and now more rapid release of carbon since the onset of the industrial revolution has facilitated the release of previously unknown levels of energy and heat, making life as we have known it increasingly vulnerable both on land, and in the sea. The sea, which has had to do more than its fair share of absorbing the unwanted levels of heat and energy may be in greater threat than life on planet earth's land masses.

So, having become aware, how is it that I became more than an interested, if not anxious, bystander? In 1998 I attended the Lambeth Conference of bishops in Canterbury UK along with approximately 800 other bishops from across the worldwide Anglican Communion. Before the conference began the Archbishop of Canterbury, George Carey, invited us to choose a theme which would be the focus of our study in small groups and from which we would contribute to the plenary sessions. Most bishops choose to be part of the sessions on human sexuality and gender equality. The ordination of women as bishops and the treatment of people of homosexual orientation were the hot issues of this conference, demanding the attention of the secular as well as ecclesiastical press.

I chose not to go with the mob but focus on the topic of environmental responsibility. A modest 50 or so of us made this choice. Shamefully I did not make much preparation before the conference began, assuming I would be able to rely on the knowledge and expertise of those more informed than I, and that as a consequence I would be able to keep a low profile. In the preparatory material I noted that a bishop from the Philippines was to chair the section. I do not have a clear recollection of the sequence of events that transpired after our initial introductions, but in the absence of the Filipino bishop, another chair had to be appointed. My story is that I went out for a pit stop and that when I returned, I found I had been voted in as the chair. I blame the very able Bishop of London, Bishop Richard Chartres, for this choice. Somehow, largely with his drafting skills and general leadership we managed to make our way through and presented the following resolution which was ultimately accepted in the plenary session. I do remember that as I presented the resolution, within the context of attention being given to sexuality and gender, I drew the attention of the gathered assembly to our resolution by saying that 'if this conference and the world generally fail to take environmental responsibility seriously, gender and sexuality will be irrelevant in 50 years' time'!

The resolution read: This Conference:

a. reaffirms the Biblical vision of Creation according to which:

> Creation is a web of inter-dependent relationships bound together in the Covenant which God, the Holy Trinity has established with the whole earth and every living being.

  i. the divine Spirit is sacramentally present in Creation, which is therefore to be treated with reverence, respect, and gratitude;

  ii. human beings are both co-partners with the rest of Creation and living bridges between heaven and earth, with responsibility to make personal and corporate sacrifices for the common good of all Creation;

  iii. the redemptive purpose of God in Jesus Christ extends to the whole of Creation.

b. recognises:

  i. that unless human beings take responsibility for caring for the earth, the consequences will be catastrophic because of: overpopulation, unsustainable levels of consumption by the rich, poor quality and shortage of water, air pollution, eroded and impoverished soil, forest destruction, plant and animal extinction;

  ii. that the loss of natural habitats is a direct cause of genocide amongst millions of indigenous peoples and is causing the extinction of thousands of plant and animal species. Unbridled capitalism, selfishness and greed cannot continue to be allowed to pollute, exploit and destroy what remains of the earth's indigenous habitats;

  iii. that the future of human beings and all life on earth hangs in balance as a consequence of the present unjust economic structures, the injustice existing between the rich and the poor, the continuing exploitation of the natural environment and the threat of nuclear self-destruction;

iv. that servanthood to God's creation is becoming the most important responsibility facing humankind and that we should work together with people of all faiths in the implementation of our responsibilities;

v. that we as Christians have a God given mandate to care for, look after and protect God's creation.

c. prays in the Spirit of Jesus Christ:

i. for widespread conversion and spiritual renewal in order that human beings will be restored to a relationship of harmony with the rest of Creation and that this relationship may be informed by the principles of justice and the integrity of every living being, so that self-centred greed is overcome; and

ii. for the recovery of the Sabbath principle, as part of the redemption of time and the restoration of the divinely intended rhythms of life.

With Bishop Michael Marshall, Lambeth, 1998.

Reading the resolution 20 years later I am saddened that the Church at large has little if any knowledge of it and saddened that its insights do not undergird the urgency of the Church's mission today.

Having accepted the baton of responsibility for environmental stewardship, it seemed logical that when the Anglican Consultative Council decided to add the environment to their list of international networks that I should be prepared to become its inaugural convener. This was a great privilege and pleasure from 2002—2006.

Being the convener meant being a nuisance, first to the institutional Church, doing all in my power to encourage environmental standards at a local, Diocesan, and national level. It is a matter of some pride that while some aspects of Church have remained laggards, nevertheless much of the Church has taken a lead. We have seen the widespread development of recycling standards, energy conservation, green power generation and by no means least, disinvestment from companies involved in the fossil fuel industry. It has also meant being a nuisance to industries that do more than their fair share of environmental damage.

Being a spokesperson for the environment has also meant being a nuisance to politicians, especially those with environmental responsibility.[63] An example has been my interactions with Greg Hunt the federal Minister for the Environment from 2013—2016. Greg Hunt did more than most to ensure Australia had no viable energy policy. He insisted that Tony Abbott's 'direct action' plan would be the most effective and economically viable way to reduce emissions. This plan meant industries were paid incentives by the taxpayer to plant trees, prevent land clearing and make energy use more efficient, etc. This has been an unmitigated disaster and despite claims of the government to the contrary, Australia's emissions since 2013 have risen, not declined. What is so infuriating is that genuine dialogue with politicians on the right is almost impossible because white is declared to be black and black declared to be white. If anything, the situation is worse since Greg Hunt moved from environment to health. We were given a Minister for the Environment, Melissa Price, who seemed to have no knowledge of, or commitment to her portfolio. No statement of any meaning was uttered from her lips since she assumed the portfolio. If she were Minster for Mining and Environmental Exploitation it may have been a better match.

63 Appendix 8: The Climate Bishop.

Who knows who the Minister might be when we go to print, but it is currently Sussan Ley. It appears Ms Ley's first commitment is to irrigators, not the portfolio with which she has been entrusted. Her portfolio has been subsumed under a mega portfolio including agriculture.

We have come to a pretty pass in western democracies where care for the environment and a sustainable future is presented by the political elite and some sections of the media as a form of socialism, the ravings of the loony left. Why is it that those who espouse a conservative position are so dismissive of this responsibility and of the science that undergirds it? It is not unreasonable to assume that those who call themselves 'conservative' would want to conserve. The difficulty is that conservatives are so besotted with the idea of individual rights, they have lost sight of what human beings share in common. In their narrow, ideological thought bubble they have convinced themselves that caring for the environment impinges upon individual rights and is therefore a ghastly form of socialism. I developed this theme more fully in Chapter 5. At this point however I simply want to reiterate that western civilisation is heading for catastrophic collapse if individualism is allowed free rein. It is an obvious truth that most of the problems facing planet Earth require commonality of purpose and that if there is conflict between the assumed rights of the individual and the health and well-being of society, it is the latter that must prevail.

Sir Roger Scruton was, until his death in January 2020, the intellectual darling of the right—much beloved of no less a figure than Tony Abbott. In 2012 he published his: *Green Philosophy: how to think seriously about the planet*[64]. Here he espouses *oikophilia*[65] (love of home) as the way forward in face of our current crisis. Scruton does not question, indeed accepts climate science and the need to reduce emissions, however he dismisses international treaties as useless, indeed counter-productive, for he argues

---

64 Roger Scruton. *Green Philosophy: how to think seriously about the planet* (London: Atlantic Books, 2012).

65 Ibid 253.

that only those committed to a European understanding of law will keep them. To him *oikophilia* is a form of patriotism, love of one's own native land. There are two matters to observe here. First that Scruton, unlike his followers in Australia, accepts the science. However he fails to understand that *oikos* (house or home) is the whole planet,[66] not simply the land of our birth and that because the awful consequences of global warming fall on everyone, there is a clear incentive for all to uphold international treaties and to hold to account those who do not. Australian conservative politics has not accepted the science and at the same time disdains international cooperation and the upholding of international law. It is for these double reasons that we are rightly looked upon as environmental laggards, or worse, as international white-anters by much of the global community.

On 7th February 2009, Black Saturday, devastating and unprecedented bushfires swept through the state of Victoria. One hundred and seventy-three people lost their lives, four hundred and forty were hospitalised with significant burns, and two thousand and twenty-nine homes were destroyed. Temperatures on the day reached 46 degrees Celsius. Of some 200 separate fires some were lit by arsonists, many were caused by falling power lines.

While Australians are used to regular fires and floods, this was unprecedented; messages of empathy and support came from all over the world. Prime Minister Rudd had business to conduct in the UK soon after the fire and with encouragement from the vast army of expat Australians living in the UK, decided to seek permission for a memorial service at Westminster Abbey. Following messages from the Dean, John Hall, and the Prime Minister's daughter, Jessica, I agreed to be the preacher at the service which was conducted in the presence of Prince Charles and the Duchess of Cornwall on the 31st March 2009. The Abbey was absolutely packed, the verger had to use his rod to cut a swathe through the crowd to enable me to reach the pulpit!

---

66 Appendix 9: Change needed for our Planet.

This is what I said in the eight minutes allocated to me:

Westminster Abbey, March 2009.

To this Abbey Church of St Peter, we come today, as many thousands have before us, to grieve enormous pain and loss, to remember those who have so tragically died and to affirm they will not be forgotten. We also come to testify to the hope that lies within us that through God's grace we will triumph over tragedy, that our communities will be strengthened, that the trees will again sprout, the song of the bird will again be heard and the ashes which have covered us will in their own way wash down and nourish the life that is yet to be born. Here in London the days are lengthening, and signs of spring are all around us, yet in the Victorian hills the evenings are now shorter, the temperature is cooler, the immediate threat has passed, and space is emerging for rest and the long haul of restoration has begun.

The two readings chosen for today speak profoundly to our situation. The first, was originally spoken out of a situation of unbearable tragedy and humiliation—the great exile. So many had been killed, identity was lost and vision in ruins. Yet out of this tragic environment the prophet imagines the emergence of a servant leader of restoration whose bearing is not arrogant or triumphant, he does not trade in bravado or certainty, but wears the ashes of tragedy on his face and clothes. He appears like the first fragile and yet beautiful mauve tips of new life on the scarred gum trees, his bruises and burns are his badge of honour, the service and building of his people his mission, his imagination for a newer, gentler, more harmonious community his driving force. The Christian Community has long seen this figure to be the first inspirational window into the coming Messiah—Jesus, the one whose crucifixion and resurrection we celebrate in ten days.

The insight could also be true of the best of the Australian character, for out of this tragedy have emerged ordinary and yet extraordinary men and women: fire fighters and cooks, school-children and the elderly, who have combined to relieve the immediate danger and who have promised to remain in the long haul of recovery.

The second reading takes us to our foundations of hope. The human spirit need not be cowered by any external circumstance, as tragic as it might be. We have experienced flood and fire before, our men and women have fought and died in many foreign conflicts, our communities have been challenged to their core by withering drought, but through them all our resolve has been strengthened, our trust in God undiminished, our hope renewed in the Easter message that even death has been overcome: 'nothing can separate us from the love of God which is ours in Christ Jesus our Lord'.

As we move forward, we take with us the memories of these terrible events and we are changed by the learning that comes from them. We can build houses that are more fire resistant, we can give better warning to people, we can learn more about the cycles and rhythms of which fire is an inevitable, and in the right circumstances, a life-giving part. But there is something else we have learned; it is that extreme conditions are likely to occur more frequently and here and throughout the world we are all more likely to be threatened. Weather patterns are changing, and the human footprint is a major contributor. I am therefore grateful and proud that the Australian Government has made a significant commitment to reduce the Australian contribution to the adverse effects of the human footprint. That we can and should do more, few with knowledge would argue against, that we should do less, only the foolhardy, the self-interested or the reckless would even contemplate.

We dare not contemplate a future without learning the lessons this experience has taught us. We Australians live in one of the most wonderful continents on earth. And yet we must live on it in humility not arrogance, in a spirit of stewardship not exploitation. We need to understand its vulnerability, for it is a vulnerability we share. We need to work with its rhythms rather than impose our own and to walk its song lines as generations of people have before 1788.

We come to this Abbey in gratitude for our heritage and in
thanksgiving for the generosity shown to us from peoples across the
globe. In quiet resolve, like the servant figure of the Isaiah passage,
we shall strive to ensure that on our continent, and on our watch, a
bruised reed will not be crushed nor a dimly burning wick of hope
ever be put out.

The following day the *Australian* newspaper savaged me, first for daring
to link the Victorian bush fires to climate change, and second for hypocrisy
in flying from Australia to the UK for the service. In a letter to the editor it
was pointed out that I was living in the UK at the time, but predictably no
apology was extracted. As always with the Murdoch press, the line they wish
to promote is more important than any facts that might substantiate it.

The disdain in which I have been held by the Murdoch papers for some
years is more than reciprocated by the total lack of regard in which I hold
News Limited and its proprietor, Rupert Murdoch. My antipathy is twofold.
First, I am appalled by the way this news outlet attempts to increase their
market share through scurrilous, exaggerated, and misleading reporting.
This is often unrelenting, as much for political figures such as Kevin Rudd,
as well as ecclesiastical figures such as Peter Hollingworth. Credit is not
given where it was due: in Mr Rudd's case for fiscal measures that prevented
Australia falling into recession with much of the rest of the world in 2008,
and in the case of Governor-General Hollingworth for his years as a
champion of justice for the poor. It shamelessly derides those on the wrong
side of their preferred right-wing stance whilst protecting and defending bad
behaviour by conservatives, often without talent or merit, simply because
they are politically and economically neoliberal conservatives.

But equally shameful is their cavalier attitude to truth that is
inconvenient to the commercial interests of their readership, or the ideology
of the paper proprietor. While the papers might claim an open mind on the
issue of climate change or even be a supporter of science, this is not borne
out by the volume of articles and opinion pieces that express a contrary view,
nor by the print space provided to those in power who have done all they can

to prevent Australia having a workable energy policy, nor by the absence of serious reporting of statements from the IPCC and other reputable bodies.

It is simply not good enough to argue that there are respectable arguments to counter climate science. There are not. Climate science makes it indisputably clear that:

- burning of fossil fuels and the release of carbon is slowly but inexorably increasing the density of greenhouse gases in the atmosphere and the acidification of the oceans;
- increased density of greenhouse gases traps more heat;
- the trapped heat equals increased climate changing energy; and
- increased energy is almost certainly going to add to the frequency and intensity of severe weather events.

We have now reached an increase of 1.1 degrees above pre-industrial levels. Within five years we will have used up the carbon budget which would keep us blow 1.5 degrees. Two degrees will almost certainly destroy coral reefs.

Opinions need to be tested. My opinion that rugby is the purest form of football might be obvious to me. But it is legitimately open to question by those unexposed to the glories of the game played in heaven! However, that leaves fall from trees and tides ebb and flow are facts that do not need testing, any more than the proposition needs further testing that increasing the density of greenhouse gases increases warming, whilst decreasing the density would facilitate cooling.

In the early 2000s my views on impending disaster caused by cavalier human behaviour more interested in profit than sustainability, brought the late Robert Carter of James Cook University to my house in Canberra. Dr Carter along with Ian Plimmer (director of multiple mineral exploration and mining companies) were two of the most high-profile Australian climate deniers who claimed to argue from a scientific background.

In my lounge room Robert Carter somewhat condescendingly informed me that carbon dioxide is not a pollutant. Tony Abbott, the prolific spruiker of this line from the climate sceptics' lexicon, probably appropriated it from him. I know of no climate scientist who refers to carbon dioxide as a pollutant. In the biblical creation narrative, all animate and inanimate matter is described as good for in its appropriate and right place everything contributes to the well-being of the whole. However, everything is potentially a pollutant. It depends where it is, the volume it is in, and the speed with which it can be dispersed. Even water can be a pollutant as those suffering the aftermath of a flood will tell you. Excess carbon has been stored underground in fossil fuels for millennia, contributing to what we have known as the 'Holocene', in the period of stable climate which has followed, humanity has flourished. Yet, in the space of 200 years since the commencement of the industrial revolution, large proportions of this carbon have been released (most in the last 50 years) potentially tipping the climatic balance. Dr Carter, as fellow scientists have shown, bases his position on spurious arguments.

Whilst one might assume environmental responsibility to be the orthodox stance of those professing the Christian faith, sadly this is not the case.

In 2008, while in the UK, I was invited by the then Archbishop of Canterbury, Archbishop Rowan Williams, to brief representatives of UK Dioceses gathered at Lambeth Palace on the work of the Anglican Communion's environmental network of which I had been the inaugural chair. After my briefing, opportunity was afforded for questions. One gentleman rose to question, in the politest of English tones, why environmental responsibility should be on the Christian agenda at all, let alone a priority. After proclaiming that saving souls was the highest responsibility for Christians, a statement I was not going to debate without nuance, for which this was neither the time nor place, he went on to say that the end of the world was in the hands of God, as was the weather and all forces of nature. He contended that humans have no role in that which belongs to God alone and that to do so is an arrogance if not a blasphemy.

Meeting as we were in Lambeth Palace, I should have been a little more circumspect in my response, but being outraged, I threw caution to the wind. I agreed that Jesus is the alpha and omega, that the beginning and end of all things are in the hand of God. However, I also pointed to the biblical reality that human action and inaction has consequences; indeed, that these consequences can be apocalyptic in scale.

I agreed it is arrogant for human beings to 'play God'. However the whole prophetic tradition calls on human beings, and particularly those in positions of power, to take responsibility for their actions, knowing that we are all accountable. In relation to climate change and environmental responsibility I pointed out that we can no longer claim the defence of not knowing. We do know, in fact the fundamentals of climate science have been known for more than 100 years. We know that, unchanged, human behaviour that continues its current trajectory will have dire consequences for future generations and particularly for the poor of the world. I pointed to the reality that even now there are millions of climate refugees, a phenomenon which will only increase in years to come. I also made the point that human beings depend on healthy diversity within the natural order. God's covenant following the Noah epic was with the whole of life, with all life that emerged from the ark, not just with human beings. We are now seeing animal and plant extinction on a scale not previously known in the lifetime of *homo sapiens*, and probably not since the last epoch-making mass extinction, that of the dinosaurs 66 million years ago. Nowhere is this more apparent than in Australia.

The more I spoke, the more I observed some awkwardness around the room. I discerned that the awkwardness had little to do with the content of what I had to say, but clearly another factor was in play. Over lunch I discovered what that factor was. A fellow sandwich muncher casually asked if I knew who the person had been who had taken me to task over the importance of placing environmental responsibility high on the Christian agenda. On revealing my complete ignorance, I was informed that the speaker was one of the most powerful laymen in the Church of England and secretary of their General Synod. Had I known this before I responded to him, would this have altered what I had to say—probably not?

A further example of permission being given to Christians not to take climate change and environmental responsibility seriously can be illustrated by the very public exchange that occurred between myself and the then leading Roman Catholic cleric in Australia, Cardinal George Pell of Sydney. The context was a meeting of the General Synod of the Anglican Church in Australia held in Canberra in 2007. Journalists were sniffing around looking for some story that might carry in the national press. The resolutions of General Synod were, overall, of little interest to any, other than devotees of ecclesiastical law. It was soon after Easter. Cardinal Pell had chosen to say in his Easter message that Jesus had nothing to say about climate change. The Cardinal's scepticism (or denial) of climate science was well known. But his implication that climate concern is akin to some form of 'new age' religion was and is thoroughly and irresponsibly scandalous. Scandalous because it insults science and continues the same arrogant stance of the Church, so familiar to Galileo, Darwin, and scientists of the past. But scandalous too because of its implication that people like myself have gone off the rails as far as orthodox faith is concerned and therefore are not to be taken at all seriously by people of faith.

I responded that he would find the Bible to be silent on most of the dogmas so dear to latter day Roman Catholicism and to have nothing to say about Cardinals. Worse, on examination, the clericalism which has been at the very core of some of the most tragic abuses of recent Roman Catholic history cannot be drawn or defended from the sayings of Jesus or the Bible. The idea that certain persons become ontologically superior in their status to that of others through ordination is anathema to scripture which insists that leaders are to take on the persona of the lowliest they serve.

On the other hand, scripture is clear about the role of human beings in relation to the created or natural order. We are part of 'nature', not apart from it. The created order is not there for us to exploit as we will; we are to be stewards, or priests, of its good. It is salutary to be reminded that indigenous people generally and the Aboriginal people of Australia in particular, have a profound sense of this reality. Caring for country being not simply the primary responsibility of the people, but the source of their fulfilment and well-being.

It could be said that the overriding biblical principle which undergirds environmental responsibility is sabbath. The keeping of sabbath lies at the heart of biblical ethics. What I mean by this is that the sabbath principle is the principle of giving appropriate space to the honouring of God, the natural order, others, and oneself. Scripture spells this out in practical terms. The sabbath day is not simply a day of rest from work, but a day of celebrating the life-giving balances inherent in creation itself. The day probably had its origins in the waxing and waning of the moon and particularly the period of darkness between the waning of the old moon and the rising of the new.

As Jesus pointed out, religious fanaticisms relating to the seventh day, obscure sabbath's true nature. This is as true now as it was then. I first understood sabbath's rhythm through a long-established agricultural habit on the farm in Sussex as I grew up. Fields were to be given a year's rest in rotation. The rhythm urgently needs rediscovery as land is over worked. But other sabbatical injunctions are also in need of urgent rediscovery like 'do not take the mother with the young' (Deut 22:6). This is a lesson the modern fishing industry has yet to learn and apply as it over-fishes and stocks run dry. It is spelt out in the principle of jubilee that debts are to be forgiven, intergenerational poverty is verboten, and personal ownership is always to be understood in the context of communal responsibility. No, Cardinal, I am afraid you are wrong on both counts, some of the ecclesiastical doctrines you hold have no foundation in scripture, whilst environmental responsibility lies at the core of belief.

In their desire for economic advantage, governments the world over continue to prioritise short term financial gain, over environmental responsibility. Large companies exploit resources even when exploitation causes large scale pollution. Financial and development transactions are entered into outside the wider arena of their consequential impact. How else could government on either side of politics approve the Adani development in Queensland's Galilee Basin?

As convener of the Anglican Communion Environment Network I chaired a conference of the network in Lima, Peru, in 2005. As part of our visit we were taken to a lead and copper mine high in the Andes, otherwise a beautiful and pristine environment. As we came close to the site, the pollution was clearly visible to the untrained eye. Arsenic and other toxic substances used to separate the ore were leaching into the watercourses which ultimately found their way down to Lima itself. The mine had a temporary injunction imposed upon it because of pollution and the danger this posed to the health of the local community. The community was tragically divided. Despite the obvious health issues, a significant proportion of the community understandably wanted the mine reopened because without it, employment opportunities were scarce. The local Catholic priest ably led a pressure group seeking justice and restitution from the government. He reasonably argued that his community should not have to choose between health and employment. The two should not be mutually exclusive. The mining company's home base was north American. We were told that the government always sided with the demands of the company, rather than the local community, because royalties that propped up the government would otherwise be lost. I do not know how, or if, the matter was resolved, but the problem facing this small community in Peru is replicated the world over. Those who live in precarious economic situations are too often made to choose between the long-term well-being and health of their community and opportunities for employment. No community should be expected to face this choice.

The option of standing on the sidelines in relation to climate responsibility is now past. School children, inspired by Greta Thunberg, have decided where they stand. Youngsters have recently initiated a class action against the Australian Federal Government for enacting policies that they believe put the future of their generation at risk. I have recently appreciated the privilege of standing with them, in Glebe Park, Canberra, outside the Eurobodalla Council Chambers in Moruya, and at a variety of school forums.

We know what we need to do. It is within our power, technologically and economically to act decisively. We have choices that will be denied future generations. These choices must be made now. Tomorrow will be too late.

Chapter 8
Vision or Institution?

The Story of the Beginning of the Australian Centre for
Christianity and Culture

Instead of imposing new obligations (Christians) should
appear as people who wish to share their joy, who point to
a horizon of beauty and who invite others to a delicious
banquet.

Pope Francis

When elected Bishop of Canberra and Goulburn in 1993 I realised
certain agendas came with the appointment, beyond those within Diocesan
structures. Being decentralised and provincially based, if the Anglican
Church of Australia is to have a role in the national capital, and through it
to the nation, the Bishop of Canberra and Goulburn needs to step up, or the
national Church has no role in the capital at all. Secondly, since federation
and the allocation of national sites for the major Christian denominations,
the national Anglican site in Barton, prominently placed on the edge of
the parliamentary triangle was languishing for want of a vision. With one
exception (Bishop Clements), all my predecessors had sought to build on the
site in a manner worthy of the national church and had failed. This inevitably
presented an extra-diocesan responsibility which I had no right to ignore.[67]
I could re-envision the responsibility, I could try and delegate it elsewhere,

---

67 Appendix 10: Ecumenical Service to Mark Canberra Day, 12 March 1994.

but I could not ignore it. With the rapid expansion and development of Canberra particularly its iconic parliamentary triangle, it is thoroughly conceivable that the National Capital Authority could, or should, ask the Church why it had the right to hold the lease if it was incapable of investing appropriately in it.

Bishop Lewis Bostock Radford (1915—1933) was the first bishop to accept this role. When prominent national leasehold sites were offered to the major denominations of the time, based on numerical representation within the population, he negotiated, for Anglicans, a site overlooking the yet to be built Lake Burley Griffin and on the edge of the proposed parliamentary triangle. Upon this site it was his intention to build the national Anglican Cathedral of St Mark. It is said that despite other triumphs, including the establishment of the two Grammar Schools in the national capital, his failure to build, or at least begin to build, the cathedral, was an overwhelming disappointment to him. A modest concrete cross was all that stood as a marker for the Cathedral.

Bishop Radford was followed by Bishop Ernest Burgmann (1934—1960), perhaps the most influential Australian bishop of his generation. Bishop Burgmann's legacy lives on today in what is referred to as the Burgmann vision. What is meant by this is a robust Christianity, fully, and confidently engaged with Australian life. While much Australian Anglicanism could be divided between those influenced by the tractarian movement (Anglo Catholicism) and those influenced by evangelicalism, Burgmann can not be so pigeonholed, or properly identified with either. Neither could Bishop John Stoward Moyes of Armidale, the Bishop who sent me to college in 1963. Burgmann is the Bishop who comes most easily to mind when the phrase 'speaking truth to power' is employed. It is not for nothing that he was named 'a troublesome priest', an epitaph first bequeathed to Thomas à Becket, Archbishop of Canterbury by Henry ll. I consciously modelled my episcopate on these two giants of men, the first an educator, the second a prophet. I hoped that during my time in Canberra I would continue to enhance the vision of both.

Burgmann was responsible for moving the diocesan geographical centre of gravity from Goulburn to Canberra. Burgmann wanted Christianity to engage with the nation from a reasoned and intellectually confident position. Above all he wanted the gospel to be 'brushed with Australian dust'. The Cathedral site, a perpetual lease in the name of the national church, was set beside a much smaller 100-year lease in the name of the Diocese. Burgmann raised money for the establishment of a national theological library and set about training his students with a broad and inclusive vision. Burgmann was canny enough to site the library across both leases. Following his retirement Burgmann lived in a flat beside the library and became its warden until ill health intervened. He died in 1967.

Burgmann's successor, Bishop Ken Clements, could hardly be expected to do much with the site, given his predecessor was living on it. In those years any further hopes for the site lay dormant. Clements was followed by Bishop Cecil Warren who put enormous effort into securing national Church support for the building of a national cathedral. He put various motions to the national synod but failed to gain the support he longed for. The reality is that Australia and Australians do not have the same national sense of pride in their capital that is well known in the US or Britain. It was never going to be possible to build in Canberra the equivalent of the national cathedral in Washington or Westminster Abbey in the UK. Australian identification is strongly provincial with focus given to the various state capitals. It was never likely that significant monies could or would be garnered from metropolitan Dioceses and even less likely from cash strapped rural ones. Bishop Warren's great disappointment in not securing support contributed to his early disengagement from the Diocese, assuming an appointment in the UK in 1983.

Bishop Warren was succeeded by his assistant, Bishop Owen Dowling. Dowling continued the efforts of his predecessor, refocusing endeavours through the appointment of Brisbane's Dean, Ian George as Rector of St John's Reid, later assistant bishop of the Diocese, with responsibility for promoting the national cathedral dream. Despite the obvious talent and national exposure enjoyed by Ian George, no further progress was made, although commitment in principle was given to the Canberra based Hindmarsh consortium for its construction.

I knew most of this background when my appointment was announced. I knew that the episcopacy of most of my predecessors, in one way or another, was marked by unfulfilled vision for this site. Should the site therefore be abandoned, or could the vision be reconceived?

As already recorded, as a boy, I grew up in a little English village with one Church. It was not until my teenage years that I became fully conscious that there were Christian denominations other than the Church of England. Gradually I realised that denominationalism had a lot to do with moments in history and responses made to them that subsequently took institutionalised shape, often with an ethnic or local overtone.

As a migrant to Australia I had long pondered the relevance of denominationalism in Australian life. What sense did it make for Australians to be identified with divisions and separations connected to arguments and agendas long past, and in another place, quite apart from the reality that with a divided voice it is much harder to witness to the Gospel amongst a population notoriously sceptical of religious affiliation. Would it not be more appropriate to find spiritual commonality, shaped and formed by the continent which is home to us all?

Thus, before arriving in Canberra on 30 May 1993, I formulated, in general terms, a different vision. I imagined the site being home to Christians of all denominations, and none. But not Christians only, a place where people of other faiths could gather across boundaries that normally divide us. I imagined people of no faith at all engaging in issues of deep significance, both personally and nationally. I imagined the site representing a diverse, yet inclusive, spiritual future which acknowledged and respected a common humanity under God, before prioritising doctrinal or ritual differences. An inclusive vision demands a welcoming and non-threatening space.

It requires hosting. God imagines and hosts space for all living. Christians are called to act as God acts. Thus I believed it a privilege and responsibility for Christians to host such a space as an expression of their faith and for Anglicans to do this as the natural and obvious extension of the Burgmann vision that Christianity be thoroughly immersed on Australian soil and be in tune with the reality of a multicultural, multifaith, society.[68]

Above all I imagined the site being a place of reconciliation, a place in tune with the spiritual aspirations and dreaming of Australia's indigenous people over thousands of years. I imagined that, were Radford and Burgmann alive today, this is exactly the vision they would have supported.

In 1994 we held a conference in Canberra to further envision the centre. The conference was attended by figures as diverse as Catholic Archbishop of Canberra, Francis Carroll, Professor Mike Dodson, a leading indigenous figure, Morris West, Australia's well revered writer, and Peter Hollingworth then Archbishop of Brisbane.

Morris West wonderfully captured the hopes of the conference:

> A place where men and women can range freely over the mysteries in which we all live, where they are not obliged to look over their shoulders for fear of eavesdroppers and censors, where they are free to be wrong in order to discover right ... a place where beauty resides and love resides and God resides, and the Grail-search is re-enacted in a search for truth; for new enlightenment in old truths

But would such a vision fly, would it resonate with all, whom, with justification, feel they are stakeholders in the site?

First, I sat down with representatives of the indigenous communities of Australia, chief amongst them being Dr Lowitja O'Donohue. We met on the site and were immediately inspired by the thoughts and dreams of some remarkable people. Muriel Slockee, an elder of the Yuin nation, took out a scrap of paper and drew two curved lines divided by a space—thus ( ). I asked what they signified. I was told they represented the impression

---

68 Appendix 11: Christianity's Australian Character, *Sydney Morning Herald*, 5 July 1994.

left in the sand by human backsides after two people have sat cross-legged in conversation, facing each other, probably around a fire. I found the image striking. It spoke of respect and, dialogue, openness to the mind of the other. From the outset it was obvious the symbol was diametrically opposite to that of the federal parliament on the hill nearby. Formed and shaped by the two houses the image of the federal parliament is) (. This characterisation of Aldo Giurgola's winning design aptly describes what goes on in the Australian parliament—confrontation. It was clear God was calling us to create a space of inclusion, dialogue, conversation, and respect. While the buildings to eventually emerge on the site do not carry this shape, nevertheless the original intent remains very much alive.

The first development saw the erection of the pilgrim poles. Donated by the energy company Actew/AGL, they were carved with symbols of Christian and indigenous spirituality by local unemployed youth under the guidance of Patrick Russell. They portray life as a journey, fuelled by faith, hope and love. From the outset it was important to bring onto the site the marginalised, those whose stories are seldom heard or valued. The second development was the fireplace with its twelve stone seats and seven pine trees. For me this remains, and perhaps will always remain, the spiritual centre of the site. Its indigenous overtones are obvious. Overlaid on this is an image from the Old Testament of the Tent of Meeting, outside the camp. As already hinted, Australians are not religious insiders, we are not temple people. As much as Australians express spiritual longings, and we certainly do, we do this outside the camp, outside the confines of institutional religion of which we are largely suspicious. The strong sense of Tent rather than Temple pervades the whole site and its development; indeed, it pervades its partnerships.

Theological heavy weights such as Karl Barth, and the *Swiss Reformed* theologian, Emil Brunner, have argued whether it is possible to come to Christian faith with a starting point in natural religion, or whether it is only possible through a starting point in revealed religion. If the created order reflects the glory of its creator, which it does, then it should be no surprise to find that sacrifice and resurrection are imbedded in the natural order, and that natural religion and revealed religion share a deep resonance with one another.

With the assistance of the Governor-General, Sir William Deane, we held several symbolic meetings on the stone seats around the fire, including smoking ceremonies. The twelve seats of course represent the biblical number for inclusion. When twelve are present, all are present. Four symbolises the four cardinal points of earth and three the divine. Multiplying them and we gain the inclusive number, twelve. The addition of three and four is seven. The seven pine trees represent the biblical number for wholeness, completeness, perhaps even perfection, a number only possible when earth and heaven meet. Most importantly it is the sabbath number, guarding and guiding the rhythms of life. In a moment of exquisite inclusiveness one of the black pines was planted by the Queen in the year 2000 and one of the white pines by Dr Lowitcha O'Donohue.

The next sounding that needed to occur was with secular authorities who had the right to approve or decline development on this significant site. I held informal conversations with Annabelle Pegram, then director of the National Capital Authority. All development in or around the parliamentary triangle and other significant areas such as ANZAC Parade and the War Memorial must be approved by this authority. To my joy and amazement, we received nothing but encouragement. Annabelle will forgive me for saying she had no strong connection with the faith. In a state of almost disbelief, I asked why the encouragement? The answer will stay with me. 'Every city must have a spiritual soul. Without a soul, a city lacks cohesion and depth, becoming a place only of function, not of being'. What more could I ask for!!

From the outset it was important that the site honour and extend ecological opportunities and responsibilities. Having been largely untouched by white settlement the site was custodian to native grasses and habitat common in the past, but rare in the present including the endangered Button Wrinklewort! Although a protection order on the grass meant a prohibition on this central area of the lease for building, we agreed that it be retained in perpetuity as native grassland under appropriate care and authority. While the loss of this land for building and development in the heart of the lease has been deeply regretted by some, the intended placement of buildings around the grasses with a hard face to Blackall Street, tiered down towards the lake, will give the feeling of a natural amphitheatre which can only enhance the whole site in perpetuity.

It was not long however before the 'loss' of this area was to be more than compensated by the acquisition of another.

I found myself at a function in Rydges Hotel, Lakeside on 6 February 1997 to farewell Michael Clarke, a department permanent head with whom I had been associated as a member of the Paul Keating appointed committee to review the Australian Honours system. I had a previous appointment that evening which necessitated the wearing of a purple shirt. Thus, wearing the shirt at what was otherwise a very secular event, I slipped in late and sat down at a table with seven other guests near the door. Believing that being noticed is far preferable to being ignored, I coped with the light-hearted shellacking I received from the master of ceremonies, before attempting to engage my fellow guests in conversation. One opened with 'so you would like the land'? 'Of course,' I replied, not knowing who he was, or what land he was referring to. Clarifying that the piece we were talking about was facing Kings Avenue, he then said, 'is there some other land you would like?'

My new-found friend was in fact referring to a government leasehold, then in use as an open-air car park, along King's Avenue and abutting Blackall Street and the national church site. Having clarified the piece and having clarified my interest he said, 'It is yours!' Trying not to be flabbergasted, and anxious that I was not being taken for a mug, I asked whether we could follow up the conversation the next day. He handed me his business card on which was printed his name and position, Director of Federal Real Estate. I rang Ian Nichol, a lawyer, and key member of our small development committee, to take up the issue with the government department the next day, the rest as they say is history. We excitedly took over the government lease along Kings Avenue which provided us direct access to the parliamentary triangle. One other lease remained outstanding, held by the ACT government. At the time Kate Carnell was Chief Minister. I appraised her of the transfer of the federal lease to the Church, on the understanding that the transfer was conditional on an inclusive vision beyond a simple denominational leasehold and suggested that the ACT government should do the same. Both leases were granted on the basis that the Anglican Church would pursue this inclusive vision.

If in the future the Anglican Church, which holds the lease in a custodial manner for a broader vision, is unable to continue with the vision, it has no moral or legal right to attempt to profit from the land, but would return it to federal authorities who, have overarching authority for the parliamentary triangle and its surrounds. The National Capital Authority would be obligated to determine its use in the national capital and nation's best interest.

Kate and I met in Commonwealth Park on Australia Day. She was in a very convivial mood. At the time the Diocese owed $200,000 'betterment tax' on its office block, Jamieson House, on Constitution Avenue. (The ACT government granted leases for Church or religious use at far less than the commercial rate. If the Church wished subsequently to sell or otherwise benefit from the land 'betterment' tax was owed).

I suggested to Kate that the Diocese pay the $200,000 to the ACT government thus freeing the site for commercial development in the future. Furthermore, should she deem it appropriate, in turn the ACT government return the $200,000 as a tangible gift in support of the vision, together with the lease. At the time we were considering an approach to the States for seed grants for this 'national' enterprise. Our rationale was that the States have a history of generous donations to significant denominational buildings in their State capitals, and that a contribution to an inclusive national spiritual centre was appropriate. None of this would be possible unless the ACT government contributed first, and they were unlikely to make a gift if it had to come from an already determined budget.

Kate expressed the view the vision was noble and deserved every success but doubted it could ever be achieved. Nevertheless, it was agreed the lease be handed over and the ACT government contributed $200,000 for the establishment of this inclusive spiritual centre. I suspect deep down she felt safe, that the vision would not happen and that the money and lease would subsequently be returned!

The third sounding that needed to be taken was with other Christian denominations. At that time ecumenical fellowship and support between the various Churches in Canberra was strong. We held regular 'Heads of Churches' meetings for prayer and fellowship in each other's homes. I was particularly grateful for the friendship and support of two leaders, Dr Thorwald Lorenzen of the Baptist Church and Archbishop Francis Carroll of the Roman Catholic Church. Without the support of these wise and godly men the venture would not have got off the ground. Archbishop Carroll went out on a limb within a Roman Catholic culture which under John Paul II and later Benedict XVI was becoming more inwardly focussed and far less inclined to meaningful ecumenical cooperation. He confessed to me later that he never doubted the venture was right but did not believe it was possible. Through him the largest Christian denomination in Australia was brought on board. In 1998 Church leaders decided on a journey together to Uluru entitled 'A journey to the Centre'. With Archbishop Carroll's help the journey began at our site in Canberra and with encouraging words being said by various Church leaders including Cardinal Edward Clancy. (He firmly dressed me down afterwards for having, in his eyes, placed him in a position of unequivocal support when at that stage his support was far from unequivocal)!

Because the vision needed legal authority and that authority could only come from the General Synod of the Anglican Church in Australia, the custodian of the primary lease, a request for a change in purpose was taken to the General Synod in 1995. It followed on from a motion taken to the General Synod of 1989 that the Diocese of Canberra and Goulburn be granted authority to develop the national site on behalf of the national Church. The two successful resolutions were as follows:

National Ecumenical Centre

Movers Hollingworth, P.J.

That this Synod, having in mind Synod motion 59/89 which among other things encouraged the Diocese of Canberra and Goulburn to develop the national Anglican site at Barton in the ACT, formerly the responsibility of a General Synod Committee –

(i) welcomes proposals currently emerging for a national ecumenical centre for Australian Christian life, witness and pilgrimage on the site;

(ii) considers that subject to the acceptance by all parties of a suitable ecumenical development the site currently held for the national Anglican Church by the Diocese of Canberra and Goulburn should be transferred to a recognised ecumenical body at a time and on terms agreed to between the Standing Committee and the Diocese of Canberra and Goulburn;

(iii) encourages dioceses to support the project as it is further developed; and

(iv) requests Standing Committee to continue to co-operate with the Diocese of Canberra and Goulburn on this matter.

The Most Reverend P.J. Hollingworth

Resolution year: 1995

NATIONAL ANGLICAN CENTRE
Mover Bishop of Canberra and Goulburn

That this Synod

(a) directs the Council of the National Anglican Centre to take no further action with respect to the designing, construction or development of a National Anglican Centre in the ACT;

(b) requests the Standing Committee to bring to the next General Synod a canon to repeal the National Anglican Centre Canon 1985;

(c) encourages the Diocese of Canberra and Goulburn to develop the primary site;

(d) expresses the view that the site should be developed with the site of establishing a centre providing facilities for research, study, training and office space and to be a gathering place for witness and worship on national occasions, available to the whole Church of God in Australia, for empowering a Christian witness in the national capital and to the life of the Australian community; and

(e) requests the Standing Committee to co-operate with the Diocese of Canberra and Goulburn, in such manner as the Standing Committee deems appropriate in the development of the primary site with a view to associating the national Church in the fulfilment of that aim.

The Bishop of Canberra and Goulburn,

Resolution year: 1989

And so, the vison met with approval, more than approval, with enthusiasm. But how on earth to bring a vision to reality, was the hurdle yet to be attempted. I have come to understand that the difference between triumph and failure is the intersection of right vision, right time, and right people. Through God's good grace, those intersections occurred.

Since the 1970s I have appreciated the friendship and advice of a remarkable Australian, Everald Compton. I put it to Everald that this vision could not be driven by, or its governance dispensed from, the Anglican Church. This would undermine the vision and give the appearance of being a piece of denominational grandstanding. Nor on the other hand could it come under the direct governance and direction of the Australian Council of Churches. Complex and often urgent decisions involved in the project could not wait to be made by a body dependent upon confirming decisions of its member Churches. There had to be another way.

Everald suggested that we enter a relationship with a university, which, he suggested, would give us several advantages. First, we would be associated with a respected body within the community with strong governance practice. Secondly, we would overcome the problem of tax deductibility, coming under the university's tax-deductible status. Thirdly we would be associated with a body that would have the capacity to promote and resource many of the outreach initiatives we had in mind, including research, the arts, interfaith dialogue, and ecumenism, to name a few.

A relationship with Charles Sturt University made a lot of sense because we had already developed a school of theology within that university from the adjacent site of St Mark's National Theological Centre. A conversation with Cliff Blake, the Vice Chancellor, and Professor Ross Chambers, the Dean of the Faculty of Arts, soon ensued. Little were we to know at that stage what a pivotal role Ross Chambers was to make, and indeed still makes. The University agreed to the partnership, the details of which needed to be thrashed out over a period of time. The University gained a prominent campus in the heart of Canberra, together with research capacity at the highest level. The Centre acquired the administrative, academic, and investment capacity of the University.

Furthering a symbiotic relationship between Church, its vision for the Centre, and the appropriate ambitions and goals of the University was to become the pivotal role of the Centre Board. Quite appropriately, University investment must produce enriching outcomes for the University. Clearly there are huge advantages for the University in having a campus so strategically placed on the edge of the parliamentary triangle. The Centre also gives the University engagement with wider Australian society, investment in ecumenism, reconciliation, the arts, and the capacity for linkage across disciplines.

The Church, with a shrinking resource base, is challenged to grasp its missional responsibility of significant engagement with Australian society. Partnerships, in this case with the University, enable the Church to enter the marketplace of ideas, invest in cultural engagement, make linkage with government, dialogue with secular organisations, share meaningful communion across denominations, and engage with interfaith groups. Without partnership, none of this would be possible. At a time when parochial survival demands so much energy and attention, the Church can, at times, be too distracted to stay with a broader vision. Feeding, nurturing, encouraging, believing in, and investing in this partnership will remain a challenge to Church authorities. Together we can, alone we certainly cannot.

Several years later, at a function to honour Cliff Blake on his retirement as Vice Chancellor, I asked him why he had agreed. His reply was typical of his entrepreneurial character, he said: 'I had no idea what you were talking about, but I liked the people doing the talking'! The potential for both the University and the Church in the partnership remains enormous if both, particularly the Church, is capable of a Burgmannesque vision. It means continuing to accept responsibility, in Christ's name, to be a transformative influence in Australian life, beyond the increasingly restrictive boundaries of denominational and institutional life.

The second intersection to prove vital was the proactive involvement of the Governor-General, Sir William Deane, as patron. Later, when his term as Governor-General ended, he joined the Board. From the outset Sir William (Bill) was enthusiastic about the vision and used his considerable influence to promote the Centre. A committed Roman Catholic, Bill and his wife Helen are by their own confession Christian first, and Roman Catholic second. Sir William was not the darling of all shades of political life because he was fearless in standing up for the rights of the vulnerable. In the manner of his life as much as by his words, 'he spoke truth to power'.

In his time as Governor-General, Sir William became the gatherer, and voice, of the nation in times of crisis. Sadly, there were many. The Thredbo disaster, the Black Hawk disaster, the Swiss canyoning disaster were three such events. I usually heard of the disaster from Sir William who would ring to say we needed to hold a memorial service and gather the nation around shared grief for the victims and their families. I would then gather Archbishop Francis Carroll, Dr Thorwald Lorenzen and other church leaders to arrange the service. I believe this to have been a most appropriate role for the Governor-General, but it has not been replicated since. Political leaders are very jealous of their exposure, image, and status. Even though the conservative side of politics espouses undying loyalty to the monarchy, they would prefer the Queen's representative to be in the background and themselves in the foreground in events that command national attention.

Sir William was very enthusiastic about the concept of spiritual inclusiveness in what has become a genuinely multicultural, multifaith society. But at the same time, he was thoroughly unapologetic about the Centre being Christian in its foundations and values. It was of course his influence that brought the Queen to the site and the symbolic planting of a black pine. It was his influence that secured the Great Cross that dominates the site, replacing the much smaller concrete cross marking the site on which the Anglican Cathedral of St Mark was to be built. If it were not for Sir William the cross would not be of the dimension we have come to appreciate. The rest of us would have been far more timid! He insisted that the cross is not simply at the heart of Christian faith, but that the sacrifice it represents should be at the heart of the whole society—at its best. It was his persuasiveness that secured funding from the Roman Catholic founded Southern Cross Club. It was his influence that secured a bevy of Australian luminaries including Sir Gus Nossal and Sir Ninian Stephens to the Council of eminent Australians who supported the centre. It was his influence that brought to the site the memorial to Australians who have lost their lives while working for humanitarian causes overseas. Having been president of Care Australia he was particularly keen that Margaret Hassan who was kidnapped and murdered in Iraq in 2004 be honoured in this way. It was his influence and insistence that kept the centre rooted in indigenous history and culture, as a place of reconciliation across all boundaries that divide. He commissioned the painting of the Holy Spirit that now hangs in the National Gallery. Created by Hector Jadany of the East Kimberley, the painting depicts his totem, the white owl, as the Holy Spirit connecting earth and heaven, time, and eternity. The painting, wonderfully portrayed and enlarged on tiles, has created the mural wall of the Holy Spirit adjacent to the chapel.

Above all it was Bill's influence and friendship that kept me focused and maintained my belief in the possibility of the centre despite the obvious challenges inherent in its inception. In my 1999 crisis it was his loyalty, encouragement, and sagacity that gave me the strength and humility to stand up and dare to believe that what lay ahead could be richer, not poorer.

The third significant intersection was the new millennium. Mr Howard's government advertised funding for significant proposals to mark the new millennium. We had some inside running in our bid for a grant through Margaret Reid, the President of the Senate and a significant supporter. Margaret's contribution and commitment cannot be understated. A proud Canberran, with a sense of pride in the national capital, she was in no doubt that a national centre, expressing the spirituality of the nation, laid with Christian foundations, was a void that needed filling.

There is no doubt she used her considerable influence, in the cabinet room, being one of the most highly respected members of parliament. Before centre-governance was settled, we had a small but energetic working group commissioned with responsibility for furthering the project. We held our meetings in the office of the President of the Senate. Margaret's generous hosting of us in this way was more than symbolic. It gave us a toe hold

Sr William Deane at the Centre

at the very heart of national political life. Along with Margaret we had
influence in the Prime Minister's office through Arthur Sinodinos, the Prime
Minister's chief of staff. Arthur was appointed by Archbishop Stylianos,
the Greek patriarch in Australia, to be his representative on the board of
the centre. While he was never an active member of the board the door of
his office was always open to us. Arthur is a most astute and capable public
servant, turned politician, in the traditional liberal mould. I retain a high
respect for him. His appointment as Australian Ambassador to Washington
is highly appropriate.

Everald Compton was the other figure who exercised influence at the
highest level to secure the grant. A lifelong member of the Liberal Party, he
enjoyed ready access to government figures from the Prime Minister down.
When our submission had been presented, he arranged a lunch appointment
with the Prime Minister to push our case. He reported back in his iconic
style, not wanting the facts to spoil a good story. His account is that the
Prime Minister asked: 'who is the primary figure behind this proposal'.

Queen Elizabeth II at the Centre.

His reply: 'Bishop Browning'. He claims that the Prime Minister then exploded 'isn't he that left-wing socialist who meddles in politics'. Everald claims he then responded: 'no you have him entirely wrong, he is to the right of Genghis Khan'! I would not dare dispute Everald's account, but in late 1998 when I was on a visit to Melbourne, I took a phone call from Margaret Reid saying our submission had been successful and that the government grant would be $5m. This grant enabled the building of the chapel.

A fourth intersection was the agreement of Dr Dawn Casey, then executive director of the National Museum on Acton Peninsula to oversee construction. Dawn was extremely generous with her time and professional skill. As a result, in construction of a significant building on Kings Avenue, we met all the accounting requirements of the grant. Not all members of the parliament were laudatory. Peter Costello was to complain on more than one occasion that the native grasses were an eyesore. I beg to differ. We have extended the grasses from the gazetted area into and onto the campus of buildings. Dawn's contribution was significant and because of our friendship I enjoyed the great privilege of 'blessing' the National Museum one Sunday morning live on 'Macca'. She arranged for a surplus and ancient sedimentary rock from Western Australia be delivered to the site. This rock forms the centre piece of the labyrinth. The signage states the rock to be from the WA Hammersley Ranges and its age estimated at 2.7 billion years. This sign came under fire from fundamentalist Christians who insist the world was created a few thousand years ago!

Elsewhere I have mentioned the contribution of Dame Elizabeth Murdoch who enabled the project to get off the ground, including the cost of running an architectural competition. In similar breath I should mention the generosity of the Fairfax family.

Early in the project's life Sir John Overall gave splendid advice. He said, 'while you may lack the resources to properly develop the whole site, use a bulldozer and put your footprint everywhere so that there is no danger the national capital authority can claim you have under-invested on the site'. Walking over the site today the visitor will observe evidence that this advice has been taken. The three buildings, the pilgrim walk, the bible garden, the great cross, the labyrinth, the fireplace, the mosaic wall, the poles, the memorial to those who sacrificed their lives in humanitarian work on foreign soil and the area reserved for native grasses make very good use of the whole site. There is plenty of space left for future investment. The 'great space' will await its own convergence of people, time, and vision. I would like the visitor who walks on the site to rub up against the basic truths of the Christian faith in the landscape they traverse. Next, I would like to see a place on the site that speaks of resurrection.

The Bible Garden is worthy of comment. Before I left Brisbane for Canberra, I shared my vision for the site with various friends, largely to gauge their support. Derek Robinson, one of four brothers, clearly gave the project a lot of thought. Much later I was approached by another brother to say the family had a Bible Garden overlooking iconic Palm Beach in north Sydney and that for various reasons it was not being kept as it should. We were asked whether it might be transferred to Canberra. The family were prepared to sell the Palm Beach site and invest the money in a trust for the purpose of a Bible

Garden in Canberra. Professor James Haire and I made the journey to Sydney to view the garden. It was a truly spectacular site overlooking Palm Beach, but the garden was not in a state that could attract visitors and appropriately honour Beatrice, the missionary member of the family in whose name the garden gained its inspiration. We concluded it would be possible to erect the garden in Canberra and that with resources available from the sale of the Palm Beach land, there would be enough to maintain it. In due course arrangements were settled and the garden, created in the wonderful menorah design that the visitor can enjoy today, was established. While the bible garden with its plants and landscaping occupies a specific area, it was concluded that the whole site should in fact be understood as 'a bible garden'. The Robinson trust is a considerable and ongoing contributor to the Christian, biblical, credentials of the site.

The Australian Centre for Christianity and Culture is quite unique in that it challenges both religious and secular boundaries of division. It speaks, as it should, of truth however inconvenient. It is one of the few instruments of religious faith in Australia that has the right to speak truth to power without accusation of partisanship or self-interest. Its ongoing flourishing or decline will be a good barometer of Christianity's tenuous hold on the life and culture of 21st century Australian life.

The Centre is now 21 years old. Its mission and engagement have developed along the lines of the original vision, receiving generous support from the University. It is now about to enter a new phase in its third decade as a remarkable collaborative venture that involves church, academy, and public society. Imagination, faith, and courage are the required ingredients for the future. Will the Church, or the University, lose its belief in the opportunity partnership offers and chose rather to settle back into the diminished space of its own cloister? Or will University and Church retain a vision that the mission of both is best fulfilled through partnership on the site, enabling a precious instrument of light and transformation within wider Australian national life.

Chapter 9
Can the Vulnerable be Heard?

The Nakba: the Colonisation of Palestine

*Not all evils can be rectified, but ongoing evils surely
should stop*

Noam Chomsky

In 1971, while vicar of Warialda, I received a phone call from Canon
John May, the Warden of St John's Theological College Morpeth, asking me
to consider an appointment on the college academic staff. At that point I had
barely been in the Parish two years. The invitation and offer were flattering,
but totally unexpected. In as much as I had any sense of future ministry,
whatever skills I might have, I considered them to be pastoral, not academic.
I sought advice from my then spiritual director Richard Borthwick SSM
who advised me not to accept. His opinion was that Morpeth was in a fragile
state and could close. Also, I had been in the Parish such a short time and
such a move would have been unwise for me and the Parish. I declined the
offer and happily put the matter out of mind.

The following year I received the same invitation, this time to join the
staff as Vice-Warden and Lecturer in Old Testament studies, a subject in
which I had shone as a student. This time I sought advice from Bishop Ken
Leslie of Bathurst whom I knew had received a similar invitation many years
earlier when he was the Rector of Alice Springs. I was somewhat daunted

by the thought I would be teaching at a tertiary level to students, amongst whom some were already university graduates and many older than myself. While I had achieved 1st class honours as a student six years earlier, I had left school at 15 without any qualifications and I most certainly had not attended a university. I put my misgivings to Bishop Ken. His response was: 'Don't worry about that George. When I was invited to the college as vice warden, I was asked to teach New Testament. I asked what I would be teaching in the first semester and was told—the synoptic problem. At that stage I did not realise there was such a problem!' With this rather dubious and less than convincing support I accepted. Margaret, three little boys and I set off for Morpeth in 1973 for me to become a noticeably young and unqualified teacher of students, and mentor of future clergy. Little did I expect that within 12 months I would find myself in charge of the college.

My main aim in the first year was to keep at least one week ahead of the students, an ambition I seemed largely able to fulfil! Indeed, several of the students have become lifelong friends and, as far as I know, they all passed their Old Testament exams.

The Old Testament challenge became infinitely more acute with the arrival of three bright Palestinian students. Because of Australia's long involvement with Palestine and Palestinians through Archbishop George Appleby, Archbishop David Penman, and Brother Gilbert Sinden, arrangements were made for Palestinian Anglican students to train in Australia. Morpeth was deemed the most appropriate college. It became immediately obvious to me that teaching Old Testament to them would be like someone from China teaching me about Australian indigenous history, or perhaps a Muslim teaching me Reformation History. I was teaching them about a land on which they and their ancestors had resided for thousands of years. Indeed, their ancestors were present in Jerusalem at the time of Pentecost. As they read the pages of the Old Testament they had absolutely no difficulty in exegeting the hand of God, however they had considerable difficulty in reading a history which seemed to blot them out of existence and conveyed, in the interpretation of some, the idea there had been an unbroken Jewish narrative over the land to the exclusion of others for three thousand years.

At this early stage I had little understanding of the prevailing situation in Palestine. I was aware of the 1967 six-day war and vaguely aware that Palestinian territories were now occupied, but that really was the sum of it. In my ignorance I had swallowed the prevailing view that Israel was 'like us' and therefore in the right, confronting aggression on all sides. I began to have a different understanding when the students would only speak of matters close to their heart when they were in the open quadrangle. They refused to speak about matters of confidence while in a building, so conditioned had they become to expecting surveillance and of being reported to Israeli authorities. I was soon to learn of the terrible plight that Palestinians have faced since 1947 and how much worse this situation had become since the occupation following the six-day war. To my shame I had not appreciated how badly they had been let down by Britain, and by Australia which had not only been amongst the first to recognise Israel as an independent state following the 1948 Arab Wars, but 50 years on had done next to nothing to ensure the establishment of a Palestinian State. When this matter is raised with Australian politicians, which it is, the excuse is always 'it is a matter for the parties concerned'. If it was left only to the parties concerned there would have been no partition proposal in 1947 and now it is totally unreasonable to assume that the bullied child in the playground can negotiate a future with the dominating bully—Israel. There must be pressure from the international community to ensure that justice prevails. Israel should understand the price it must surely pay for its continuing disregard of international law. This price is far more than ongoing insecurity and international condemnation, it is the undermining of its own national sense of morality.

Let me sketch a very brief recent history from the eighteenth century.

Haskalah (reason or intellect) was a movement in the late 18th to early 19th century that attempted to acquaint the Jews of East and Central Europe with both Hebrew and European languages and with secular education and culture as a supplement to Talmudic studies. The movement borrowed much from the European Enlightenment and was called the 'Jewish Enlightenment'. When it began most European Jews lived in ghettos, the result of centuries of isolation and segregation. The aim was to make Jews more mobile and integrated. An early leader of the movement was Moses Mendelssohn (1729-1786) the grandfather of Felix Mendelssohn.

Orthodox Judaism strongly opposed the Haskalah movement seeing it as a dilution of Jewish culture and more particularly of its religious rituals. The obvious consequence of this opposition was to choose continuing isolation. Logically this implied that Judaism cannot prosper if its adherents are integrated within the dominant cultures of the diaspora. Herein lies a fundamental difference with Christianity that from the second century, when true to itself, has claimed no citizenry of its own, but sought to be an agent of life-giving transformation within the various cultures of the world. Its failure to do this, most notoriously in the crusades, has been the cause of its greatest shame.

It is a sad inevitability that cultures which refuse to integrate within the broader communities within which they find themselves will be treated with suspicion. In the case of Judaism, this has been a breeding ground for shameful antisemitism. It should be no surprise that many American Jews who have long been well integrated within American society are alienated by modern Israel's aggression towards Palestinians.

Zionism, Jewish nationalism and colonialism, is the reverse of the Haskalah movement. It began in the 19th century in reaction to the years of antisemitism, isolation and ghetto living. It concluded that Judaism could only be free of interference in a distinct homeland, a homeland cleared of the influence, even the presence, of others. Zionism gains its name from Zion the sacred hill usually understood to mean Jerusalem. The implementation of Zionism has meant the expulsion of countless Palestinians from their homes, the perpetuation of Palestinian refugee camps, now spanning four generations, oppressive segregation and the continuing annexation of Palestinian land and property.

From the outset it needs to be said that many Orthodox Jews opposed the Zionistic philosophy. They argued that God does not call his people into a materialist, militarist state like other nations. This is of course the same argument used in the books of Samuel against the establishment of a Jewish State in approximately 1000 BCE. They argued that for such a state to come into existence violence would have to be perpetrated against others, and for the state to continue, that violence would continue. They argued that the establishment of the state would damage Jews who chose to remain part of the diaspora. Further, they argued that virulent Zionists provoke antisemitism in order that they can present themselves as its saviour. The secular and militarist nature of modern-day Israel confirms these fears.

While modern Israel seeks validation from 'religious history' stretching back to Abraham, the reality is it is a nation that does not reflect the values and virtues of its religious history, especially the prophetic tradition which demands the respect and honouring of others. Zion, as depicted in the Old Testament, is a sacred hill to which all are drawn without distinction, in peace and harmony. The vocation of 'God's chosen people' is the privilege of being the conduit for this universal peace and harmony. If not this, then what? What vision of God justifies 'chosen people's' existence through the ethnic cleansing of others?

The United Nations mandate which envisions Jerusalem as an international city, home to all and a sanctuary for Judaism, Islam, and Christianity, comes close to expressing the biblical image of 'Zion'. It is ironic that modern day Israel images Zion as an exclusive citadel rather than an inclusive sanctuary, while an international and secular body is closer to understanding this vision. In the prevailing situation one might well ask what vision of God is being served here, or whose God is being honoured. John Newton's hymn *Glorious things of thee are spoken Zion City of our God*, envisions Zion as no longer sited in a place, but in a person, Jesus the Christ, in whom both Divinity and Humanity perfectly dwell.

The Judaism of modern Israel, aside from the Ultra-Orthodox, is cultural (perhaps ethnic) rather than religious. Christians make a serious mistake in assuming that through uncritical support of Israel they are somehow supporting God's intention as revealed in the pages of scripture through a consciously religious people. (President Trump announced in August 2020 that he moved the US embassy into Jerusalem to please US evangelicals, not to support Israeli ambitions!) This evangelical obsession with Israel is rank nonsense. Not just nonsense, it is de facto cruelty and injustice, veiled with a false piety. Such support condones injustice on a scale completely condemned in the prophetic tradition and is in opposition to the teaching of Jesus. New settlers who are religious, especially from the US, are supported by Christian pre-millennialism, belief that God intends Israel to occupy the land from the 'river to the sea' as a precursor to the return of Christ. This reveals a barely hidden intention that Palestine is ultimately cleansed of all Palestinians.[69] It justifies a continuing expulsion of Palestinians from homes, land, and heritage that has been theirs and their ancestors for generations.

Theodore Herzl (1860-1904) is in many respects the father of modern Zionism. He was born in Hungary but grew up in Austria. He initially felt that antisemitism was a social problem of assimilation. If Jews could move away from their ghettos, then antisemitism would disappear. He moved to Paris as a journalist and was shocked to find deeply rooted antisemitism,

---

69 Anshel Pfeffer. *Bibi: the turbulent Life and Times of Benjamin Netanyahu,* 2018. Pfeffer quotes a conversation with Netanyahu while spending months with the Netanyahu family 20 years ago. 'In the next war, if we do it right, we'll have a chance to get all the Arabs out', he said. 'We can clear the West Bank, sort out Jerusalem'.

of which the Dreyfus affair[70] was an example. He became convinced there was no alternative other than for Jews to have their own State. He moved from seeing the problem as social, to being political. In his 'Jewish State' written in 1896 he called for the establishment of Israel. He travelled to Constantinople to meet the Ottoman Sultan and ask for Palestine to be so declared. Although there for 11 days, he failed to meet the Sultan.

He went to England to encourage support for a Zionist congress. He intended to call it in Munich, but the Jews there were largely assimilated and opposed it. It was held in Basel and attended by approximately 200. After, he wrote in his diary:

> 'If I had to sum up the Basel Congress in one word—which I will not do openly—it would be this: at Basel I founded the Jewish State. If I were to say this today, I would be greeted by universal laughter. In five years, perhaps, and certainly in 50, everyone will see it'.

The other main Zionist champion was Chaim Weizmann (1874- 1952), who was born in Belarus. His aptitude for science was observed early on. He went to Germany and Switzerland to study chemistry; from there he went to England where he became professor of Chemistry at Manchester University.

He is however better known for his political ambitions for Zionism. With others he secured the Balfour declaration. In 1917 Arthur Balfour, the British Foreign Secretary, wrote to Lord Rothschild as follows:

Foreign Office

November 2nd, 1917

Dear Lord Rothschild,

I have much pleasure in conveying to you on behalf of His Majesty's Government, the following declaration of sympathy with Jewish Zionist aspirations which has been submitted to, and approved by, the Cabinet.

---

70 In 1894 Alfred Dreyfus, a French military officer of Jewish descent, was falsely accused of treason and passing French military secrets to the Germans. The real culprit was a German spy, Ferdinand Esterhazy. Dreyfus was finally acquitted and exonerated in 1906.

His Majesty's Government view with favour the establishment in Palestine of a national home for the Jewish people, and will use their best endeavours to facilitate the achievement of this object, it being clearly understood that nothing shall be done which may prejudice the civil and religious rights of existing non-Jewish communities in Palestine or the rights and political status enjoyed by Jews in any other country.

I should be grateful if you would bring this declaration to the knowledge of the Zionist Federation.

Yours,

Arthur James Balfour

The declaration was not about creating modern day Israel, but about winning the Great War. Britain was desperate for Woodrow Wilson to bring America into the war. This declaration was designed to bring American Jewish pressure, through the Zionist Federation, to lean on the President.

The Balfour Declaration was one of three incompatible promises made by British interests to three distinct groups for expedient reasons relating to the war. The Arabs had themselves already received what they understood to be a promise of autonomy after the war if they would assist Britain in the overthrow of the Ottomans. The Ottomans were of course part of the German alliance and Britain was fearful that, unless they were overthrown, allied shipping through Suez could be cut off.

In 1915 Sharif Hussein received from the British High Commissioner in Egypt, Sir Henry McMahon, the following correspondence which clearly indicates that some territorial reward was promised:

'We declare once more that His Majesty's Government would welcome the resumption of the Khalifate by an Arab of true race. About the questions of limits and boundaries, it would appear to be premature to consume our time in discussing such details in the heat of war ...' (August 15, 1915).

Hussein was of the belief that he was being promised an autonomous Arab state from Yemen in the south to Syria in the north should he bring

Arabs into the war on the side of Britain and its allies. He and his fellow Arabs had no desire to remain under Ottoman sovereignty.

The Arab revolt followed, and the Ottomans were ultimately overthrown. The battle of Beer Sheba and the charge of the ANZAC Light Horse Brigade had nothing to do with the establishment of Israel and everything to do with the overthrow of the Ottomans. The people fighting alongside the ANZACS were Palestinians, not Israelis. The 100th anniversary of this battle attended by the Australian Prime Minister, Malcolm Turnbull, in 2017 was scandalous in its brazen support of Israeli imperialism with soldiers on horseback carrying Israeli flags to the total exclusion of any reference to Palestine and Palestinians. The Palestinian President, Mahmoud Abbas, was not invited. It was in fact a re-writing of history.

Promises of post war territorial acquisition were also made to the French, to be fulfilled in the creation of Syria and Lebanon. As Boris Johnson was to write in the *Churchill Factor*[71], 'Churchill sold the same camel three times'.

In 1917 Weizmann became head of the world Zionist organisation. As Arab nationalism grew and the formation of a Jewish State in the 1920s and 1930s seemed no closer, he experienced resistance from Zionist extremists and was voted out. In the late 1930s he resumed control of the organization and was appointed the first president of Israel following its establishment in 1948, a position he held until his death in 1952.

The failure of the Russian Revolution of 1905 and the wave of pogroms and repressions that followed caused growing numbers of Russian Jewish youth to migrate to Palestine as pioneer settlers. In addition to Palestinian Jewish people who had been in Palestine for centuries, by 1914 there were about 90,000 Jews in Palestine. 13,000 settlers lived in 43 Jewish agricultural settlements, many of them supported by the French Jewish philanthropist Baron Edmond de Rothschild.

---

71 Boris Johnson. *The Churchill Factor: How One Man made History* (Hodder and Stoughton: London, 2014).

In the following years Zionists built up the Jewish urban and rural settlements in Palestine, perfecting autonomous organisations and solidifying Jewish cultural life and Hebrew education. In March 1925, the Jewish population in Palestine was officially estimated at 108,000, it rose to about 238,000 (20 percent of the population) by 1933.

If Zionism has its roots in a proactive response to antisemitism and the oppression of Jewish people, it was about to receive an enormous boost, not from within the Jewish community, but from the corporate guilt felt by nations in Europe following the Holocaust. Some events are so horrendous they have consequences beyond their immediate impact. The terrorist attack on the twin towers in New York and the Pentagon in Washington on September 11, 2001 brought about the invasion of Iraq and Afghanistan. The former has proved to be a catastrophic decision from which the Middle East and the world is yet to recover, while the latter has been the longest military engagement ever to enmesh the US and its allies. The suffering, distrust, and alienation left by the war in Iraq, outstrips in magnitude the suffering and terror inflicted upon the cities of New York and Washington and indeed upon all American people.

The same is true of the Holocaust. The Shoah, as it is known in Judaism, is aptly called one of the most horrendous acts of evil ever to be perpetrated by human beings on their fellows. There are no words to adequately describe this evil. However, the consequences have had a rippling effect far beyond the evil itself. The Jewish people have, over the course of history, every reason to feel abused and to perceive antisemitism to outstrip any other form of ethnic or racial discrimination. How much their chosen isolationism contributed to this prejudice and misunderstanding is quite another matter. However, the consequence of responding to the Holocaust with fortress Israel, the consequences of believing they cannot trust others to come to their aid, that they alone are victims and that any activity however cruel and unjust can be justified on the grounds of 'security', has meant 70 years of grievous pain suffered by Palestinians.

The United Nations partition plan of 1947 was rejected by the Palestinians for very understandable reasons. Why should they agree to the loss of slightly over half their territory, territory which had been their land for centuries if not millennia, simply because foreign powers so dictated? However, their failure to agree was very costly. The Arab war which ensued, and which lasted for more than 12 months, ended in a ceasefire from which Israel emerged with 78% of the land while Palestinians emerged with only 22%. In the ceasefire Gaza was to come under the administration of Egypt and the West Bank under the administration of Jordan.

The Holocaust is an evil unlike any other. Nothing compares to its obscenity. However, in the living memory and psyche of Palestinians, the Nakba or 'catastrophe' holds, for them, a similar place. Over 700 thousand Palestinians were driven from their homes and villages to become refugees in Jordan, Lebanon, and Syria, while others became internal refugees in their own territory of Gaza and the West Bank. Some families have now been refugees for four generations with no hope of restitution or return. Those in Lebanon have few rights. No right to work. No right to access health or education services. No right to own property. No right to services such as electricity and water. All because Lebanon treats them as people in transition back to their homes, a transition which Israel, supported by the US has not allowed. They are the Middle East's nobodies. This is not a situation they chose nor is it a situation born out of actions on their part, it is a situation forced on them by the superior power of their aggressors.

Many go to sleep with the key for their long-lost front door under their pillow. Under what circumstance or condition of international law can this be termed acceptable? The Shoah, as unbelievably shocking as it was, is in the past, please God, never ever to be repeated. The Nakba on the other hand continues in the present. Every day Israel encroaches into more and more of the little Palestinian land that remains. Every day more houses and olive orchards are bulldozed. Palestinians in many areas are not allowed to build new houses, while many others exist under demolition orders.

In 1967 it became clear to Jordan and Egypt that Israel was subverting resources, especially water, that did not belong to them. Hostilities began to heat up. In a spectacular preemptive strike Israel took out the Egyptian airforce and within six days the war was over. Consequently, the Egyptian and Jordanian administrations in the Palestinian territories ceased, they became occupied by Israel—as they have remained ever since.

Under international law the occupier cannot move its civilian population into occupied territories. In fact, Israel has now moved more than 700,000 of its citizens into settlements on the West Bank, illegal under international law. This aggressive form of colonisation has been increasing in volume and virulence in recent years under the leadership of Prime Minister Benjamin Netanyahu. Ayman Odeh, the leading Arab/Israeli politician claims 90% of Israeli aggression against Palestinians has been instigated by Benjamin Netanyahu and 10% by all his predecessors combined. Israel makes no secret of its intention to have one million settlers in Palestinian territories as soon as possible. The aim is clearly to make much of the West Bank a no-go area for Palestinians.

Under international law the occupier is responsible to care for the security and general well-being of the people it occupies. The reverse prevails. Israeli soldiers deployed in the Palestinian Territories 'protect' the illegal settlers and consequently place unbearable burdens on the Palestinian civilian population. Thousands of Palestinians have been jailed for protesting this privation. Research shows that almost all stone-throwing and aggravation occurs within a few hundred meters of the settlements. The international community needs to understand that these acts of aggression from Palestinians are an inevitable consequence of settlements being prioritised over Palestinian culture, economy, and freedom. This aggression is called terrorism by Israel and its supporters. How can such terminology be justified when those involved are doing no more than trying to safeguard that which belongs to them? When visiting Palestinian children facing charges in an Israeli court in 2017, I spoke with parents of a young lad from Hebron. They said, 'Please tell the world the Settlements are choking us'.

Under international law the occupier must withdraw as soon as it is safe to do so. The Palestinian territories have now been occupied for more than 50 years. Many members of the Israeli Knesset are on record as saying not one inch of soil will ever be ceded to Palestinians, that there will never be an autonomous Palestinian State. The consequences of leaving people without hope are dire; dire for the people without hope and dire for those who cause this privation. As many in the Gaza strip have said, and are increasingly saying, it is better to die protesting than to live like this. Violence is almost always counter-productive, nevertheless it is not hard to understand the reason for the violence. Severe and prolonged injustice almost always provokes violence. Those initiating the violence are named terrorists, meaning they are responsible for the unrest. However, responsibility really resides with the oppressor, with the one who places his boot on the neck of those whose property he intends to appropriate.

It is dire too for those perpetrating the suffering. What kind of people have you become when your existence and prosperity has been achieved by knowingly treading others into the ground? What kind of person moves into the house of someone who has been removed against their will, eating in their kitchen, drawing vegetables from their garden, and sleeping in their bedroom? What kind of person are you who can purposefully stop a pregnant woman at a check point from gaining medical attention and watch her die without needed medical support? What kind of person are you who can forcibly take a child from his or her home at 2.00 am. because, without evidence, you believe they threw a stone at police who allowed settlers to harass them?[72]

In the last 50 years there have been many 'peace initiatives', mostly mediated by the US which cannot be considered an impartial broker. The most well-known of these initiatives were the Oslo agreements of the 1990s. The photo of Prime Minister Rabin shaking hands with Yasser Arafat in the presence of Bill Clinton is well known.

---

72 Appendix 9: [Arch]bishop warns US Israel more terror will come, 13-15 September 2003.

The Palestinian leadership are often maligned with the assertion that they will never miss an opportunity to miss an opportunity. While undoubtedly there have been many failures in negotiation from the Palestinian side, this is a gross misrepresentation. It has always been in Israel's interest and their covert intention, never to finalize an agreement, but continue the status quo during which they have been able to alter 'facts on the ground' in their favour. The Oslo agreement established the Palestinian Authority, a de facto instrument of the occupation not trusted or admired by most Palestinians. It lacks the ability to do anything other than manage the status quo, during which more and more Palestinian land and Palestinian rights are lost. It acts as Israel's agent.

The Oslo agreements established a five-year time frame in which there was supposed to be an Israeli withdrawal from Palestinian Territories and sustained progress towards a Palestinian State. As I write, that was 27 year ago! This has been a tragic and unmitigated failure, not because of Palestinian reluctance, but because of Israeli prevarication and desire not to make a final settlement. The agreement divided the West Bank into three zones, areas A, B and C. Area A, under Palestinian civilian and security control covers the cities of Ramallah, Nablus, Hebron, Jenin, Bethlehem, Tulkarm, Qalqilya, Jericho, and 80% of Hebron. Area B covers 400 Palestinian villages and approximately 24% of the West Bank. It is under both Palestinian civilian control and combined Israeli/Palestinian security control. Area C, approximately 60% of the West Bank is completely under the control of Israeli forces. It is an area pocked with check points, settlements, and Israeli only roads which impose severe restrictions on Palestinian life.

Israel has announced its intention to annex the whole of the Jordan Valley. Israel's political leaders have often expressed the desire to control as much land as possible with the smallest number of Palestinians possible. Many Palestinian homes, including those built long before the 1967 war have demolition orders hanging over them. It is reasonably obvious that without enormous pressure and sanction from the international community it is Israel's intention to restrict Palestinians to what will be disconnected Bantustans in areas A and B. Even in these areas there are illegal and provocative settlements, most notably in Hebron where a few hundred illegal settlers are protected by 2000 Israeli troops. In their task of protecting settlers, they restrict and humiliate the Palestinian population. What had been the primary market street of Hebron, Shuhada Street, has been closed since 1994. The current market has a settlement overshadowing it from which garbage and excrement is poured on the shops below, despite a netting set to capture the worst of it. All of this happens in clear sight of the army observation towers the occupants of whom do absolutely nothing to stop it.

The picture painted above has been confirmed by the January 28, 2020 released 'deal of the century' from the White House. Trump's idea of a Palestinian State is a series of non-contiguous Palestinian bantustans lacking any capacity for genuine freedom and independence, forever relying on the whim of Israel for its economy and basic services. It also envisages a greater Israel which annexes as much Palestinian land as possible while absorbing as few Palestinians as possible. The 'capital' of Palestine is suggested as Abu Dis, not East Jerusalem, but an under privileged suburb outside Jerusalem's security boundaries.

Considering this situation, what is the obligation of the international community, especially the Christian community?

The most urgent obligation for Christians is to understand facts on the ground and to be clear where theology and missiology intersects with these facts.

Conservative (evangelical) Christianity is terribly misinformed on two counts. First it is influenced by a false millennialism that justifies and accepts the oppression and suffering of a whole people as collateral damage of its bizarre doctrine. If this sounds too harsh then the only other conclusion to be drawn is that this brand of conservative Christianity is either totally oblivious of the suffering meted out to the Palestinian people by Israeli policy or simply does not believe it possible. Either way such ignorance is inexcusable and an affront to credulity.

Millennialism focuses on the 'rapture' and return of Christ in the foreseeable future and believes a precursor to these events will be Israel's occupation of the ancient lands of Canaan 'from the river to the sea'. Thus, Israel's total occupation of the West Bank and Gaza is not really about Israel, but about a misconstrued Christian apocalyptic. Those who hold this belief oppose any rapprochement between Israel and Palestine and similarly oppose any ceding of land. In a trip to Israel and Palestine in late 2018 I sat down for an evening meal in the St George visitors centre, Jerusalem, with a pilgrimage group from the US. The group had great difficulty in coming to grips with the fact that as an Anglican Bishop I support Palestinian rights. At one point I was asked if I really thought that if Palestinians were 'given land' they would have the ability to manage or govern it. The truth that this land is Palestinian historical homeland which is being progressively stolen from them appeared beyond their ken.

This group and others like them are very influential in US domestic politics. Without their support President Trump would not hold power. The US comes to any proposal for peace between Israel and Palestine with its own domestic politics in the forefront of its mind. Thus, the US can never be accepted as an honest broker in any peace deal between Israel and Palestinians. The US is and always will be compromised by its internal domestic realities. Tragically the tentacles of this bizarre Christian apocalyptic reach beyond the boundaries of the US into the thinking of Christian communities in Australia and other parts of the world.

Secondly, conservative Christianity is misled in believing that somehow the actions of modern-day Israel are an expression of the will of God. Giving divine imprimatur to policies and actions of the Israeli government is condoning actions that are contrary to the ethical mandate inherent in both Old and New Testaments.

Judaism and Christianity are monotheistic religions, they are founded on belief that all living are indivisibly related under the sovereignty of God. No human being has rights that are superior to other human beings.

The Jewish and Christian scriptures contain many expressions of covenant between God and God's people, but arguably the foundational, universal covenant, assumed by all later covenants, is the Noah covenant enacted between God and all living following the great flood. In this covenant God blesses all living in its life-giving diversity. The covenant follows the narratives in Genesis 1 and 2 in which human origin and the relationship of all humanity with God is described. These narratives, fundamental to Christians and Jews alike, make no distinction or value judgement on one group or ethnicity over another. We are all humans together. We are all 'Adam'.

Later covenants of particularity, made with Abraham and David, assume the early covenant. They unfold God's intention to honour specific groups with the responsibility of being agents of God's life-giving grace. In other words, those who feel in some way they are God's people only have the right to this status in as much they are channels of the justice, peace and harmony that is God's intention for the whole world. Shalom does not exist in isolation, it can only blossom in its fullness when all are embraced by the grace of God. We might well greet family friends and associates with an expression of peace—shalom, but it is only when we express this greeting and intention with strangers, even those with whom we are alienated, that God's blessing might fall on us.

Currently the State of Israel shows no sign of this divine vocation, or right, and has therefore ceded the right to be known as God's chosen people. Many Jewish people have that right, particularly brave souls who stand up for justice and equity within a culture which disdains such sentiment. It is particularly galling to be named anti-Semitic when standing for the rights of Palestinians. It must be even more galling to be named a self-hating Jew for doing the same thing.

In the Gospels Jesus challenges his followers to be salt and leaven. In other words, followers are called out of the safety and security of group identity (religious, cultural, or ethnic) to be a source of blessing in the wider ocean of humanity and the extended order of creation. For most of their history Jews have been part of a great diaspora which began with the fall of the Kingdom of Israel to the Assyrian king Sennacherib in 721 BC. The relatively short periods in which Israelites have enjoyed their own sovereignty have been marked by all the evils common to other nations. With very few exceptions the kings of Judah and Israel were judged as having fallen well short of any divine vocation. Thus, if a corporate sense of being known as *God's chosen people* is to be taken seriously, then perhaps it is only possible within a diaspora. This being the case, Christian approval of modern Israel as God's instrument is thoroughly misplaced. It should be far more important for Christians and Jews to work harmoniously with each other and people of other faiths to achieve justice, respect, and harmony within all cultures and peoples throughout the world. It should never be the aim of any religion to create a theocratic state, least of all through the oppression of its indigenous people. Israel stands condemned by the Balfour declaration which specifically excludes such action.

In 2018 President Trump broke with international consensus and moved the US embassy to Jerusalem. The two US clergy invited to be present for the ceremony and offer a prayer were two of the most well-known exponents of misplaced millennialism in the US today, Robert Jeffress and John Hagee. Their presence confirmed, if confirmation were necessary, that US policy of being totally in step with Israel, is more to do with US fundamentalist evangelical ideology than it has to do with Israel itself. Indeed, both men are on record for including Catholics, with Muslims, Jews, and Mormons as those who can never enter eternity. The embassy was blessed by two men who perceive Israeli expansion in terms of God's plan for Jesus' return.

How is this situation to be reversed? Are there any realistic grounds for optimism?

I would dare to venture three grounds.

First, truth and justice are always on the side of the oppressed and history teaches that ultimately truth and justice will prevail. Right resides with Palestinians and its truths must be told.

But it is not easy. President Trump has made an art form out of calling all information detrimental to himself 'fake news'. The Israeli propaganda machine is very adept in making international media self-censor when dealing with the Israeli occupation. The price paid by hard-working journalists who dare provide facts uncomplimentary to Israel is high. Pressure is exerted, print space is demanded for alternative facts or perspectives which are never permitted in reverse. In Australia, the Murdoch Press' groveling support of Israel and its denunciation of Palestinian 'terrorism' is well known.

The supposed existential threat hanging over Israel, used as an excuse for extreme oppression, needs to be challenged. Israel is a nuclear power and has been since the 1970s. This fact was revealed to the world by Mordecai Vanunu in 1986. Mordecai came to Australia and converted to Christianity at the Anglican Church of St. John's Darlinghurst. His later journey to Europe, seduction by a Mossad agent, his drugging, and jail in Israel for 18 years, is well known. He is still restricted by house arrest, unable to travel overseas or resume normal life. Israel's army, the 11th most powerful in the world can deal with any incursion that might come from Gaza, Lebanon, or Syria (there is no threat from Saudi Arabia, Egypt, or Jordan). Indeed, minor incursions, especially from Gaza are used as an excuse for a disproportionate response. Members of the Hamas military may well verbally threaten Israel's right to exist, but their potential for action is virtually zero. In stark contrast, members of the Israeli Knesset and cabinet who say that Palestine will never exist have considerable influence and means to ensure their words are not empty. Every time one Israeli loses their life, hundreds of Palestinians lose theirs. These are not reported. Palestinians frequently suffer corporate punishment for the actions of an individual.

The threat from Iran is harder to measure. Iran is not responsible for the terror events experienced by the West, such as 9/11. Ideology and resources that originate in Saudi Arabia are responsible. Iran would not be foolish enough to launch a full-scale attack on Israel. The consequences for their country would be annihilation. Palestinians have no reason for an alliance with Iran which is Persian and not Arab, Shia and not Sunni. Iran's struggle is not fundamentally with Israel, but with Saudi Arabia, they are the two great powers of the Middle East.

The separation wall built by Israel almost exclusively on Palestinian land and used for the daily disruption of thousands of Palestinian lives is excused as a security necessity. If this is the primary reason for the wall, why are an increasing percentage of the Israeli population being placed on the other side in burgeoning illegal settlements? The demolition of Palestinian property and population in the Galilee is supposedly based on reasons of security. The true reason is an outrageous land grab.

For reasons of security and safety, visitors to Israel and Palestine are discouraged from visiting Palestinian areas. Again, nothing could be further from the truth. Having been a frequent visitor to Palestine I have always felt completely safe amongst Palestinian people and in Palestinian territories. I have never seen a weapon in a Palestinian home. I have had a gun pointed at me on more than one occasion, by settlers and the Israeli police, but never by a Palestinian.

Another untruth is that Christianity is threatened by Islam in the Palestinian territories. This is untrue. In 2017 I attended the Palestinian Parliament in Ramallah. When our discussions concluded I was taken to the steps of the parliament overlooking the city and asked to pray over the city and for the parliament. Those doing the asking were Muslim members of parliament. Before I left, the same parliamentarians impressed upon me the need for a Christian presence to remain strong in Palestine. They argued that it is through a Christian voice to the wider world that they are more likely to be heard. For reasons we all understand it is harder for a Muslim voice to be heard. Since 1948 the Christian presence in Israel/Palestine has reduced from over 20% to a barely measurable figure. Because the occupation is so oppressive, many Palestinians have sought to migrate. It is much easier for Christians to migrate than it is for Muslims. In 2018 I visited the remaining Aramean speaking Church in Bethlehem using an Aramean liturgy. I met a

Church elder whose wife and family have already migrated to London. He has now migrated himself although his heart remains in Bethlehem.

The privations imposed upon Palestinians in their daily lives are too numerous to catalogue. The settlers enjoy water to wash their cars and keep their lawns green. Palestinians are allowed barely enough to drink, cook, and wash themselves. Settlers enjoy first world housing, unlimited power, and ease of movement. Palestinians are refused permission to build, have their houses demolished. Many enjoy electricity for an indeterminate number of hours per day, have impositions on their travel, and are often denied access to crucial areas for employment, health, and education.

Any attempt to resist the oppression is described as terrorism with severe punishment, even for children. Many are held without charge. Families are denied access to those imprisoned while financial aid given to families of those imprisoned is referred to as aiding and abetting terrorism.

The facts I have outlined are dreadful and deserve to be better known. As they become better known, public perceptions will change, we are already seeing some signs of that. Fair-minded people, anywhere in the world, when accosted with this knowledge will be appalled and will want to use whatever small influence at their disposal to influence pubic and international opinion. In Australia we are often told that Australia and Israel share the same values. Even with all our shortcomings, I want to scream 'no, we most certainly do not'!

Palestinians are very resilient and entrepreneurial, engagement with the rest of the world is the key to their release from decades of isolation and entrapment.

My second ground for hope is in the knowledge that Israel, for all its strength and bluster, is as vulnerable as any other nation on the planet and with appropriate influence can change course.

Israel can be hurt, and this hurt can be achieved through what is known as BDS (Boycott Disinvestment and Sanction). BDS is a peaceful form of protest, supported by well-informed organisations and community members worldwide. *Change of behaviour almost always occurs because of a carrot or stick.* BDS has negligible impact economically but has significant impact on reputation and public image. Israel's paranoia about BDS is a reasonable indication that it works. More nations, companies and individuals need to sign on. Boycott is the most well-known arm of the movement. There have been cultural, sporting, and academic boycotts. Boycotts of certain products and companies, especially those working in, or helping to construct, the illegal settlement have been highly successful. Boycotting companies involved with technology used to oppress Palestinians is essential, including those involved with telecommunication. On the other hand, supporting various Palestinian representatives and teams should be encouraged and great fuss made when their visas are denied.

It is harder for ordinary citizens to become involved with disinvestment. If portfolio shares are held, investigation can be made into their investment holdings. Large banks have been successfully targeted in relation to environmental justice and global warming; similar efforts can be made in relation to human rights violations.

Sanctions were successfully employed against South Africa to end apartheid. The situation in Palestine can only be described as apartheid. If it is not, those who find the word objectionable must be asked what word better describes the situation. Rights are not equal. Restrictions are placed on Palestinians that do not apply to the settlers. Palestinians are treated under military law whereas Settlers are treated under civil law. Settlers enjoy unrestricted movement (except in area A) but Palestinians under certain circumstances cannot even cross the road to reach their farmland. On what grounds was it appropriate to place sanctions in South Africa, but it is not appropriate to place them in Israel?

My third ground for hope is that a younger generation with no personal memory of past hurts and trauma is less likely to carry historical grievances into the present. Because of social media, the younger generation is far more global in their outlook than their forebears. Young people, not unreasonably, want to get on with their lives, to live as others live—Israeli and Palestinian alike. Many of these find the most logical solution for Israel/Palestine is equality without boundaries. There is absolutely no reason why Palestinians and Israelis cannot live harmoniously together, indeed flourish together, in the lands currently known as Israel, Gaza, and the West Bank. Those who resist this notion are either captive to fears and prejudices which should have been long left in the past, or they have an underlying racist disposition. Such disposition is roundly condemned in countries that support Israel, including Australia. Why is it permissible in Israel?

The time has come for Israel to decide whether it wants a democratic state or an exclusively Jewish state, for surely it cannot have both. It also needs to choose between being an autonomous state that depends for its existence on the subjugation and oppression of others or being confident enough in its Jewish identity to embrace difference, knowing that difference will not be a threat but an enhancement to that identity.

Palestine and Palestinians must abandon fractious and divisive political allegiances that have no place or usefulness in the present and insist on full membership of a bi-cultural society in which the giftedness of the Arab population and the giftedness of the Israeli population create a diverse and vibrant society which could be the envy of others.

Chapter 10
We are the Company we Keep

*The fundamental law of human beings is interdependence. A
person is a person through other persons.*

Desmond Tutu

In 1969 I began to keep company with two young men, talented and
troubled in equal measure. They lived at Warialda Rail, about 7 kilometres
south west of Warialda, my first Parish. The early settlers did not want the
dirty railway running through their town, or indeed to suffer the indignity
of needing to rub shoulders with railway labourers, hence the settlement
out of town. Early days of white settlement in Australia were far from
egalitarian.

The 'Rail' was a small settlement of substandard housing, home to
disadvantaged people including many children. I met them as a teacher of
RE at the school and became aware that few facilities were available to them.
I decided to start a branch of CEBS (Church of England Boys Society) at the
'Rail'. Having disseminated the necessary information through a letter box
drop, there was considerable interest. On the first night almost every young
boy in the Rail arrived to be enrolled. We met in a disused tin shed with a
curved roof that reached the ground. It was utterly chaotic, I had absolutely
no control. Twin brothers Peter and Jonny were ring leaders. After about

half an hour I decided I must do something and sent the twins out. For the rest of the evening they rained rocks on the roof!! It was like the blitz! At one level it was very funny, but at a practical level it was intolerable.

After that abortive night I drove out to the Rail and picked up the boys who wished to continue, including Peter and Jonny, in the Parish car and took them into the main group in town. I will not confess how many I often had in the car. On the first and subsequent nights I asked the boys where they lived and where I should deliver them home. I was stunned by Peter and Jonny telling me that they did not know where they were staying. Physical abuse and alcohol marked the lives of most adults in their family. The boys would often scratch food together for themselves while all the adults spent their time and money at the pub. On any given night they might be at one of their grandparents', an uncle's place or indeed the home of one or other of their parents. I learned very quickly that dysfunctional behaviour almost always has a reason, that a judgmental response exacerbates the problem and that building trust and respect is an exceedingly long term endeavour. I often think of the boys and wonder how their adult lives have unfolded. I am grateful for their extraordinary athleticism at Diocesan sports days. As long as these boys came, we invariably 'cleaned up'! I count it a privilege to have kept their company for a short time, they have contributed to the many faceted mosaic that is my long life.

We are the company we keep has long been a favourite adage. It is both a good and a bad reality. The company we keep can make us deeply racist, prejudiced and narrowly ideological, or it can make us generous, empathetic, welcoming, and open.

Negative company keeping can be illustrated from Australian contemporary political life which is judged poorly by the general population. Politicians tend to emerge from a narrow ideological nursery, beginning careers as political staffers with loyalty to a party and its ideology. This has led to partisan politics rather than consensus building around transformative policy.

Similar negative formation can be illustrated through the incarceration of Australia's first nation people for minor infringements. The company kept in this incarceration makes recidivism almost inevitable. A cycle inclusive of drug taking develops that is almost impossible to break, for the bonds of friendship made in these circumstance override potential motivation for changed behaviour.

I speak English because this is the language of my parents. I am an anglophile because I have imbued the culture of my birth and the smells and texture of the land upon which I was raised. My faith is deeply and personally owned, but its expression is comfortably lived and clothed within the liturgy, music, and culture of my tribe—the Anglicans. I am an adopted Australian. I have been here long enough to enjoy and defend its culturally open inclusiveness, and the contrasting features of droughts and flooding rains. I live where I have chosen to live. I wear the 'guernsey' and barrack for Australian teams against any foe including the poms.

I have long known however that as wonderfully blessed as I have been by the company I keep, there are millions of others whose lives are lived differently, whose struggles I have never known and who see the world through different lenses. I know that my life would be immeasurably deepened by travelling their path, even for a little while, for travelling in the company of another, even for a short while, is to be blessed permanently. We all know that a chance encounter can be life changing.

Thus began a major feature of my tenure as Bishop of Canberra and Goulburn, bi-annual youth pilgrimages to the developing world. Tourists and pilgrims are deeply contrasting travellers. Tourists observe from the safety of their air-conditioning. They take photos and seek to be entertained, not intending to engage or be vulnerable to the people and cultures through whom they pass. The reason for a pilgrim's journey is the reverse. It is to engage, to be vulnerable and to allow something of the dust of that place to remain, long after the journey has come to an end.

A pilgrim's purpose is also quite different to that of an aid worker. The latter has a specific task of reconstruction, education, health, or other charity and leaves when that task is completed—not always to the benefit of the recipients. A pilgrim sets out with a different purpose; to see with new eyes, to walk in the company of those who live differently. Visiting the developing world, it is necessary to accept vulnerability, indeed, to share the vulnerability of those amongst whom you walk. Unlike tourists or aid workers, a pilgrim is prepared to live as the people live, to sleep where they sleep, to eat what they eat, and live with the privations that they endure, albeit for a short time. To become immersed in others lives is to be changed. Indeed, many of the young people returning from the pilgrimages found settling back into the seeming triviality of life at home more difficult than the outward journey of living in an Asian or African slum on the outskirts of a major city. Each pilgrimage lasted for five weeks and comprised about 20 young people aged from 16—25. My theory was that any shorter time and the participants could 'hold their breath', not allowing themselves to become vulnerably engaged.

The idea began out of a generous experience afforded Margaret and me by the then Primate of Australia, Archbishop Sir John Grindrod. At the time I was one of his Brisbane regional bishops. He was asked by Bishop George Kyaw Mya of the Diocese of Hpa-An in Myanmar if he could supply a bishop to confirm and ordain members of the Karen people who had fled from his Diocese across the border into Thailand and had in 1984 formed a large refugee camp at No Bo (Mae La).

This was a deeply transformative experience for both of us. We had never entered or experienced a refugee camp. My formal duties of ordination and confirmation of large numbers was an honour above words. But deeper was the experience of sharing the lives of people whose poverty became our riches. We were fed out of rice rations that had been tithed in previous weeks. Our security was provided by the volunteer Karen Freedom army. Our bamboo shelter had been erected specifically for our visit. We were in the company of a dignified, generous, beautiful people whose struggles and pain are almost unimaginable and yet who met us with joy and generosity. In 2019, the camp remains the largest concentration of ethnic Karen in Thailand. In company with many others, they remain the forgotten people of the world. Margaret and I came home with their spirit grafted within us. Theirs has been a gift to us beyond measure.

Our first Diocesan youth pilgrimage took us, not to a formal refugee camp, but to a large unauthorised settlement of poor and displaced people on the outskirts of Manilla, the Philippines, and to a rural community to its north. Our shelter in the settlement camp enjoyed minimal hygiene. To enter, we stepped over an open sewer, and contributed to it with our ablutions which drained outside from the floor in the corner which we allocated for this purpose.

Soon after our arrival we went to the market to purchase food. Our western sensitivities prevented us from purchasing anything much, except rice. The offerings of meat, entrails and insects seemed to subdue the appetite of even the most intrepid. When we took our rice back to our shelter to cook, we became a source of amusement to the crowd who gathered outside. They quickly dispersed but returned with delicacies that made short shrift of our sensitivities. Kabab sticks held chooks heads, pieces of chook's intestines, and blood. It was all quite tasty! A much bigger test was to come. Next morning, we heard the cry 'balut', 'balut', heralding a marketeer on a pushbike selling fertilised (duck) eggs which had been incubated for 14 or so days and steamed overnight. I am ashamed to say this favourite Filipino food was a test I failed.

In the evenings I and my male companions joined the men in companionship around a bottle of gin, bulag, the cheapest gut-rotting brand available. It was consumed culturally, tagayan style, out of a single glass passed around the group, to be drunk in one gulp, and filled by the lead man. To provide some protection to the stomach it was followed by a chaser of water. I have no idea of the alcohol content, but I do know my stomach was on fire all night. (Filipinos are the largest consumers of gin in the world).

I have two abiding and conflicting memories of my stay. First of the Deacon appointed to the settlement by the Diocese. A highly intelligent, compassionate, and gentle evangelist. His lodging was tiny, fitting his bed and enough room for his few clothes. No kitchen, bathroom, or lounge area. The total floor space would have been less than that of the spare bedroom in one of our houses. He ate out with his neighbours and parishioners in the settlement, who also did his washing.

My second and contrasting impression was of Diocesan hierarchy who were aghast that I was staying in the settlement. One of the tragic assumptions of the institutional Church, learned from the West, has been that those in authority or positions of power no longer live as parishioners live. It is a common reality in Australia that clergy expect a standard of housing which is frequently above that experienced by most of their parishioners. At Lambeth conferences African lay people confided that their bishop expected them to carry their luggage and pay their bills.

This pilgrimage reinforced the centrality of the Christian Gospel for those who, by choice or election, become exemplars of Christ in leadership: 'He (Jesus) did not count equality with God a thing to be grasped, but emptied himself taking the form of servant, being born in human likeness' (Phil. 2: 6-7).

Before leaving the Philippines, we visited the Catholic Cathedral in Manila, the Minor Basilica and Metropolitan Cathedral of the Immaculate Conception. It is a most imposing edifice. Unfortunately, I left when it became clear that in order to enter, I needed to pass a receptacle with a sign which indicated that sums deposited would count towards a treasury of merit and contribute to a deduction of necessary days spent in purgatory. I was shocked that that such a brazen, mercenary, and deceitful piece of medievalism was being practiced on a faithful good hearted and generous people. Given that what you are prepared to walk past, you are prepared to accept, I left. Despite being deeply entrenched in the institutional Church throughout my whole adult life, I find any practice which places the institution, its needs and survival, above the service and care of people, utterly repugnant, and frankly, self-defeating.

Our next pilgrimage took us to Ethiopia and the Holy Land. Ethiopia was an easy choice for we were to be hosted by my sister Val who has lived amongst the Afar people in the great Rift Valley of Ethiopia since the 1970s. Her story is wonderfully chronicled in *Maalika*[73], the account of her remarkable life.

At that stage Val had a house in Addis Ababa. She welcomed us in typical Ethiopian style with a coffee ceremony, music, dance, and other expressions of Afar culture. Visiting the Afar, or indeed most of the poor of the world is to encounter hospitality on a different level to that experienced in the West. Our hospitality is polite, perhaps even a little tokenistic. Their hospitality is total. Of course, we can fit ten of you in! Everyone sleeps on the floor! Everything in the house is at your disposal! It is taken for granted that a visitor, or stranger, will be embraced and treated as a member of the family, for as long as they need to stay.

With Sister Val in Afar, Ethiopia, 1998.

73 Valerie Browning and John Little. *My life among the Afar nomads of Africa* (Macmillan: Sydney, 2008).

We stayed in Addis for a couple of nights before journeying down to Afar country. For a special meal, a party of boys went down to the market and bought a goat. Thanks were given over the goat which was duly slaughtered outside the front door. Its flesh was garnished with garlic and herbs and stewed on an open brazier for the evening meal. Gratefulness to the animal for the gift of its life is totally absent from western culture. It is no wonder we westerners consider ourselves outside, even above, the natural order. It was good to experience the immediate relationship between food and the source which provided it. Our western experience is that food arrives covered in plastic, later abandoned to become one of the planet's worst sources of pollution.

We travelled down to Afar via the Awash valley, the site where Lucy's skeleton was discovered in 1974 and estimated to be 3.2 million years old.[74] She is believed to be an ancient ancestor of modern humans. In a visit to her skeleton in the National Museum of Ethiopia, it was good to be reminded not only that we humans share a common ancestry, but we have always shared space with other life on this planet.

Despite sharing common ancestry, humans are racist. We need the humility to recognise it. Throughout my adult life I have needed to address racist stereotyping and assumptions that have accompanied the privileged start in life that I have enjoyed. Racism generally remains subterranean and passive, to emerge in times of crisis or threat. In some, it is active and aggressive as observed in the conversation of shock jocks and their political patrons. Xenophobia diminishes those who hold such views, as well as abusing victims of those views. In my lifetime ethnic cleansing has occurred on all continents and amongst a variety of societies.

---

74 Lucy is the nickname for a remarkably complete (40 percent intact) hominin skeleton found in 1974, and dated to 3.2 million years ago. The specimen is usually classified as *Australopithecus afarensis*. It is argued that with long arms, short legs, an apelike chest and jaw, and a small brain but a relatively humanlike pelvis, bipedal locomotion preceded the development of a larger (more humanlike) brain in hominin evolution. Lucy stood about 3 feet 7 inches (109 cm) tall and weighed about 60 pounds (27 kg).

We made camp for the first time on open stony ground, typical of Afar country. Stones needed to be moved to create a reasonably smooth place for a swag. As we settled in, the prayers of our hosts and guides, facing east to Mecca, reminded us that we were a group of western Christians, among a people of reverent Islamic faith. The respectful honouring of each other's faith was one of the important learnings of this journey. It was made visibly apparent to us through the marriage of Ismael, a Muslim, and Val, a Christian. There has never been any attempt to try to 'win' the other over. Indeed, the value or virtue in each faith is best demonstrated in and through the respect and honouring it shows the other. Val maintains the home, as best she is able, as an Islamic home, providing space for prayer and honouring festivals such as Ramadan. In turn Ismael acknowledges that the foundation of Val's extraordinary service of the Afar people as 'mother', is her Christian faith. Val is completely intolerant of evangelistic groups whose aim is to 'save' individuals with no thought to the consequences of their actions upon the societal structure to which the individual belongs.

On a later visit to Awash I ran into the local Imam. He quickened his step to greet me, kissed me on both cheeks and said: 'Brother George, you must come quickly to my home, since we last met I want to know where you and God have journeyed and what you and God have discussed'. I do not remember being asked a similar question by a fellow Christian, or indeed asking another Christian a question of that depth and beauty.

Val and Ismael have found many commonalities through their faiths. Hospitality, care of others, respect for the environment, a keen sense of justice, prayer, fasting, and charitable giving are but some examples. Millions of Christian and Muslim adherents have a long journey ahead to catch up.

From our camp we observed Ismael, in the distance, holding court. Clearly a grievance needed to be settled. The discussion appeared to continue for many hours. Towards the end there was a loud clap or drumbeat. When he returned, I asked Ismael what that was all about. He said there had been a dispute between families, one had been injured by the other. He said the first part of the meeting was airing and determining the facts. Secondly it was negotiating agreement over recompense. The loud noise was the end of the matter when he said it shall be spoken of no more. I felt the western court system had a lot to learn from this straightforward approach!

It was a privilege to share the company of nomadic people, folk for whom treasure lies in their herds and children. If the ultimate goal of life is contentment, then our pilgrims were confronted with the reality that the Afar people may have arrived at a destiny which eludes many of us in the west, whose striving for material well-being contributes to missing the real goal. Val told us that loneliness let alone serious mental illness is virtually unknown amongst these nomadic herdspeople. We became aware that our way of life was not only foreign to them, but that it had a detrimental impact on them. Climate change, largely the effect of first world emissions, has caused the two main rainy seasons to become unreliable, causing great distress and putting at risk a total way of life. It has also meant that neighbouring tribes, like the Oromo, try to enter Afar country as their own territories no longer support their herds. It is a tragic reality that the world faces a growing number of environmental refugees.

The female members of our party joined the health attendants as they visited expectant mothers in their nomadic homes (deboitas). They learned that giving birth can often be long and complicated. Fistulas, still births, and maternal deaths are far too common. Responding to this situation through education, training, and changing some cultural practices, is clearly an opportunity for foreign aid to make real difference.[75]

On our way to Asayita, what was the capital of the Afar region, we passed a salt mine. The Awash river eventually disappears into the desert, this part of the Great Rift Valley being below sea level. The mine is foreign

---

75 This challenge has been taken up by Dr Andrew Browning, his charity Maternity Africa, and the Barbara May Foundation which funds hospitals in Mille Ethiopia (Afar Region), Bahirdar Ethiopia (capital of Amhara region), Kivulini (Arusha Tanzania) and Juba, South Sudan.

owned and cherished by the government for its royalties. The Afar receive no benefit from the mine, despite it being in their territory. This phenomenon repeats itself the world over, as foreign ownership and national governments combine to harvest resources with no attention being paid to a denuded landscape and diminished local lives. In 2019 Ismael spent some time in gaol because he stood against those who profited from the mine at the expense of the Afar people. No charge was ever laid, but such is the fate of people the world over who stand for their people against powerful international conglomerates and politicians who support them.

We journeyed from Ethiopia via Egypt to Palestine/Israel. The inquisition at Ben Gurion airport, entering and leaving, made it clear that Israel automatically viewed with suspicion any traveller who chose to be present among Palestinian people. Every effort is made to ensure that Christian pilgrims stay in Israeli accommodation, are guided by Israeli staff, and spend money which boosts the Israeli economy, not the Palestinian economy. Reinforcement is given through travel advice which warns that it is unsafe to travel or stay in Palestinian territories. Nothing can be further from the truth, but more of that later.

We enjoyed a memorable stay in Nablus hosted by the local Anglican congregation. Nablus is an ancient Palestinian town on the West Bank about 49 kms north of Jerusalem and situated between Mount Ebal and Mount Gerizim. It was here that we first tasted the threat and intimidation that the illegal Israeli settlements cause to the Palestinian people. The Settlements are ubiquitously present on the hills above the Palestinian communities. Their security fences, green lawns and modern architecture stand in contrast to the Palestinian villages below. We walked with our Palestinian friends outside the boundary of the town and were confronted by settlers who barred our path. Their guns were pointed at us. It was intimidating. They made it clear that they had the power. Because of their intimidation it has been necessary for an international, ecumenical group of accompaniers to give three months at a time to stay in the towns and villages of the

West Bank to accompany children to school. The settlers have electricity 24/7, Palestinians experience intermittent supply. Settlers have water to green their lawns and wash their cars. Palestinians have barely enough water to drink and wash their clothes. Even in towns notionally under the oversight of the Palestinian Authority, services are delivered at the whim of Israeli authorities.

From Nablus we learned how difficult it is for Palestinians to visit family and friends, go to hospital or even reach their farms. The settlements and their connecting infrastructure have been purposely designed to make life as difficult and intimidating as possible for Palestinian people. The ugly dividing wall, built on Palestinian land, speaks loudly about Israel's ugly mindset. For Israel to exist with this mindset, Palestinians are forever to face intimidation and punishment. Those who support Israel in these actions are fellow right-wing governments like Hungary and Brazil, but oppression and colonisation should forever fail the humanitarian court of international opinion. It need not be this way. It used not to be this way. In past times Avraham (Hebrew), Ibrahim (Muslim) and Abraham (Christian) played very happily together in the streets of Jerusalem—and they could again.

We visited the Samaritan community on Mount Gerizim. This devout Palestinian community traces what it claims to be 3,600 years of worship on this mountain. They accept only the first five books of the bible, the so-called books of Moses, as canonical. They have a tradition and way of life that needs and deserves protection, which UNESCO in part provides.

We visited Jacob's well, one of my favourite holy sites, favourite because it has not had a Church built over it and the visitor can sit beside the well and imagine being part of conversations that have occurred around it for millennia. I especially imagined myself sitting in on the conversation between Jesus and the Samaritan woman (Jn. 4: 1-26).

It is a sad reality that Christian presence in the Palestinian territories is now almost too small to count in a census. Most Christian Arabs who live in the Holy Land, live in Israel. The intimidation felt by Palestinian

Christians is so intense that migration becomes an easy choice. Intimidation for Palestinian Christians is magnified by treatment from fellow Palestinian Muslims. As life for Palestinians becomes more oppressive, it should be no surprise that frustration is expressed through a stricter Muslim identity, which together with settler harassment makes life almost impossible. The Anglican parishes we visited on the West Bank comprise devout and faithful parishioners, but this faithfulness comes at a cost unlikely to be experienced by western Christian pilgrims. In 2019 we visited a friend who for some time was the Anglican priest in Nablus. He is now parish priest for a Palestinian community east of Haifa. He makes no secret of the fact that he encouraged parishioners in Nablus to migrate.

Reaching the Jordan River today is a disappointing experience. Israel controls the aquifers, while above ground water has been massively over exploited. Little if any water now reaches the Dead Sea with the consequence that it is rapidly shrinking, while that which remains is ever more salty. The Jordan River has always symbolised transition in the journey of life, transition from captivity to freedom, from death to life. Unsurprisingly, the sacrament of baptism remains rooted in symbolism associated with the Jordan River. The baptised enter from one side, are immersed, and emerge on the other side, clothed with new life in Christ. It was a thrill to baptise one of the

The Baptism of Robert Stockee in the River Jordan.

Baptism of the Indians in the River Jordan.

pilgrims in the Jordan on the first pilgrimage to Palestine and then baptise a contingent of Christian pilgrims from India who said they had been waiting a day for someone to baptise them. On the second pilgrimage one of the pilgrims was baptised in the waters of the Dead Sea.

Today the Jordan River is the boundary between Israel and the Hashemite Kingdom of Jordan. While the West Bank of the river is part of the Palestinian Territories, it is being progressively annexed by Israel. Crossing the Jordan at the King Hussein Bridge (Allenby Bridge) is frequently a nightmare of humiliation as Israeli border forces randomly hassle and turn back visitors. Crossing the Jordan is no longer a joyous transition, but an experience of disrespect and intimidation.

Most Christian pilgrimages take their pilgrims to various sites associated with the life, ministry and death of Jesus. It is a moving experience to visit these sites, but seldom is any thought given to the living stones, the remaining Christian community amongst the Palestinian population. To live with them, pray with them, break bread with them and share their pain and struggle means returning home with a transformed life, not just a few photographs.

It is deeply distressing that many western Christians hold on to a false assumption, namely that Israel somehow epitomises all that is good and godly, and Palestine or Palestinians represent terrorism and hatred. This view is fostered through a well-resourced and highly efficient propaganda machine. It is so important for all Christians to stand for justice, for freedom for the oppressed and for respect and dignity across ethnic, religious, and cultural divides.

Twice our pilgrimages journeyed to the Republic of South Africa, one to Mozambique and one to Rwanda. In South Africa we kept company with those who had recently been released from apartheid and although still poor, were finding their feet.

A visit to the Apartheid Museum in Johannesburg was confronting, not simply because of the reality of its inhumanity, but also the mindset required in those of us who wish to contend with its ugliness. The inscription on the entrance wall reads:

> To be free is not to cast off one's chains, but to live in a way that respects and enhances the freedom of others.

Likewise, the Hector Pieterson[76] Memorial, erected in Soweto close to where the young man was shot in 1976, is also confronting, not least in that it draws attention to the role youth take in many of the world's ethnic struggles. He was shot when he turned around to try and pick up another stone, protesting the enforced teaching of *Afrikaans in the black community*. The police opened fire on students, thus igniting the climatic struggle that ended apartheid and saw the release of Nelson Mandela on the 11th February 1990.

> To honour the youth who gave their lives in the struggle for freedom and democracy.

While spending 10 days in Soweto we spent nearly a week visiting the HIV AIDS hospital where nurses and doctors shared the same virus as their

---

76 Hector Pieterson was born in 1963. He became the iconic image of the 1976 Soweto uprising in apartheid South Africa when a newspaper photograph by Sam Nzima—of the dying Hector being carried by a fellow student—was published around the world. Hector was one of the first casualties of the 1976 uprising against the sole use of the Afrikaans language in schools.

patients. Families were expected to meet the basic needs of their family member, including the collection of the deceased. My most memorable moment came from attending the compulsory therapy session (a bit like alcoholics anonymous)—one group for men and another for women. In my group men rose, not to speak about their virus and their commitment to a more disciplined sexual life, but to speak about their sexual exploits, which were proudly revealed as testimony to their manhood. I found it difficult listening. I thought to myself: there is a war on here, many are losing their lives and you talk about your sexual profligacy!

One man remained silent until almost the end of the meeting. He eventually stood and said: 'I am gay'. 'I became HIV positive when I was raped as a 15-year-old schoolboy. I have remained celibate'. Then turning to the men in the room he said, 'Your sexual prowess does not and should not define your manhood. Your most important organ is your brain and clearly yours is exceedingly small. Your manhood is defined by the example you set, the discipline you accept, the respect you show. You must redefine what you mean by your manhood, and if you do the curse of your virus will lessen'. I have often shared that story, especially with my Christian fundamentalist brothers and sisters and asked, 'from this group of men whose company would you most like to keep'?

While associated with the HIV hospital we took our turn handing out condoms at the adjacent massive bus terminal. Here we were largely keeping company with grandmas who were the main distributors of these instruments of sexual hygiene. I am not sure whether they took them for their husbands, their sons, or their grandsons. Probably all three. What is salutary is that responsibility was being taken by women, not by men. That this is the case in various areas of leadership across the world is a wake-up call to men who seem far more dislocated by the changes of the modern world than women. The same observation was clear from a visit to Diepsloot, the appropriately named township (deep ditch) outside Pretoria. It was created to house asylum seekers from Zimbabwe and other southern African countries. In this most desolate of places the women were pregnant or suckling a child, gathering water, trying to cook and clean. Men were standing around as if in a daze, not knowing what to do, or where they fitted.

The phenomenon of female responsibility and leadership was also clear from our one-day visit to Manenberg, a coloured township of about 50,000 from the apartheid era. Our bus left us on the outskirts of the town, leaving us to walk in, because it was deemed too risky for the bus to enter the township. Rife with unemployment, the youth of the town find an outlet for their frustration through gang membership. Violence and theft are common. The grounds of the Anglican Church of the Reconciliation were deemed a sanctuary by the rival gangs, a place of refuge, a little like the cities of refuge in the Old Testament. Lawless, and with no obvious police presence, grandmas stood up to fill the vacuum. Wearing orange t-shirts, and respected by the youth, they were the primary source of law and order. Catching one of their own grandchildren, they would take him by the ear and send him home.

Before leaving South Africa, I must note with some shame that a young female pilgrim was held at gunpoint in Soweto and relieved of her phone and a small amount of money. It was a traumatic experience and should not have happened had I been more attentive to security issues for the youngsters as they walked with fellow young Africans from local churches. In the debrief that followed it was pointed out that the person with the gun almost certainly meant no personal harm. His robbery was probably linked to his poverty. What was stolen allowed him to feed his family for a couple more days. While this truth is cold comfort, if poverty is to be addressed in a meaningful manner, it is necessary to walk a day's journey in the shoes of the poor. It is important to realise that the demeaning nature of poverty is that it strips the sufferer of choice.

Our visit to Mozambique was inspired by the desire to keep company with one of the living saints of the Anglican Communion, Bishop Dinis Sengulane of Maputo. Bishop Dinis is one of the longest serving bishops in the Church. In 1988 it became known that he was interceding between the combatants in the brutal Mozambican civil war. When the war came to an end, he launched his 'swords into ploughshares' project which enabled 600,000 weapons of war to be surrendered for items of domestic use, sewing machines, bicycles, tractors, spades, etc. The project, inspired by verses from Isaiah 2: 3-4, was a huge success, carried by the charisma of this extraordinary man. Many other places in the world would be well served by a similar plan but lack the personal leadership to implement it. Another great passion of the bishop is the anti-malaria campaign. (I was later to attend a conference in Johannesburg at which his participation was cut short by a bout which confined him to his bed). It was a privilege for the young pilgrims to keep company with one for whom the gospel came alive through his imagination that emancipation, peace, justice, and care of the poor are possible through the grace of God. Unlike many bishops the world over whose accommodation exceeds the local standard, Bishop Dinis lived in a small flat, in a multi-storied apartment.

We left Mozambique for Rwanda to keep company with another bishop who had the wit to imagine another miracle of grace—the fostering of orphans of genocide. The Rwandan genocide of 1994 shamed the world.

The Rwandan genocide memorial.

Some of the remains of Tutsi, as well as Twa and moderate Hutu,
carried out between 7 April and 15 July 1994.

It was watched as if in slow motion on the television with the world doing nothing to intervene and stop it. Seemingly and shamefully nothing got in the way of Hutu anger and bitterness towards Tutsi neighbours. Clergy and bishops were implicated, some of the worst atrocities happening within the walls of Churches. When the blood shed was eventually over, some clergy and bishops were so implicated, they could no longer return to their work. One is left pondering what it might take for any human being to become so tribally focussed that any atrocity becomes possible.

Bishop Alexis Bilindabagabo, Bishop of Gahini, believes he survived the genocide by a miracle of God. He was instrumental in establishing the Barakababo Foundation which fosters the orphans of the genocide. On our visit, we met many of the children. One young girl stands out in my memory because of her extraordinary self-sacrifice. As a young teenager she headed a household of five including herself. She stayed at home to allow the others to go to school. She contributed to the sustainability of the house through management of the garden and production of food. The Foundation's work is not solely about the placement of children, and care of widows, but about sustainability.

We visited the genocide memorial in the capital, Kigali. This memorial alone contains the remains of 250,000 souls. (Remains from recently recovered unmarked graves are continually added). Shelves were dedicated to skulls, others to limb bones while the bottom shelves housed shoes the folk were wearing when they were cut down. In recent years, an amphitheatre has been constructed and the wall inscribed with names of the slain continues to grow as further remains are identified.

In those days I used to run every morning, no matter where I was. I ran only for one day in Rwanda. As I ran people who had been walking, enjoying the cool of the morning suddenly ran away in panic. Clearly the trauma of the genocide was associated with the memory of running. I had no desire to be part of that memory.

Following the genocide, reconciliation became an urgent necessity; for Tutsi and Hutu continued to live beside each other. While those slain were Tutsi, and the perpetrators Hutu, we were to learn that the division was largely an outcome of colonisation. People were slain because of what was written on their identity card, not because of ethnic difference. The inscription on the wall of the memorial links reconciliation with forgiveness, justice, and peace.

Sadly, both Rwanda and Burundi appear unable to develop a political culture devoid of strongmen and the alliances that follow them. These alliances appear to draw in Church leadership on one side or the other.

We visited the Archbishop of Rwanda in Kigali, Emmanuel Kolini, who graciously and warmly received us. He had recently joined the Anglican Archbishop of Sydney in an alliance of Churches opposed to those who accept LGBTQI into their midst. I found it then, and still find it now, extraordinary that a Church that had less than a decade before been implicated in a genocide should feel it was in a moral position to cast judgement upon churches throughout the world which opened their arms to members of the gay community.

I met and was inspired by Bishop Bill Godfrey of Peru when he visited St Francis College Brisbane in my time there as Principal. When he moved from Uruguay to Peru, I wanted to call on him and share his ministry for a short time. So it was that the final youth pilgrimage visited the Anglican Church in Peru, before walking the Inca trail to Machu Picchu.

Our first ten days were spent at various missions of the Diocese amongst the poor on the outskirts of Lima. On this pilgrimage we took a young 'street kid' from Canberra whom I met at an Anglicare run school in the city for youngsters for whom main-stream schooling simply did not work. She specifically asked to come. 'You do those overseas journeys for young people' she reminded me. 'I am coming on the next one'. 'Well', I replied, 'if you are determined, you will'. Her costs were largely met by Rotary International.

In one community, nestled under what looked like a wall of rock and mud capable of sliding down at any moment, she asked, 'Is this where people live, or is it where they keep their animals'? Coming from one who was used to living tough, this was quite a question! Poverty as we understand it in Australia is a relative term. What took the attention of some of the pilgrims was the 'duck programme'. Families were provided with tools, as basic as they might be, to make their lives self-sufficient and independent. The ducks, supplied by the Church, provided a ready supply of meat and eggs.

The worshipping life of the Church was an integral part of the life of the wider community. One Sunday I was asked to preach, through the good favour of a Spanish interpreter. With the interpretation, the sermon probably went for about half an hour. When it came to an end there was a stunned silence. They were not used to such a 'short' delivery. They were determined not to be sold short and so after the singing of a hymn I started again!

In keeping with the title of this Chapter, I was quite moved to be keeping the company of this young pilgrim from Canberra. It was not until we arrived in Cusco that I became a little more aware of the struggles she was facing. We were there for two unforgettable experiences, both unplanned. The first was an earthquake which shook a restaurant where we were enjoying lunch. (Friends and family at home heard news of the earthquake almost before we rang them to say we were all fine). The second was front row seats for the Sun festival, a spectacular Inca tradition held annually on the 24th June to coincide with the winter solstice. In Cusco, the young lady became unwell, her sickness not associated with a guinea pig meal, but with the consequences of withdrawal from the drugs to which her body had become accustomed. We had two days to make up our mind whether she would join us on the trek to Machu Picchu. The Inca guides left the decision to me. She came—but I was responsible for her welfare. On the first day she and I arrived at camp at least an hour later than the next slowest. The next day I said, 'We will not be last'. The journey ahead took us over 'Dead Woman's pass' with snow on the ground and an altitude of 13,828ft. She was the first female in our party over the summit and from there did not look back. After we returned to Canberra she was reconciled with her parents and I was invited to her 18th birthday. Feeling a little out of place amongst so many vibrant young people I took my leave. But not before her mother took me aside and said: 'I did not expect my daughter to live until she was 18, just look at her now—thank you so much'. It was one of my most cherished compliments and gave me energy for many months to come. Above all it strengthened my commitment to keep company with those on the edge of my peripheral vision.

Before leaving Peru and the Incas, a brief comment about their culture which has important lessons. It is not possible to know everything about their culture, because much was destroyed by the Spanish. However, we know that for them, life was understood as a journey through a triple decked universe, symbolised by the snake, puma, and condor. The underworld for them was not a place of darkness and evil but a place of origins symbolised by the snake. The snake was associated with new life and wisdom. The puma symbolises earthly life, its struggles, strengths, and weaknesses; while the condor is the most sacred of the three, symbolising the afterlife. These symbols could have been a rich foundation upon which to graft a South

American indigenous Christianity. But no, they were bent on crushing this ancient culture. In Lima we visited the Museum of the Inquisition. The instruments of torture were almost beyond looking at. It is beyond belief that such torture and cruelty could be inflicted in the name of Christian mission. I am so grateful that when Pope Gregory sent Augustine to England in 595 that his instruction was to 'celebrate the local accent'.

We were blessed in seeing a condor soar above us at Machu Picchu.

We Christians have not learned a great deal over 2000 years. We are not to impose anything on others, but to live with them, without partiality, in love. I have been particularly struck by the fifth chapter of the anonymous letter to Diognetus, one of the earliest known Christian writings:

> Christians are not distinguished from other men by country, language, nor by the customs which they observe. They do not inhabit cities of their own, use a particular way of speaking, nor lead a life marked out by any curiosity. The course of conduct they follow has not been devised by the speculation and deliberation of inquisitive men. They do not, like some, proclaim themselves the advocates of merely human doctrines.
>
> Instead, they inhabit both Greek and barbarian cities, however things have fallen to each of them. And it is while following the customs of the natives in clothing, food, and the rest of ordinary life that they display to us their wonderful and admittedly striking way of life.
>
> They live in their own countries, but they do so as those who are just passing through. As citizens they participate in everything with others, yet they endure everything as if they were foreigners. Every foreign land is like their homeland to them, and every land of their birth is like a land of strangers.
>
> They marry, like everyone else, and they have children, but they do not destroy their offspring.
>
> They share a common table, but not a common bed.
>
> They exist in the flesh, but they do not live by the flesh. They pass their days on earth, but they are citizens of heaven. They obey the prescribed laws, all the while surpassing the laws by their lives.
>
> They love all men and are persecuted by all. They are unknown and

condemned. They are put to death and restored to life.

They are poor, yet make many rich. They lack everything, yet they overflow in everything.

They are dishonoured, and yet in their very dishonour they are glorified; they are spoken ill of and yet are justified; they are reviled but bless; they are insulted and repay the insult with honour; they do good, yet are punished as evildoers; when punished, they rejoice as if raised from the dead. They are assailed by the Jews as barbarians; they are persecuted by the Greeks; yet those who hate them are unable to give any reason for their hatred.[77]

There is little doubt that I meet others as a privileged person. Privileged because of the colour of my skin and the place of my birth. Privileged because of an opportunity for education and a lifetime of full employment. Privileged because of the opportunity to travel. Privileged because of the offices I have held. Privileged because choices have been available to me that are denied others simply through no fault other than accident of birth and all that has subsequently flowed from that. I should not feel guilty because of that privilege but I must guard against any sense of entitlement. It is a brutal reality that millions of us who are privileged, live out of a sense of entitlement that diminishes and enslaves others.

We have built a world in which the individual reigns supreme and nationalism is on the rise. This is not the world of Christianity. The world of Christianity is the world of journey, of sandals, a walking stick and the willingness to greet every stranger along the way, for by chance, you may indeed be entertaining angels.

---

77 Letter to Diognetus, https://www.christian-history.org/letter-to-diognetus. html. This is one of the earliest extant Christian writings.

Chapter 11
COVID19 and an Opportunity to:

Find out what God is doing and do that

Because God has made us for Himself, our hearts are restless until they rest in Him.

St. Augustine

'Look busy, Jesus is coming' is hardly an acceptable mantra for a well-directed life!

In 1970 I found myself yarning to men around the bull ring at the annual Warialda show, in northern NSW. After a while I noticed another man standing somewhat to the side. I apologised that I had not previously noticed him. This triggered an absolute blast! 'That is typical' he asserted, 'you priests are all like that, you are rude, uncaring and simply look after yourselves'. I was quite shell-shocked, not least that he was publicly lambasting me. Fortunately I had the presence of mind to say 'I would like to follow up the conversation, may I pop out to see you sometime next week' 'You would not have the guts' he retorted.

About three days later I found myself driving up to his house on the Bingara Road. I confess to being a little nervous. When I knocked on the front door the farmer's wife came out looking somewhat disconcerted. 'He is not here', she said. I asked where he was. She informed me that he was ploughing and that he would not welcome an interruption. I felt however that this was too important to let go, so tramped out to the paddock he was working. It was obvious he had seen me but refused to stop and kept ploughing. I thought the only thing to do was to stand in front of the tractor and make him stop. This he did—eventually. I was the first to speak. 'You began a conversation at the Show Ground; I want to have the opportunity of finishing it'. He was clearly shocked that I had made him stop. Remaining sullen, but not quite as aggressive, he repeated what he had said before—'you are all the same'. I asked for clarity about the 'you'. Then tumbled out a story which obviously was continuing to consume him internally. A clergyman three before me had been very judgmental when one of his sons had died. Apparently, the cleric had refused to take the funeral. The hurt this had caused continued to fester. Piercing this ulcer was so important. I am unaware that I said anything wise, I simply listened, stood my ground, and did my best to absorb his pain. In the remaining months before we left the Parish, he and his wife returned to Church. I would not say we became close, but I learned an especially important lesson; when matters are clearly out of kilter, they must be addressed otherwise the pain will continue. Addressing the issue is what God does, it is the way of the cross.

On the other hand, and despite accusations of divine culpability, it is not hard to see, or have pointed out to us, what God is not doing.

God is not involved in conflict and warfare. Sure, many who have claimed to be followers of mainstream religion have been totally and appallingly involved. The inquisitions, the holocaust, the Balkan conflict, Northern Ireland, 21st century religious extremism, forced 'evangelisation' of indigenous people, are scandalous examples of activity with human self-interest being played out with covert divine sanction. As Jonathan Sacks points out these actions are: *Not in God's name*.[78]

God shows no partiality. British are not favoured over Germans, or Sinn Fein Catholics over Protestant Ulstermen, or Orthodox Serbians

---

78 Jonathan Sacks. *Not in God's name: confronting religious violence* (Hodder and Stoughton: London, 2015).

over Bosnian Muslims, or Israelis over Palestinians, or heterosexuals over homosexuals. Israel Folau[79] was totally wrong to assume he knew who met with divine favour and worse, those who were condemned to final and permanent rejection.

God does not intervene to stop us fighting, or contracting cancer, or messing up the planet. We all have the capacity for triumph and tragedy, and we all live in a transient world in which being born, decaying, and dying is common to all. Looking at human history, inclusive of our lifetime, we seem more skilled at tragedy than triumph. We can all chose to hate or love. Intercessory prayer is not asking for divine intervention, it is focusing or channelling the energy of divine love and compassion on this person or this place. As spiritual beings we all have the capacity to be conduits of healing grace. Those who have been prayed for will know how powerfully transformative this can be. Like the men with their paralytic friend, we are lowering this person or this circumstance at Jesus' feet (Mk. 2: 1—12).

God does not exclude or punish. Exclusion, exhibited by many religious adherents towards people of female gender, and others of homosexual orientation, or even of ethnic origin, is not taken from the divine 'to do list'. Justification for male power or control is falsely engineered as mirroring divine 'headship' or order. There is no headship in God, just a great deal of feet-washing. This truth is proving somewhat inconvenient to those who uphold male 'headship' but go on to discover that outstanding spiritual leaders are often female, while some of the most creative are gay.

God has not deputised to cardinals, priests, ministers, pastors or Sheiks, Imams or Rabbis, exclusive access to divine presence. It is alarming that many religious leaders are followed as if they are themselves the voice of God. It is tragic that the official position of the Roman Catholic Church remains

---

79 Israel Folau, one of the highest profile members of the Australian Rugby Union team, the Wallabies, infamously proclaimed in 2019 that homosexuals, and people who are not 'born again' were going to hell. He belonged to a Church run by his father out of a mansion in Sydney called 'The Truth of Jesus Christ Church'.

asserting their sacerdotal life is the only real channel of Christian grace and therefore ministries of other Christians are in some way invalid. Nicodemus was told that 'the wind blows where it will, you hear the sound of it, but you cannot tell where it has come from or where it is going' (Jn. 3:8).

We know that any activity of God cannot embrace the foregoing because of what we know about the nature of God. The nature of God revealed to us in Jesus is the antithesis of the actions just described.

According to the Catechism of the Catholic Church: The Fathers of the Church distinguish between theology (theologia) and economy (oikonomia). 'Theology' refers to the mystery of God's inmost life within the Blessed Trinity and 'economy' to all the works by which God's nature is revealed. Through the observed activity of God, the nature of God is revealed to us; but conversely, the nature of God illuminates the timeless activity of God. So it is, analogously, among human persons. A person discloses herself/himself in actions; the better we know a person, the more we understand their actions and hopefully respond with less judgement or acrimony.

It is more than a little interesting to note the etymology of 'economy' is embedded in the concept of household (oikonomia). Human or divine economy is best understood as that which builds or diminishes households. All the activity of God is directed towards communion, the unity of the household, the establishment of community, the achievement of 'oneness'. This is of course what we believe to be the ongoing work of the Spirit, the Lord and Giver of Life, who constantly forms and reforms us in community. So, if this is what God is doing, then surely this is what we should be doing! Christians should be in the business of nurturing and forming community. The activity of God, the Divine Economy, is all about creating and redeeming, holding all thing in one communion and fellowship.

If this is the economy of God, in what way does the human economy align. Well of course it does not. In Trump's America the human economy, monetary wealth, is more important than community health and Trump thrives on confrontation and division. In Morrison's Australia economic investment is more important than social investment. In Xi's China economic well-being is tied to totalitarianism. Loss of individual liberty is the price to be paid for fiscal gain.

So, being a little more specific, where is God to be found in a world beset with so much rancour division and danger, and how might we respond?

Anecdotally I would say God is always surprising. Most of the transforming experiences of my life have happened without plan or intention on my part. I have never applied for a position. I have often found myself entirely outside my comfort zone based on previous experiences. Even the great CS Lewis speaks of being '*Surprised by Joy*'.[80] In early chapters I have recounted moments which I can only understand as divine encounters. But on a subject as important as this, anecdote is not enough, a bit of substance would be helpful.

Soon after my arrival in Morpeth as Vice Principal in 1973, I agreed to run a Pierre Teilhard De Chardin study group in the local city of Maitland. Chardin (1881–1955) was a polymath, Jesuit priest, philosopher, and scientist. Looking back, I wonder what on earth possessed me to think I was competent to do that! Like many free thinkers before him, Chardin was viewed with suspicion from within his own Church, the Roman Catholic Church. He suffered the same fate as many scientists and religious before him who thought outside the square. Even before his writings became well known, he became a persona non grata within the Roman Catholic Church, which claimed he refuted the doctrine of original sin and taught a form of universalism. Within a Church which disallows doctrinal ambiguity, this position is understandable, but suppressing ideas is ultimately more harmful to the one doing the supressing, not the one with the ideas. Like all thinkers Chardin is fallible, but his ideas have had the capacity to give flesh to many dry bones.

---

80 CS Lewis. *Surprised by Joy* (Harper Collins: London, 2012). '*A young man who wishes to remain a sound atheist cannot be too careful of his reading.*'

Chardin's most well-known book is the *Phenomenon of Man,* and his most well-known idea—the Omega Point, belief that everything in the universe is fated to spiral towards a final point of unification. Teilhard's theory attempted a coalescing of Christian theology and science. The outcome was that his theory was not perfectly scientific as examined by physicists, and not perfectly Christian either. Not perfectly scientific because it is not and cannot be a proven scientific theory, and not thoroughly Christian because biblical Christianity insists on the possibility of human rejection, the refusal to love, the refusal to belong. Interestingly another scientist theologian, Professor John Polkinghorne,[81] asserts that for him, an understanding of the development of life through the prism of evolution reveals a God more worthy of belief and devotion than a God who predetermines absolutely everything.[82] A risk the creator appears to take is that we can become what we choose to become, ironically love requires nothing less. If, to a certain extent, we become what we choose to become, God can hardly be held accountable for human foibles, or worse, gross acts of human evil. Early biblical narrative, attuned to the omniscience of God, made God responsible for good and bad alike.[83]

While not wedded to Chardin's theory as the centrepiece of my personal theological journey, I am drawn to it for two reasons. First it is one of the many paths through which teachers and students can explore the

---

81 John Charlton Polkinghorne, KBE FRS (born 16 October 1930) is an English theoretical physicist, theologian, and Anglican priest. A prominent and leading voice explaining the relationship between science and religion, he was professor of mathematical physics at the University of Cambridge from 1968 to 1979, when he resigned his chair to study for the priesthood, becoming an ordained Anglican priest in 1982. He served as the president of Queens' College, Cambridge, from 1988 until 1996.

82 'God didn't produce a ready-made world. The Creator has done something cleverer than this, making a world able to make itself.' John Polkinghorne.

83 For example: 'The Spirit of the Lord departed from Saul and an evil Spirit from the Lord tormented him.' (1 Samuel 16: 14-15).

complementarity of science and faith. Without such paths each generation will be filled either with bigots considering science to be incompatible with faith, or cynics holding that nothing has value unless it can be seen and touched. This is a world of dualism condemning its citizens to a half world experience. Bigots will not properly engage with the world, often retreating into conspiracy theories to defend irrational positions, while cynics live in a world devoid of spiritual narrative. As covered in a previous chapter, it is a deep sadness that faith is increasingly contributing to anti-intellectualism, disallowing proper attention to matters as critical as climate change. This is giving atheists an easy ride. Religious fundamentalists and atheistic fundamentalists are defending and attacking the same shallow house of cards. Biblical Christianity does not believe in the God that Dawkins and Hitchens say they do not believe in.

Secondly, I am drawn to the theory because it offers a path into the exploration of biblical Christianity without the religious jargon which is so off putting to those outside a personally owned spiritual narrative. Biblical Christianity is about Christ being all in all, about God being the community into which we are destined to be drawn. Chardin helps us approach this truth without religious language and baggage. If we can get a handle on the destiny to which we are travelling, we should be able to get a handle on what God is up to and do that.

Teilhard argued the idea of an Omega Point is deeply embedded in Christian thought. Embedded in belief that the divine Logos, Christ, draws all things into himself. In the words of the Nicene Creed, he is 'God from God', 'Light from Light', 'True God from true God', the one 'through him all things were made'. [84] In the Book of Revelation, John the Divine thrice

---

84 'Lord Jesus you are the centre towards which all things are moving: if it be possible make a place for us all in the company of those elect and holy ones whom your loving care ones liberated one by one from the chaos of our present existence and who are being slowly incorporated into you in the unity of the new earth.' Teilhard De Chardin. *Hymn of the Universe* (Collins Fontana: London. 1973): 70.

declares Christ to be: 'the Alpha and the Omega, the beginning and the end' (Rev. 22:13, 1:8, 21: 6-7). The Book of Revelation is popularly understood to be about the end times. To read the book through this lens is unhelpful, indeed read this way it has been the subject of various pseudo spiritual conspiracy theories in almost every generation. It is not about the end times in a chronological sense, but about the end (τελός) person, the one in whom all things are fulfilled. Having taken human form, Christ (the lamb), died risen and ascended, gathers humanity with him into divinity. Now, this is an omega point worth aiming for!

This insight has been of profound significance to me, which you could have deduced in dribs and drabs throughout previous chapters. What God is doing is fundamentally and always about linkage, connection, community, redeeming, making whole. This is hardly surprising given we Christians believe in a Trinitarian God. It is ironic, but distinctiveness is most wonderfully complete when it is part of the whole, like colours in the rainbow, instruments in an orchestra or hues in a painting. Distinctiveness that asserts itself disproportionately is always out of place and ugly. If all being united in Christ is an apt credal articulation of the Christian faith, then the path of life for individuals, groups and generations is always to find new ways in which connections can be made and community built. This task has never been more urgent, or perhaps more difficult. In our age too many nations and leaders have come to believe that security and well-being is to be found in separation, and worse, in inflicting damage on others, diminishing them that they themselves might increase. Sadly, many of the leaders who promote self-interest at the expense of a harmonised global community claim Christian allegiance, and in the case of the US, rely on Christian patronage at the ballot box.

Chardin and Polkinghorne sought to show that faith and science are not only compatible, but necessary windows into an understanding and appreciation of the other. In like manner, it is necessary that faith, and particularly Christianity, engage more fully with evolving 21st century societal norms at both a national and international level. It is a matter of concern that the political right wing has falsely appropriated faith to justify neoliberal individualism and an economic system which increasingly preferences the advantaged against the disadvantaged. Judaeo-Christian values upon which western civilisation is said to be built are incurably socialistic. That is to say, these values are committed to equity and justice. It is important to understand that well-being is only partially achieved through one's own efforts; it is primarily experienced through shared goals and aspiration and commitment to common good.

Through the work of the Spirit, it is the vocation of Christians to build community in every aspect of life. *The Church is the only institution that exists primarily for the benefit of those who are not its members.*[85] The primary duty of Christians is to be points of connection through which community and fellowship might be a transformative experience for all. For most of human history community was forged tribally, conflict with other tribes being the norm. Relatively recently tribalism has given way to nationalism in much, but not all the world. Nationalism does not build community, although it might do so negatively by developing a demonising narrative towards others. (Leaders find it easier to build support by describing what they are against rather than a vision of what they are for). What is desperately needed is growth of positive, life-giving societal norms on a global footing. We will not be able to meet the challenges of 21st century life on this planet otherwise.

If forming community—drawing the whole created order to a common point—is what God does, then we do not need to look much further to discover what we should be doing. This is a huge challenge, made more acute in a post COVID world. COVID19 has forced us into various levels of isolation, but, unsurprisingly, the more we are isolated the more we long to break free, to relate, to belong, to live a societally cohesive life at the centre of our being. How are we going to do this? What might shape the way forward?

---

85 William Temple.

In the space of a few short weeks COVID19 has brought the human financial economy to its knees. There is a global recession that has the capacity to replicate the Great Depression. Millions are out of work. Investments have been decimated. The road to recovery will be long and arduous. But is it possible that this moment of global disruption is also an opportunity for a refiguring of the human enterprise? Is it possible that we have seen 'what matters' in a new light, that previous priorities are no longer important and that we may have stumbled across a path to fulfillment, contentment, harmony and peace that has eluded us in our years of prosperity? Is it possible that henceforth the human economy will serve the divine economy rather than attempting to replace it to become the 21st century's most sophisticated idolatry?

As we noted in Chapter 6, the 21st century human enterprise has tended to understand human value in monetary terms. Those countries that have done best to navigate beyond COVID19 have put human health above economy.

In religious tradition, new insights are most likely to occur through the experiences that are like a lockdown, not in times of regular and well-rehearsed routine. Retreats, fasts, periods of isolation, exiles, times in the desert, stillness, meditation, contemplation, Ramadan, Lent, Jesus' 40 days in the wilderness, the Hebrews 40 year sojourn in the Arabian desert, all are examples of environments through which real learning and transformation occur.

The COVID19 shut down, globally but not universally imposed by national governments, feels unnatural. Its necessity has made for compliance, but it became quickly clear that most could not endure it for long. Humans are made to relate, we are fulfilled through our belonging. A supreme irony has been playing itself out. Those who have complied, who have contributed to the diminishment or demise of the virus have contributed to the hope of a stronger reemerging community. Those who have not complied because of a sense of personal entitlement have caused the freedom they have longed for to become more tenuous, for themselves and for others. It is an irony that no one is free while others remain captive. Community, and unity building is God's activity, it is also human desire. As in every aspect of life we humans do not sit well with paradox. The more we seek to secure something for ourselves, the more likely we are to see it slide out of grasp. As Jesus said: 'What we hold onto we lose, what we give away we keep'.

Chardin gave ample clues as to what being drawn towards a point of communal convergence meant for him:

- **We are not human beings having a spiritual experience, we are spiritual beings having a human experience**

What an extraordinary and radical way of turning thought about what we like to call 'human nature' upside down. I began the chapter with a quote from Augustine: 'Because God has made us for Himself, our hearts are restless until they rest in Him.' We are caught between 'doing' things because we are human and 'being' something because we will always be more than the sum of our doing. It is our being rather than our doing that draws us into community.

John Cleese[86] appears to be devoting what remains of his life to the exploration of what awaits after death. His driving theory is that consciousness is not tied to the brain, which would condemn knowing to mortality and gift death with the final victory. He argues the brain is merely a transmitter of consciousness, consciousness which is not limited by mortality. Unfortunately, he does not appear to have the same capacity as Chardin to connect his secular exploration to religious experience.

- **Love is still the most powerful, untapped energy in the world.**

We know that love and fear are the two strongest motivators of human behaviour. It is a sorry reflection of the human condition that so much of our living is motivated by fear.[87]

- **The age of nations is passed. Now, unless we wish to perish, we must shake off our old prejudices and build the earth, our single home.**

---

86 Co-founder of *Monty Python* and star of *Fawlty Towers*.

87 Appendix 6: Let Love Triumph over Fear, 7 November 2004.

To have said this in the 1950s was extraordinarily insightful. The statement was made before the recent pandemic. It was made before the threat of irreversible climate change became an immediate reality. It was made following the debacle of German nationalism which led to the Second World War, but before the dangerous rise in nationalism that has accompanied the beginning of the 21st century.

- **The future is in the hands of those who can give future generations valued reason to hope.**
- **Above all trust in the slow work of God.**
- **Someday, after mastering the winds, the waves, the tides, and gravity, we shall harness for God the energy of life, and then, for a second time in the history of the world, men will discover fire.**

If only this were a realistic hope! Here I am afraid Chardin departs both from the reality of human history and theology's reflection on the human condition. 'I do not do the good I want, but the evil I do not want is what I do' (Romans 7: 19). We will not harness for God the energy of life; we are too flawed. However, drawn by the Spirit into Christ we will indeed discover fire for the second time.

Is it possible that, as we navigate our way through to a post COVID19 future, we might have no ambition to return to what we thought was normal, but embrace a very different, more gracious, more hospitable, more livable future? Or will the human propensity for failure, for self-interest, for winners and losers, prevent the economy of God from breaking though in a fresh manner? Will fear prevail?

The following are offered as old insights that have been strengthened by the COVID19 experience.

We are as strong as our weakest link

I met Tabitha when she was approximately seven. She came to my Aspley, Brisbane, door with her grandmother who had cared for her since she was born. She was physically frail and wafer thin. She suffered many physical disabilities, including an inability to orally consume food. Her difficulties had become too much for her parents to manage—hence being cared for by her grandmother.

After a few preliminaries she came straight to the point, 'I would like to be confirmed'. Tell me about that, I rather meekly responded. 'Well' she said, 'I love God and I know God loves me. I have been baptised and I would like to be a full member of the Church'. What more was there to be said! Later grandma filled me in with a little more detail about Tabitha's precarious health, the fact she was not expected to live into teenage years (in fact she did) and that her love of God was a feature of who she was.

We arranged a confirmation service that subsequently occurred at St George's Church, Eumundi, on Queensland's Sunshine Coast. Tabitha chose the music, she chose the readings and she and I shared the homily, sitting cross-legged together on the sanctuary step. During the homily I asked her what it meant to die. 'Oh! Bishop' she said, 'that is easy, it is to have a cuddle from God'. Tabitha will never know the contribution

Sharing the Homily with Tabitha on the Sanctuary step.

she made to my life and ministry. The vulnerable are not a burden, but a gift to be cherished.

About the same time Margaret and I had a home at Montville also on the Sunshine Coast. After working in the garden, I started the journey home to Brisbane and came immediately on an accident that had occurred seconds before. A little boy had run across the road from his cubby house, straight in front of an oncoming small truck. The little fellow was horribly injured. I had an early mobile phone (brick) and rang the ambulance and then rang a prayer chain I was associated with. He was tended to on the side of the road and then rushed to the Nambour Hospital before being air-lifted to Brisbane. The prognosis was grim. I visited him a couple of times in the Brisbane Children's Hospital, but he remained in a coma and, shamefully, I soon forgot about him.

Some months later I received a call from his mother, 'Bishop George, would you come to Tasman's coming home party!' Realising this was the Tasman I met on the side of the road, 'of course I would love to come to the party', I joyfully responded. The family lived in a typical Queenslander in Lutwyche, one of the inner northern suburbs of the city. Having climbed the steps, I could see straight through the hallway to the backyard where a young boy was playing on a trampoline. 'Tasman, Bishop George is here', shouted his mother. Tasman hopped off the trampoline straight through the house and jumped into my arms for a hug. 'You were with me on the side of the road when I had my accident' he blurted. 'Yes', I responded, 'I was'. 'Did you know I saw God' was his next stunning statement. 'No, I did not know' I inadequately replied, 'what is God like'. 'He is like a miracle with sparkles' was his retort; a description of God that in my view remains unmatched from any learned theological treatise that I have come across!

The vulnerability of Tabitha and Tasman was a priceless gift.

Vulnerability is often shunned, not tolerated. The vulnerability of the indigenous people of Australia receives little empathy, nor is their history and culture cherished. Instead, we tolerate indigenous prison representation at more than a quarter of total incarcerations. It is why health and longevity data show a gap between indigenous people and the rest of the population. It is why a request for indigenous voice in the parliamentary process has been summarily dismissed by the government's political leadership. In the COVID19 pandemic we have gone out of our way to protect the vulnerable, amongst the aged and the health compromised; post COVID we must embrace all who have been historically vulnerable, not simply for their sake, but for all our sakes. Living on this continent will never be what it should be without their knowledge and culture.

In response to COVID, government doubled the job seeker allowance. Post COVID19 it should remain at a livable level. It has been unconscionable that the wealthy have retained generous tax provisions such as negative gearing and tax-free superannuation income, while those without income have been denied the dignity of a living allowance.

Finally, arguably the most vulnerable on the planet are the stateless. Unfortunately, in every western country there is a right-wing rump, often vulnerable themselves, some who are given to conspiracy theories, some who enjoy a fundamentalist religious culture, some who are poorly educated, for whom racism is never far from the surface. It does the political class absolutely no honour to court these voters through the victimisation of others. Trump shamelessly does it, as does Pauline Hanson, the notorious Australian leader of 'One Nation', but so does Peter Dutton, the politician in charge of Australia's border security. It is beyond shameless that historical boat arrivals are still held in detention offshore. It has become even more reprehensible in light of the fact that countless numbers arrive by air, making their claims after their arrival. It is years beyond time that asylum seekers held offshore were absorbed into Australian society and provided with ongoing care to deal with the mental anguish that long years in incarceration have doubtless inflicted.

We are dependent upon those who serve us

The dark and sombre days of COVID19 have highlighted how central to the life of the wider community are those who are employed in various forms of service. Doctors and nurses have put their lives on the line for the wider community, some paying the ultimate price for doing so. Teachers and child-care workers have had to adapt to a different mode of delivery in order that education might continue, and children kept safe. Those who work in supermarkets have had to suffer the slings and arrows of pent up stress and anger from the wider community.

And yet how are they remunerated? Immediately prior to the pandemic outbreak, almost daily headlines told the story of people, already on low wages, not receiving their proper remuneration. The problem is made worse by the fact that many are not permanent employees, lacking the safeguards that permanency offers.

Now is the time to reassess the value attributed to various forms of work though remuneration. In May 2001 I wrote in the *Anglican News*, the monthly paper of the Diocese of Canberra and Goulburn, 'I have spoken before of the obscene salaries and separation packages being commanded by senior executives. why do we condone such misappropriation of public or private money'? Nothing has changed—if anything it is worse.

Neoliberal capitalism honours those who are deemed to be creating monetary wealth, while treating those who work in service of others as second-class citizens. When he was Australian Treasurer, Joe Hockey coined the expression 'lifters and leaners'. Lifters were those who accumulated wealth, leaners those on social benefits and those who chose to build social capital rather than financial capital. But what is wealth? Surely the wealthy are the contented, the healthy, the well-adjusted, the educated and those at ease with their place in life. Various service industries work to build this true wealth and should be compensated accordingly.

As mentioned elsewhere, one of my predecessors, Bishop Burgmann, argued that no one should be remunerated at more than seven times the remuneration of the lowest paid. The true wealth of a nation should not be calculated on the stock market or 'exponential growth' but on the strength of the community to be generous, hospitable, inclusive, and forgiving.

Communication and intimacy with loved ones is our greatest source of grace and strength

In February 1942 Singapore fell to the Japanese and 80,000 allied troops became prisoners of war—what Churchill described as the worst British military defeat in history. Amongst the Australian troops taken captive was the young Captain Adrian Curlewis. The following years of terrible privation were made bearable for him through the loving correspondence which took place between him, his mother, Ethel Turner, (author of *Seven little Australians*) and his wife and family. This correspondence, together with Sir Adrian's diaries has been beautifully published by his daughter Philippa in *Of Love and War*.[88] I had the privilege of presiding at Sir Adrian's funeral at St Andrew's Cathedral Sydney, in June 1985.

The exceptional life and character of Sir Adrian Curlewis was cherished and nourished through his family.

Our world has made great technological advances since 1985. Standards of living have greatly increased, the middle class to which most aspire, enjoy privileges and luxuries that even the wealthiest in past generations could barely have dreamt. And yet this wealth has proved to be no panacea for happiness, let alone contentment. Fragile mental health has become a wrecker of family life. Suicide amongst the country's youth, its farmers, its returned soldiers, and amongst many stressed professionals, has become its own pandemic. Domestic violence is in plague proportions from which no ethnic, economic, or social grouping is immune. What are we doing, what pressures are we putting people under, that these phenomena are so ubiquitously characteristic of modern life?

Currently judgement about success or failure is made in terms of material wealth and ladder climbing. The success or failure dial needs a radical reset. Its current setting presupposes a competitive, if not combative modus operandi. In the late 1990s I preached, as I often did, at the valedictory service for Canberra Grammar graduates. I took as my text

---

88 Philippa Poole. *Of love and war* (Sydney: Lansdowne Press, 1982).

Isiah 42. 3 a 'bruised reed he will not break and a dimly burning wick he will not quench'. From a Christian perspective the text is assumed to be prescient of the coming Messiah, Jesus.

I suggested to the young, there was little doubt that, because of the privileges they had enjoyed, many would become phenomenally successful professionals, some would hold high representative office, while others would run successful businesses. But on current national statistics too many of them would also treat their partners badly and some of them would abuse children. I asked on which basis would they prefer to be judged to have lived good lives. Would they prefer that judgement to be based on material wealth, entrepreneurial success, and fame, or on the basis that their lives had nurtured and enhanced the lives of others? The two are of course not mutually exclusive, but they become exclusive if the drive for one is made at the expense of the other. Australia's political class must look seriously in the mirror and ask if their combative style, so awfully demonstrated in parliament, contributes to the kind of society we would all prefer to enjoy.

The natural environment restores us as we breathe its air, swim from its beaches, walk in its parks and dig its gardens.

As previously recounted, my mother was convinced that open air was the cure all for almost everything. The first few months of life for her eight children were not spent in protective isolation, wrapped inside an artificially heated home. No, on the contrary, each spent a few hours each day in their pram pushed out into the garden.

Britain has been progressively establishing, and then implementing, an 'Accessible Natural Greenspace Standard'. This standard includes areas of:

- at least 2 hectares in size, no more than 300 metres (5 minutes' walk) from home;
- at least one accessible 20-hectare site within two kilometres of home;
- one accessible 100-hectare site within five kilometres of home; and
- one accessible 500-hectare site within ten kilometres of home; plus

- a minimum of one hectare of statutory Local Nature Reserves per thousand population.

Until 2020 Australia had experienced 28 years of unbroken economic growth. But had we? What was included and what was excluded in this calculation? What was not included in the calculation was a value on environmental loss. We have refused to put a price on carbon, expecting future generations to bear the cost of our profligacy. Every year more productive land is lost through the expansion of housing and infrastructure. Every year more species become extinct putting sustainable diversity at risk. Every year more demand is placed on water, and the rapacious appetite for mining is met at the expense of water resources and sustainable aquifers. We now know that the loss of substantial areas of the Great Barrier Reef is almost inevitable in the lifetime of people already born. In addition, our economic growth, so named, has only been possible because of increased migration, without this increase it would not have been sustained. This is not sustainable. The world population now stands at 7.8 billion.

Economic systems that are dependent upon population expansion will ultimately crash. There will be a time, near or far, when population exceeds resource availability, or worse when the size of population collapses sustainability. It is estimated that a population of 10 billion could only be sustained if most of the world were vegetarian. The problem is that the growing middle class aspires to be omnivore. Land space, water, and resources required for domestic animals will be prohibitive with a human population of this scale. COVID19 has given us a taste of what we can expect with humans and animals in proximity to each other.

In Chapter 7 I canvassed the role opinionated ignorance has taken in preventing responsible environmental practice, thereby putting at severe risk the lives of future generations. We cannot say we did not know, to plagiarize the title of Sophie McNeill's 2020 book.[89] Further blockages on environmental action by legislators should now be open to charges of criminality.

---

89 Sophie McNeill. *We cannot say we did not know*, (Harper Collins: Sydney, 2020).

Individuals need society and everyone must play their part in society's well-being.

The dreadfully coercive side of communism is all too apparent in modern China. Its lies, lack of transparency, intolerance of any criticism, and shocking cruelty of minorities has been on display for all to see. At the same time, the worst of capitalism has also been on display in the US. How a democracy could have elected such an inappropriate, divisive, and dangerous leader in Donald Trump is almost impossible to understand. But at least in the US voices of criticism are heard and institutions do their best to counter his corrosive leadership. Of the two, it would be preferable to be a citizen of the US.

However, there must be another way. When the war in Europe came to an end in 1945, Churchill was rightly the hero of the British people. But his status did not protect him from an ignominious defeat at the ballot box. The British people wanted more than simply a victory over their enemy, Germany, they wanted a caring society. The National Health Service and the welfare state were born, at a time when economists might well have argued 'we cannot afford it'.

Whatever gifts and skills we may be fortunate enough to possess, under God they are not to provide maximum advantage to ourselves, but to provide maximum benefit to society which nourishes us all. This view which lies at the heart of Christianity is as much a critique of neoliberal capitalism as it is of communism. Nothing could paint this picture more clearly than the spectre of Trump, as COVID19 takes hold in the US, seeking financial control of any vaccine that might emerge.

We all benefit from a legacy of past discoveries, of poets, artists, and musicians, of pioneers and adventurers and of course of unsung carers and nurturers. It is the vocation of all human beings to contribute according to the gifts and capacities with which they have been blessed.

Leadership is best expressed through shared responsibility and consensus.

When I became a regional bishop under the leadership of Sir John Grindrod, the Archbishop of Brisbane, in 1985 he led a short retreat for me prior to the episcopal ordination. I asked him what he wanted me to do. His answer was 'put yourself about'. He went on to say that what I did was of far less importance than how I enabled others to do what they were fitted to do. My role, he explained, through the authority the Diocese gave me in the office of bishop, was to remove barriers and create pathways which enabled the clergy and through them the laity to be effective ministers of the Gospel.

I could not have received better advice. My role was fundamentally to act as servant to the servants, the same role should be in the head of all leaders in a democracy. Throughout my quarter of a century in active episcopate I tried to respond to little things on the day they arrived and bigger things as soon as resources were available to deal with them.

Opening new pathways requires imagination, creativity, and courage. Failure is always a possibility, but failure implicit in not using the authority delegated in leadership to strike new paths is infinitely more serious.

It is also the role of a leader to gather people who are more able than you are. A person who wishes to be top dog is not fit to be a leader. It has been my good fortune to be surrounded by people who have made initiatives, remedies, outcomes, and new ideas possible. It is inexcusable for a person in high office to hold that office surrounded by fawning incompetence. It is a matter of delight to me that virtually all my senior staff in the Diocese of Canberra and Goulburn went on to become bishops in their own right.

Currently the world and many of its institutions are in serious decline because of failure in leadership. This is in no small part due to the competitive ladder climbing required to reach the top rung. Having arrived, staying becomes the top priority, infinitely more important than the motivation of service which presumably was the reason for wanting to be there.

To find out what God is doing and do that is a lifetime journey of discovery that requires the constant mindset of a servant, a servant of the Creator, Sustainer and Lover of all.

Postscript
Looking Forward, Looking Back

We do not think ourselves into new ways of living, we live
ourselves into new ways of thinking.[90]

I am deeply sorry that my generation has not left the world a better place, worse, has squandered opportunities and resources leaving future generations with fewer options in the human quest to live more harmoniously with God, with everything else, and with ourselves.

My generation has been willfully blind to four catastrophic failures of thinking, acting and living: economics, politics, environment, and religion.

I will not rehearse details already covered in previous chapters. Economic failure is rooted in a philosophical blunder, namely belief that human progress can or should be measured materially. This has justified and legitimated human exploitative action on a gigantic scale. This has been lauded as a great achievement by many—but at what price?

The most obvious victim has been the environment which has suffered degradation on a monumental scale, with consequences that are now almost impossible to reverse. As nations around the world announce their annual GDP and calculate percentage growth, environmental cost and loss is never included. The blunder has been accentuated by the failure

---

90 Richard Rohr. *The Wisdom Pattern* (Franciscan Media: Ohio, 2020): 58.

of religion, all religions, to live in such a manner that they could convince their communities human life is but one component in the complex web of the natural order and does not stand above or outside it. It is not the mission of humanity to 'conquer' nature, but to live appropriately within the whole created order, always working for its redemption and renewal.

Ironically, economics has failed because of the exaggerated importance attributed to it. In countries like Australia, economic well-being is always assumed to be of greater importance than social well-being; economic capital more important than social capital. In the good times politicians invest in more exploitation rather than social well-being so that bad times become further alienating. This has led to a world in which an increasing number of young no longer wish to participate. Why be part of a world in which the few control and own infinitely more than the many, and in which anxiety seems to be an unavoidable state of being?

The failure of politics is fundamentally a failure of leadership. It is quite easy to point to failures of tyranny, corruption, ineptness, and self-interest exhibited in what has been called the 'third world'. It is easy too to point to failures in the communist world where the flourishing of individuals has been secondary to the primacy of the state. But I am not talking about these areas of human struggle, but of the world of western democracies in which I have lived and voted all my life. The failure of western democracies lies deep within an adversarial modus operandi. The few occasions when this adversarial system has been relegated to second place has been when there has been a national disaster like COVID19 or an external military threat. Normally political energy is expended in defining a position to the left or right of the opposing party, rather than in the building and implementing of good consensus policy that serves the well-being of society as a whole. Western democracies are shaped by policies designed to attract voters around that to which they are opposed, rather than being committed to the much harder task of shaping the world in light of what is in the best interest of all. I am ashamed to say that in Australian politics, this situation has become infinitely worse in the last 20 years. It may be a little early to make a judgement, but there are signs that when female leadership arises, adversarial politics diminishes.

Environmental or ecological failure is made the more reprehensible because we cannot say we did not know. We have known for most of my lifetime that more and more species are becoming extinct or endangered. We have known for decades that largescale burning of fossil fuels is changing the atmospheric equilibrium upon which modern humans have been able to build civilizations and prosper for more than 200,000 years. We also know that the sea is absorbing more than its fair share of the earth's human generated pollution and because all life is dependent on the oceans, their currents and the weather systems they generate, the changes occurring do not simply impact life at sea, as serious as this is, but also life on land. We have known for the same period of time what we must do to redeem this situation. But we still refuse to do so, not because we lack the capacity, or because doing so is too costly, but because doing so is presumed to negatively affect the financial well-being of those invested in the status quo, who, through their wealth are able to influence and effect political indecision.

Most would consider religion irrelevant at best, and the source of the world's ills at worst. I do not agree with the first assertion, I strongly beg to differ. However, I agree in part with the second. Religious tribalism and extremism are well known. No religions are immune from this blight. Violence perpetrated under a religious banner is, as I have earlier said, usually motivated by economic injustice, but nevertheless its association with religion is shameful. Violence is equally perpetrated with no religious motivation.

What leads me to agree in part that religion is the source of the world's ills is not the terrible things that are done, but that religion has been an abysmal failure at being what it is called to be, a transformative power for good in a broken world. People who claim religious faith have not lived in a life transforming manner.

For much of its history Christianity has condoned violence, the Inquisition and the Crusades being two of the most shameful periods of its history. Islam still has work to do in relation to explicit violence in its sacred texts.

In most institutions, religious and secular, the promotion and defence of identity appears more urgent than the mission of love and service for which they exist.

After over 50 years in Christian ministry, including more than half that time in senior leadership, I have to say that Christianity has become something that Jesus did not intend—an institution. Serving and defending the institution, its power and wealth, is something of which I have been part. At times I have found this a struggle for I have been an insider, while living with the heart of an outsider. Most business conducted by the Synods and Councils of the Church has been 'insider business', which I have never found particularly fascinating. The annual meeting of national bishops was for me three days to be endured, rather than three days of mental and spiritual stimulation.

So, what is the problem?

Richard Rohr[91] puts it better than I might:

We worshipped Jesus instead of following him on his same path.

We made Jesus into a religion instead of a journey towards God and everything else.

This shift made us into a religion of 'belonging' and 'believing' instead of a religion of transformation.

So, what are we to do? Where does the future lie? Has my generation lived the best of days leaving the next generation the crumbs?

Jesus' use of 'leaven' and 'salt' as metaphor gives us a significant clue as to his intent. He did not expect all to become his followers, but that his

91 Richard Rohr, OFM, is an American author, spiritual writer, and Franciscan friar based in Albuquerque, New Mexico. He was ordained to the priesthood in the Roman Catholic Church in 1970. He has been called 'one of the most popular spirituality authors and speakers in the world.'

followers would be agents of transformative energy in the rest of society though their living. Further, it was not his intention that his followers spend most of their time with one another but that they become the presence of Christ in their family, within their neighborhood and throughout the network of connections that life afforded them. There is not a lot of point in attending weekly worship, or being part of a Bible Study group, if this is essentially about being an insider with a ticket to heaven. I began with a quote from Bishop Leslie Newbiggin: 'You do not believe anything unless it makes a difference to the way you live your life'.

It is concerning that many clergy now find themselves being chaplains to ageing congregations who seek personal, comforting, assurance, rather than energy or vulnerability to be agents of transformation. In any case, if a congregation is drawn from a single age quartile, capacity to influence a broad spectrum of society is severely limited. An early shock to my years as a bishop occurred when the first young man I ordained, and in whom I had significant hopes for effective ministry, quickly resigned his ministry. Seeking feed-back he responded: 'I find it easier to talk of eternal truths to the trawler men on the wharf than the faithful members of my congregation. The latter want weekly assurance given to the childlike affirmation they learned in Sunday School and have not grown beyond'.

COVID19 has forced Margaret and me into the formation of a house Church for an indefinite period, in support of the local Parish which can no longer hold Sunday services in the traditional manner. Our home is not large enough, nor the restrictions broad enough, to allow all to come every Sunday. It has made me wonder whether Jesus intended people attend a religious institutional service once a week, or whether meeting semi-informally around word, food, hospitality, bread and wine, would be more life giving. Those who have come to our place have enjoyed the opportunity to contribute to discussion, to know one another more intimately and to enjoy the social interaction. A friend has observed the gathering has the hallmarks of the popular *Alpha* course, without the Nicky Gumble video!

If this is to be part of the new 'normal' it will mean the times of corporate worship when all groups come together must be celebratory, meaningful, and inspiring. The Parish institution must enable broader connectedness, connectedness which is vital to warding off insularity and complacency.

Traditionally clergy have been trained to 'do God for people', rather than developing a much more important skill, namely creating a space where people and God can do their business. Developing this skill requires imaginative and creative risk taking. Conventionally congregations are 'done unto', which may suit an older generation but does nothing for a younger generation. Even children of Christian families do not easily make connections with institutional Church life.

In the years that immediately followed retirement, Margaret and I took a benefice in rural Dorset UK which included seven small villages. Once a month we developed a service conducted by members of the community who had no necessary connection with the Church, let alone its leadership. A theme was agreed upon. They were invited to choose music and readings and give a homily. The service became the most highly attended and some who attended began to slip across to the more 'normal' Church services. While I retained the right to veto any content, it was risky. For approximately 15 months I never regretted for a moment taking this risk and was always inspired by the content and delivery.

The thirty plus baptisms that occurred during this period followed the same pattern. A member of the baptismal party was expected to give a talk which traversed the following three areas:

- Speak of the values and traditions which the family hold dear.
- Speak of the future which they hope the child will grow into and say what as parents or godparent they hope to do to build that inheritance.
- Speak of God and God's grace and how that is to be cherished and nurtured.

Every family participated, some with extraordinary eloquence and insight.

It was soon discovered that meeting in this way brought another presence to the gathering, the wind or spirit of God who 'blows where he will', gently nudging along the path of life for all who give themselves to the shared experience. Our current house Church experience has the same flavour to it.

We live in complimentary spheres of existence. The world of our personal experience. The world brought to us by the experiences of others, and the greater world of unfolding history which can only be understood or made sense of through a meta story which makes sense of all reality.

As important as it is to own our story, we cannot stay in this sphere alone, we must live in the company of others, human and nonhuman. Meeting at some depth with others is an antidote to self-absorption and an opportunity to experience a more inclusive identity. Belonging is a two-edged sword. It is often deeply enriching. But it can also be a source of rivalry, prejudice, and hostility. Much religion is about exclusivity, belonging to a particular tribe that is believed to possess unique access to the divine. Through boundaries, definitions and doctrines, institutional religion has all too often accentuated tribalism, elitism, and exclusion. Too often the secular world sees and hears only of this rivalry.

But religious faith exists to celebrate and be fed by meta story which undergirds all existence and is the source of true wisdom. By its very nature, meta story is inclusive. Influenced by post western enlightenment, there has been strong resistance to the idea that there is such a story. Many in the Western world resist even the possibility of there being a meta story, reducing existence to personal observation as the only arbiter of truth. In Christianity, the meta story, has a name, Jesus, and at the centre of that name stands the cross.

It is possible that in small house Churches individuals are more likely to be drawn into all three spheres of living than they have been in conventional Sunday worship.

For most of the twentieth century the world has been blighted by declining belief in the possibility of a meta story, but somehow we have managed to scrape through. This will not be so in the 21st century. Climate change, over-population, mass human migration, pandemics, economic inequity, democratic decline, surging nationalism, squandered and reduced resources, all contribute to a world in which survival let alone prosperity will depend upon universal acceptance of and commitment to the values of a common story.

This will not be articulated by political leadership, the czars of industry, or sadly by religious leaders committed to the survival of their institution. It will be led by ordinary people who wish to live with justice, in a sustainable world characterized by harmony and peace.

The cornerstone of this story is the cross, belief that gentleness, compassion, sacrifice, forgiveness, are the signs of true humanity, because they reflect the nature of the divine whose fingerprints can be found in every corner of the created order. Winning that makes others lose builds no lasting future. The supreme irony is that the way of the cross is the way to life. Finding this way, commitment to this way will transform politics and economics, tools necessary in the maintenance of human civilisation.

Followers of Jesus in the 21st century are not called to acts of piety that flow from belief that holiness is separation. We are called, as we always have been, to engage deeply with the world for its transformation.

By our living, possibly more than our words, we need to speak truth to power.

Appendices

Oh, I don't reject Christ. I love Christ. It is just that so many of you Christians are so unlike Christ.
If Christians would really live according to the teachings of Christ as found in the Bible, all of India would be Christian today.

Mahatma Gandhi

Appendix 1

**Address given by Bishop George Browning
at the 11th National Prayer Breakfast Service,
*(Parliament House, Canberra, 3 November 1996)***

*In days to come the mountain of the Lord's house shall be
established as the highest of the mountains and shall be raised up
above the hills.*

*Peoples shall stream to it and many nations shall come and say:
'Come, let us go up to the mountain of the Lord, to the house of the
God of Jacob; that he may teach us his ways and that we may walk
in his paths.'*

*For out of Zion shall go forth instruction, and the word of the Lord
from Jerusalem.*

*He shall judge between many peoples and shall arbitrate between
strong nations far away.*

*They shall beat their swords into plowshares, and their spears into
pruning hooks.*

*Nation shall not lift up sword against nation, neither shall they
learn war anymore.*

*But they shall all sit under their own vines and under their own fig
trees, and no one shall make them afraid.*

For the mouth of the Lord of hosts has spoken.

Micah 4:1-5

'I have a dream that one day on the red hills of Georgia the sons of former slaves and the sons of former slave owners will be able to sit down together at the table of brotherhood

'I have a dream that my four little children will one day live in a nation where they will not be judged by the colour of their skin but by the content of their character.'[92]

Micah had a dream. He dreamed that one day the Lord's house would be established on the highest mountain, that all the nations of the world would be drawn to it, that nations would beat their swords into ploughshares and their spears into pruning hooks and that everyone would sit under their own vine and under their own fig tree.

The Aboriginal people of Australia have a dream, more correctly, they have a dreaming. The most well-known icon of that dreaming is the rainbow serpent which focuses creation, unity and belonging for the whole created order and for human beings within that order.

What is the dream of this House? What is the dream of this Parliament? What is the dream of this Nation?

All the dreams that have ever been, or will ever be, in some respect express the insatiable longing of all human beings to belong.

Micah's dream emerged out of his own history, his own story. Who was it who said: if you have no story to tell you have no life to live? Micah believed that Jerusalem was the place where God's presence dwelt. There, peace and righteousness would be known. He believed that where God was present life could be lived in its fullness. He therefore dreamed of a time when all nations would be drawn to this place. Being drawn to the place, they would also be drawn to God. Being drawn to God, they would also live. Living means being drawn to one another in God, sharing Gods life with one another.

Christians share the same dream. However, for us the dream is not confined to a place, for we believe that the place has been fulfilled in a

---

92 Martin Luther King. Civil Rights March, Washington, 1963.

person, the person Jesus, who has risen from the dead. We believe that we are all united to God and one another through him. We do not believe this in any triumphant sense. On the contrary, we believe that Jesus is God's way of being human. It is the emptying way, the dying way, the servant way, the giving way. It is through this way that we experience resurrection. It was C.S. Lewis who said: I believe in the resurrection in the same way that I believe in the dawn of each new day, I see everything else in its light. With this sight we are able to see all things dying, transformed into all things living. All things divided, becoming all things united. For those of us in leadership who hold this vision, Matthew in our second reading this evening had a salutary word. St. Matt 23:1 1: The greatest among you will be your servant. All who exalt themselves will be humbled and all who humble themselves will be exalted.

The Christian dream has become the Christian vision: our longing to belong has been accomplished.

In the last few months Australia has been involved in a debate that has shocked and surprised many of us. The debate has made us focus upon issues of race, issues of immigration, issues that relate to Australia's indigenous people, issues that relate to the United Nations and Australia's place within a world community of nations.

In our relationship with the world, Christians have two responsibilities, to be distinctive and to engage. To engage without being distinctive is to enter another's space without bearing a gift, to be distinctive without engaging, is to remain outside another's space in judgement.

The focus of the present debate has been on immigration. I don't want to say anything about that, except that I note with considerable sadness that we seem to have become scared of what the debate has the potential of doing to our economic position. We seem to be afraid that if the debate continues any longer we will lose tourists and foreign trade. The debate began in fear, it should not end because of the fear of negative economic consequences. It should end out of the recognition that the issues raised are morally unacceptable.

I wish however to focus upon our own indigenous people. Australia's Indigenous people, more than most, have a story to tell: and, because they have a story to tell, they have a life to live. The vast majority of white Australia has not heard that story. The vast majority of white Australia has never known how to engage. I long for that story to be heard by all Australians, not just for the sake of the Aboriginal and Islander people but for all our sakes. The land upon which we walk forms and shapes us. The longer we walk on this continent the more we shall be shaped by it and our stories will converge.

On budget day I stood with three white Australians on the lawns outside Parliament House waiting to speak at the Aboriginal Rally. I waited for about two hours to speak. In the meantime, I heard many angry speeches. The next day one of our best-known Aboriginal leaders rang me at home and spoke for about an hour. Her main message was, 'thank you for standing there and absorbing our pain'. I have never been more humbled, and I have never felt more acutely that I was standing where Jesus stands, the one who draws all people to himself.

At the heart of Christian belief is the Greek word metanoia. It is usually translated 'repentance'. Unfortunately, it has become associated with guilt, not least because of bad preaching. The word more accurately means second thoughts or, ah! now I see. It is a word associated with scales falling from the eyes. Feeling guilty about the actions of previous generations *will not help anyone*, but recognising those actions for what they were and seeing with new eyes will *change everything*. I urge those of us who claim the title Christian to be the first to experience metanoia, to see with new eyes, for when we see with new eyes we will also engage.

Peter came very strongly from his own culture and his own history, he was used to and confident in his own distinctiveness. However, this prevented him from engaging beyond his own Jewish world. It was only when he saw the basket being let down with foods that he had always understood to be unclean, and he heard the voice saying to him, 'Peter rise and eat, don't call unclean what I call clean', that he was then able to engage beyond the boundaries he had previously prescribed for himself.

As you know there is no word more central to Christian thought than the word reconciliation. We believe that on the cross, God was in Christ, reconciling the world to himself. If Jesus is God's way of being human, then our true humanity is caught up in the same action. God in Jesus took our shoes, walked our path, listened to our story and proclaimed his message through us. The process of reconciliation in Australia can follow no other path. We must enter into the story of one another. We must listen. We must listen and listen and listen and go on listening until eventually we can say 'ah now I begin to see! God has truly heard our cry'. However, we only fleetingly hear him call our name. No wonder we have difficulty hearing one another. Listening is costly, costly in time and costly in commitment.

Many have asked me whether it would be appropriate to organise a rally of people outside Parliament who wish to make a moral stand for tolerance and for the protection of our multicultural society. I would like to have your feedback on this matter.

I am afraid that many of the speeches in recent weeks may have deafened ears so that folk are now even more likely only to hear that which resonates with their version of distinctiveness, while engagement with the rest of Australian society, let alone that of the wider world community, becomes increasingly harder.

If this has happened, then the speech makers must accept full responsibility, as must those who have remained silent and failed to correct. The passage we have read from Matthew is specifically directed to Church leaders, but it is also appropriate for leaders of Christian faith, and of none, who hold public office.

In my short speech at the Aboriginal rally, I said that when we reach the year 2001, the Centenary of Federation, we may have built better roads, we may be more technologically advanced, we may have better health and educational facilities for the majority of our people, but if we have not achieved an appropriate reconciliation with our own indigenous people, I do not believe we will have the right to call ourselves a nation come of age. Reconciliation is a moral and spiritual focus for all Australians.

I come to this place today praying that a desire for reconciliation will burn within the very soul of this Government, this Parliament, this Nation.

I have a dream. I have a dream that Australia might be God's Pentecost. I have a dream that Australia might be an icon to the world of true reconciliation across the boundaries of all ethnic origin. I have a dream that Australia's chief contribution to the world community of nations will be the depth of its morality and the depth of its spirituality.

Martin Luther had a dream.

Micah had a dream.

The Aboriginal people of Australia have a dream.

God has a dream. His dream is Jesus.

St. Augustine said: 'Without God we cannot, without us he will not.'

The staggering truth is that it only takes one. 2700 years ago the one was Micah. In 1944 in a Nazi extermination camp the one was the priest Maximillian Kolbe. In 1963 the one was Martin Luther King.

In 1992 the one was Nelson Mandela.

Your calling, my calling, is to be that one in the name of Jesus who is the one.

Amen

Appendix 2

John Russel Browning and the beginning of World War 2
(John Russel Browning's own account of the early part of the Second World War)

March 35 commissioned 2nd Lieutenant in the 4th Territorial Battalion Royal Sussex regiment

1938 Promoted Lieutenant

September 1938 Migrated to Australia

February 1939 Recalled to Britain to serve as Administrative officer in my father's newly formed 70th Searchlight Regiment. RA Promoted Captain

Married Barbara May Barnes July 1939

August 1939 Searchlight regiment mobilised and stationed in Sussex.

October 1939 applied to join my original regiment, given command of 'C' coy 6th Royal Sussex. Had responsibility for the ground defence of Tangmere RAF Base near Chichester. (One soldier accidently shot another in the guard room).

February 1940 6th Battalion Royal Sussex ordered to France as part of 12th Infantry Division. (As part of a new Division we had not completed training nor were we fully equipped. For example we only had 3 Bren machine guns per coy instead of 9). We landed at Le Havre and moved to a situation near Rouen where we camped as a Brigade with the 7th R Sussex and a Bn of the Queens (Surrey).

May 1940 the Germans broke through and our brigade was ordered first to Abbeville, this was then changed to Duelens. By then our transport had left for Abbeville with our supplies.

The first Bn to entrain were waiting all-night in column of route and did not get into their train until daylight. We were the last to go. As our train approached Amiens the 7th R Sussex in the train just ahead of us was dive bombed. The compartment containing the officers was hit and the line blocked. We got out onto the top of the cutting we were in. Later we assembled in a field and tried to avoid being seen by German reconnaissance aircraft. Our colonel had a hernia and could not march. One of my men had had all his teeth extracted and could not eat the iron rations. I managed to get some eggs and he had a raw egg. The 7th Bn were attacked by tanks but we remained unharmed until our colonel arranged for a train to take us back to Paris and then to a huge chateau near Nantes. A sergeant who nearly drowned said he was disappointed when brought around as he said it had felt good! I felt rather ashamed that we had not put up some resistance to the Germans.

The roads were packed with Belgian and French refugees. Most had mattresses strapped to the car roofs to protect them from strafing aircraft.

When we arrived at our camp we learnt that we were to be used under Royal Engineer direction to unload war material for the depots being established. There were all kinds of rumours; one said that German paratroopers had landed nearby. I went with my company to search the wood where they were supposed to be, but found none. It was now into June and Paris had fallen. We were now employed in leading the war material back for evacuation. On June 15 we had orders to march the 26 miles to St Nazaire for embarkation. We marched in two files each side of the road and dived into the ditch as German aircraft attacked. We had no casualties and my men said I seemed to enjoy myself. We spent the night in the open by the docks.

A small major managed to fit into a concrete drain pipe. We had one casualty that night. We embarked on the *Floristan*. There were several RN ships in the harbour and quite a lot of AA fire. There were occasional flights of hurricanes from Tangmere. I was impressed with the calmness of the RN and how few hits the Germans scored. Unfortunately, the *Lancastria* with 7000 men on board was sunk. We had 2000 on our cargo ship and all were on deck. I had a Bren gun mounted for AA shooting. A Denier came over low and we appeared to hit it. I was impressed with the morale of our men. They all shaved and behaved in a soldierly manner. We went around for a moment as we left the harbour and we heard that France had surrendered that day, the seventeenth of June. We were lucky to get away. It took two days to reach Plymouth and we were unmolested en route thanks to the RN and the RAF. I really felt then that God was on our side and that we would win the war.

Appendix 3

Ordained Anglican members of the family

1st Generation

Robert Frank Browning	1911–2003
John Russel Browning	1913–1998

2nd Generation

Robert Derek Browning	1942–
George Victor Browning	1942–
Rosemary Jane Gillham (nee Browning)	1946–
John Clifford Davies (husband Julie Brett)	1932–

3rd Generation

Richard John Browning	1969–
David Sheath (husband Ruth Gillham)	1969–
Simon John Gillham	1970–

Appendix 4

Tony Blair and speech to Australian Parliament

(Article by Andrew Fraser, **Canberra Times** *15 April 2006.)*

'The struggle in our world today is not just about security, it is a struggle about values and about modernity—whether to be at ease with it, or rage at it. To win we have to win the battle of values as much as arms... Ranged against us are the people who hate us; but beyond them are many more who don't hate us but who question our motives, our good faith, our even-handedness, who could support our values but believe we support them selectively. These are the people we have to persuade. They have to know this is about justice and fairness as well as security and prosperity. As in truth there is no prosperity without security and no security without justice. That is the consequence of an interconnected world'.

British Prime Minister, Tony Blair.

Bishop Browning was in the gallery of the House of Representatives on March 27 when British Prime Minister Tony Blair gave Australia's federal politicians the philosophy filleted above. It came complete with references from Blair and his hosts, Australian Prime Minister John Howard and Opposition Leader Kim Beazley to Peter Thomson, the Australian Anglican priest who helped shape Blair's thinking.

Three days later, Browning, the Anglican Bishop of Canberra and Goulburn, took Blair on. He was giving a sermon to mark one of the Church's 'solemn collegial acts' the renewal of ordination vows. (It was the Bishop's 40th such renewal).

Browning told ministers young and old, 'I felt it was a good speech, but it was not beyond debate ... His main point was that there is a battle going on that we must join; we cannot sit on the sidelines.' In going back to basics it did not go far enough.

'Who says prosperity is the ultimate good? It might have sat more easily with me if he had started with well-being and used a logic such as: *there can be no well-being without respect, there can be no respect without trust, there can be no trust without forgiveness.* The logic used by the British Prime Minister is one that commences with a standard of living and moves backwards towards a moral value, the logic of most incumbent leaders in the Western world today.

The battle being fought for prosperity is not one that Christians can join, for one will either be seduced by the hope of its gain, or consumed by the fear of its loss. The headline ['Australia: you're rolling in it'] in the *Sydney Morning Herald* on the same day as the Prime Minister's visit was one of Australians wallowing in prosperity ... We have never before been able to educate children, own a four-wheel drive, pay off the mortgage and own shares—all at the same time.

'We would rather incarcerate people than invest in rehabilitation and we are so hell-bent on our prosperity that we cannot think of any restraint to assist in the rehabilitation of the environment, even for the sake of our children. In politics, we forgive absolutely everything in the lives of those who govern us, including and in particular transparent lies on significant matters of public policy, as long as our mortgages remain secure. No wonder some segments of the world find our values confusing and inconsistent.

He is just as strong in his Easter message for 2006.

He starts by quoting a former Archbishop of Canterbury, William Temple, from the middle of the last century: 'All governments rest in part on falsehood, most conspicuously through the necessary but false supposition that the state acts in the best interest of the whole community, whereas in fact it always acts in the interests of that segment of the community which is able to work its machinery.'

Browning adds in his message, 'There is no problem with wealth, as long as all have access to it. There is no argument with democracy, as long as folk do not have someone else's version of it imposed upon them.'

He admits his views often led him to being misunderstood and even take him into conflict with those who have responsibility for the worldly governments of our time.

Browning was mindful to stress that 'not all religious voice is a power for good' and pointed to more extreme elements from the Right in fundamentalist clergy. Asked what should be done now in Iraq he says, 'I wish I knew, to be quite frank, we've made a terrible mess'. And in the budget? 'I would favour fewer tax cuts or no tax cuts. In certain circumstance I could support increased taxation to increase investment in social capital for the common good'.

Appendix 5

A Noble Vision reduces our Uncertainty

(*The Way I see it*, Canberra Times, *6 March 2005*)

Much has been written and spoken about the perceived alliance between right-wing politics and right-wing religion.

I do not think all who are politically right-wing believe some of the more bizarre pronouncements of right-wing religion(s), but what seems to attract them to one another is their mutual love of certainty. In an age of so much uncertainty, it is not surprising that people seek a harbour and safe anchorage from the continual buffeting of change. But is such a harbour really safe? (Risk management and litigation have become central to the life of almost every business, organisation, or institution, but are our lives better as a result?) Nuance and ambiguity are the stuff of life.

Paradox is never far from the heart of truth. Change, apart from God, is the only constant. 'Change and decay in all around I see, O thou who changest not, abide with me'.

Apparently, the reason we went into Iraq was to deliver certainty, if not about weapons of mass destruction, then about regime change, if not about regime change, then about reducing the risk of terrorism. Even the CIA seems to admit that the risk of terrorism is now greater as a result of our involvement with Iraq.

Why shouldn't we strive for more certainty? In many respects we should. For the sake of safety we need certainty that the power supply to our house is properly insulated and that the vehicles we travel in are mechanically sound. In this sense, certainty is delivered by securing what is external to ourselves.

However in human affairs, that which is external cannot deliver certainty, it is not possible, it is an illusion or mirage. In human affairs we have to work constantly on relationships, which to a lesser or greater extent are always fickle. Security with our neighbours will not be delivered by a higher fence, or faster planes, or more weapons, but with trust, respect, mutuality, equity, compassion, etc.

The Christian faith teaches that the ultimate truth is relationship—our relationship with God and with one another. True faith is not secured by tightening dogma, or the enforcement of the law, but by abiding in grace.

It is a relief to know, thus far, that the regime change in Iraq is not going to deliver a government that adopts a religious fundamentalist code of law.

Many ask, to what extent does the drive for certainty in human affairs in the politics of the United States or even Australia, derive from a religious love for external dogma rather than an inner transformation of the human spirit?

I suspect there is considerable validity in the question in relation to the US. However I do not believe the same climate prevails in Australia.

As the weeks slip inexorably by, and Good Friday and Easter come closer, we recall again that sacrificial love and service have been the powerhouse that have driven the Christian faith and the essential ethic behind Western culture. May we continue to risk ourselves to such a noble vision.

Appendix 6

Let love triumph over fear

(*The Way I see it,* Canberra Times, *7 November, 2004*)

[*The 2004 US election was won by George Bush and
Dick Cheney over John Kerry and John Edwards. It
was a win for the hawks over those who promised a more
compassionate and just society both for humanity and for
the wider created order.*]

It is probably not surprising that Americans seem to have fallen victim to their well-known lack of understanding of the rest of the world and have voted for fear.

What is more inexplicable and somewhat terrifying is that this vote has been delivered by the vote of the Christian community. Given the size of that vote, once promised the election was probably never in doubt. But how could the Christian community vote for fear over love?

What is it that they have understood about the Christian Gospel that made them so earnest to vote for self-interest rather than a wholesome vision for all human beings on the face of the planet, who must live together in harmony and peace, putting aside personal lifestyle ambitions for this more noble goal?

The vote has now been taken. History shows that at the end of the day fear will always draw the larger crowd and produce the loudest noise. The voice of love is sadly always more muted, but thankfully in the end always more attractive. We can only hope that the vote now taken in the US will not deliver a less respectful, more polarised, more self-serving world community where might is right and the poor and marginalised are passed by.

Even more I pray that this new-found might for a conservative Christianity that links itself with fear and self-service will not become the dominant way in which Christianity is experienced or understood by the non-believing world or by the Islamic world: in the same way that the Islamic world prays that the world will not make too close a link between it and violence.

Christianity is sometimes described as a triumph of (choice for) love over fear. Fear is a very natural and understandable human emotion. Sadly, it is a tad too natural. It is essentially a closed and protective response to the stimuli that surrounds us.

Love on the other hand is an open-hearted response where concern for the other is chosen over protection for oneself and where, at the end of the day, safety for oneself is known to exist in the life-giving destiny of the other.

Fear sets up clear boundaries of division, it knows who it thinks are its friends, but more particularly it knows how to identify the enemy. Love on the other hand knows that listening is redemptive, that understanding builds respect, that respect is the building block of human community and that security can be realised only when injustice is addressed, producing a generous, diverse, self-giving, and peaceful community.

Let us pray that this election, which, whether we like it or not affects us all, will not deliver false security for some at the price of peace and justice for all.

Appendix 7

Christianity, the Forests, and the Environment

(Church Scene, *June 1996*)

World Environment Day was marked in early June. In May,
the National Conference Forest Protection Society held a
seminar at the National Convention Centre, Canberra. This
address was delivered by the Anglican Bishop of Canberra
and Goulburn, George Browning.

Is Christianity incurably anthropocentric?

On a visit to the South Eastern corner of NSW last year, I was asked: 'Is Christianity incurably anthropocentric?'

It was an excellent question, the person asking had every right to assume the answer to be in the affirmative. Those of us who are in the business of religion, and more specifically the Christian religion, have given every impression that the only thing we are interested in (and which God is interested in), is the human soul or spirit.

This is totally wrong. The prologue of the Gospel according to St. John reads:

'In the beginning was the Word, the word was with God and the Word was God. He was in the beginning with God. All things were made through him, and without him was not anything made that was made. In him was life.'

The whole created order, and the place of human beings within it, is the business of the Christian faith.

Because the Christian faith is primarily a celebration of life, it is inevitable that successive generations of Christians will warn against that which threatens life.

When Christianity was born, the main threat was the brutal and demeaning presence of the occupying Roman army. Jesus was expected to be the liberator, the one promised to set his people free. Much of the language of the Gospels is therefore the language of God's Kingdom, mistakenly misinterpreted at first as a divine equivalent of the Roman Empire.

In the Middle Ages, the great threat was pandemic, the plague, and the ever-present possibility/probability of death. In response, religious language was dominated by death, guilt, sin, etc. Some of that language has survived in the blood and thunder preachers of today's religious right.

The language of Christianity in South America for the last 30 years or so, in response to totalitarian government, has been the language of liberation, coining the phrase 'liberation theology'.

As contemporary threat to life is linked to a threat to the environment, it should come as no surprise that the environment is increasingly a focus for religious expression. Critics within and without the Church claim the environmental movement is itself a 'new religion'. No, it is a crucial expression of the old religion, belief in a creator God invested in the redemption of the whole created order. As people in every generation have been drawn to the sacred through the natural order, it is no surprise that environmental concern has become a starting point for evangelism.

When a cause becomes separated from its roots, it can lose its rationale, lack balance, and ultimately become an untruth (a heresy). The environmental movement, and the timber industry are frequently combatants. Christianity can and should ground the environmental movement in life principles that all will want to support.

In this paper I hope to underline principles that have application in your area of work and interest. I would also like to challenge the view that the environmental movement and the timber industry are necessarily incompatible in the same manner that critics claim faith and science are incompatible. They should be able to talk to each other.

The Sense of the sacred

It is a cause of grief that a sense of the sacred has been lost by large segments of global population, particularly in the West. *Sacredness attributes value to all life, calls on those who value it to walk lightly and appropriately, sets boundaries to protect harmony and well-being and elicits awe and wonder.* The Old Testament is full of environmental exhortations that underlie the sacred.

Do not plough the ground every year. Every seventh year everything should be allowed to rest. If you are collecting eggs, do not take them all, and do not disturb the mother bird. When harvesting grain, do not glean. Leave some grain for the poor and needy, the fatherless and the widow.

Most ancient people express the sacred through their traditional stories. This is particularly true of Australia's indigenous population through their dreamtime narratives.

A sense of the sacred does not mean that human activity should be excluded. On the contrary, a sense of the sacred should guide every human endeavour. To say: 'the ground upon which we stand is holy', is not to say that we should not be here, or that we cannot share this space; it means we are temporary custodians, others have been here before and others will come after us. It means our needs must always be set in a larger context of others' needs, other humans and other flora and fauna. Sacredness should inhibit exploitation that diminishes.

The Aboriginal view is that the earth is mother. Mother is the source of life's nourishment. Mother is the one above all else to whom respect is given.

Our culture is not one of respect but of ownership, of domination and individual rights. A culture of the sacred is not a culture of ownership, but its reverse, of being owned, with concomitant privileges and responsibilities.

A loss of the sacred leaves humanity on a collision course with its hope of a sustainable future.

Interdependence

In the western world, individualism has become one of our most frightening diseases. It pervades almost everything we do. It threatens shared family life. It feeds a consumerism that encourages identity drawn from what we own, rather than from to whom we belong. It puts at risk those for whom independence is difficult, the vulnerable. It threatens the environment, because the environment is all about mutuality, interdependence.

Considering the right's insistence on individual rights, agreement over uniform gun laws was an astonishing achievement. The outcome flies in the face of this dominant culture. Only a disaster of the magnitude of Port Arthur could have brought it about. We do not want, but may end up facing, a massive environmental disaster to bring about a change of attitude which will place humanity within the created order, not above it.

The various species which make up the created order are mutually interdependent. Nature is very generous and forgiving with extraordinary restorative capacity. However, there will come a moment when the balance is so disturbed that it cannot be corrected. Some would say that moment has already arrived. Species of the created order are not important just because we see them, they are important for themselves and the role they play in the intricate web of life on this planet.

While every individual life has value, (every sparrow, every hair), relationship is everything. Everyone, everything, exists to enhance the life of others. In Christian theology separation is hell. However, both collectively, as well as individually, human behaviour manifests the characteristics of separation, relating everything to self and is disposable, useful only for this time and this place.

Sustainable development

In the biblical creation narrative, the work of each day is described as 'good'. The whole is described as 'very good'. Every part of creation can only be properly understood or valued in relation to the whole. Of course, everything is in a continual state of transformation and change, but sustainability for individual parts is dependent upon the health of the whole.

For thousands of years human beings have made changes to their local environment. Many places around the Mediterranean were heavily timbered, and yet for centuries have been nothing more than rocky outcrops. Many will know the contrasting arguments relating to Aboriginal use of fire. While cultural burning is rightly lauded as a means of preventing catastrophic wildfires, others argue that burning associated with human habitation over 60,000 has changed rainforest to vast swathes of Eucalypt.

Today our capacity for change is no longer confined to local outcomes, it is global. We have the capacity to change the sustainable quality of the globe in a way that no generation has before us.

We know that there are many aspects of human life which impinge upon sustainability: economic policy, birth control, consumerist lifestyle, use of water, etc. It is my contention that we have reached a stage in human history when we can no longer continue with development, or policy, that has a negative outcome for the environment. The world must be a better place for our having been here, not a worse state as a result.

When I assumed my present position as Bishop of Canberra and Goulburn it seemed to me the Diocese was living in a manner which was unsustainable. Some institutions, some positions and some attitudes had more to do with protecting a past than securing a present and a future. Changes had to be made. Many of them caused pain.

Unless we believe we are the last generation of people to live on the face of the earth, we have a responsibility to leave it at least as we found it, perhaps we have an even greater responsibility to restore some of the damage of the past.

From principles to application

Environmental responsibility must fall first on city dwellers, many of our customs are unsustainable. Public transport must take the place of private transport. The endless building of new motorways is not building livable cities.

Despite some improvement we continue to drown in our own rubbish. Until laws are enacted which force those who make rubbish to clean it up, we will see little change to our packaging laws or our common methods of disposal. We cannot and should not export rubbish. Creators of it are responsible for it.

It is said the major crisis of the next century will be water availability. Those of us who live in cities will need to make major changes about our use of water and the way it is collected and recycled. Potable water should not be used for functions other than cooking and washing.

Responsibility falls also upon those who work on the land. Some farming practices are unsustainable. Some tracts of country should no longer be grazed or farmed. The responsibility for change is massive and cannot be borne by those on the land alone.

It is difficult to support cotton production. Water available for agricultural irrigation should be allocated to food production. Water should not be a commodity for sale on the market. Water available for environmental sustainability must be given an economic value. River systems cannot be allowed to die.

Many properties in western NSW are clearly marginal. When margins are small the temptation exists to survive at the expense of the environment. Governmental policy should encourage environmental best practice, including support of some landowner to remain unproductive to restore and rest the land.

Responsibility falls also upon those who are responsible for National Parks and Wilderness areas. Creating a National Park or Wilderness area does not necessarily mean it will remain a resource of pristine quality. Some are badly infested with feral species. Others that were used to low level burning, now denied, suffer two serious consequences. First species that require the intervention of fire for their propagation are denied this cycle.

Secondly a build-up of flammable material can and will cause massive wild-fires with enormous damage.

I am a strong supporter of National Parks and Wilderness areas. Bushwalking is one of my favourite pastimes. However, even a layman like me can see that more time, energy, and resources need to be invested for the high ideals that lie behind their creation, to be realised.

Finally, responsibility falls upon those of you who are involved in the forestry industry. I know that many of you feel you are unfairly in the spotlight. However, trees are unquestionably the focus of life on land. The forests sustain biodiversity. Trees protect the land from erosion, they control the level of water tables, they provide nutriment for the soil and health to the air, they add beauty to the landscape, and provide timber for our houses.

For most of the 200 years that white people have lived on this continent, terrible mistakes have been made. Some have been made from ignorance. Treatment of indigenous people, ill-conceived farming and forestry practices, all have suffered from presumption and ignorance. Ignorance is forgivable, especially if lessons have been learned. In the last 20 or more years there has been considerable progress in our understanding of this continent and of the way in which humans need to live in harmony with it.

The forestry industry has been part of this progress. More resources could be expended educating the wider community about changes that have been made to the practice of forestry. Undoubtedly, some still believe your practices are little changed from the crude practices of early years, it is just that they are now on a larger scale! I do believe you have a story worth telling about your attitude to the sacred, your belief in and protection of biodiversity and your commitment to sustainability.

For example, you need to tell the story of the life span of the eucalypt, of the place of fire in its lifecycle, and of best practice in its harvesting. Help people understand that ideally you will enter an area once every 100 years, but that some policies are forcing you to re-enter an area every 40-60 years.

However, some mistakes are not really mistakes! They are the result of exploitation and greed. Farming and forestry alike can ravage or rape the environment; or exist in harmony with it. Destructive practice will only be kept under control through self-regulation. Forestry is an essential, sustainable, industry; unacceptable practice does the industry great harm.

Conclusion

The Christian faith is about life celebration, about the interaction of God with humanity and the whole created order. It is therefore more than appropriate that the Christian Gospel contributes to the important social issues of our time, including that of the environment.

Firstly, *are we owned, not owners and therefore have a responsibility of stewardship.*

Secondly, *the human species lives in partnership with all living things, not in domination over them.*

Thirdly, *is this moment of history action or policy that does not build sustainability brings about our demise.*

Even though most human beings are urban dwellers, their responsibility is no less significant.

Outside of the cities there are probably three main players who influence the development or decline of this continent's vegetation. They are the farming community, National Parks and Wilderness areas, and the timber industry. The focus of attention has perhaps fallen unevenly on these players. All three have a responsibility to educate the wider community as to the changes that have taken place and are taking place. All three must learn from the mistakes that were made in the past. All three will stand condemned if further degradation continues through exploitation or greed. All three must be responsible for self-regulation.

Environmental sustainability is the business of us all. Undoubtedly further changes will be called for in the decades ahead. These changes will have drastic effects upon some local or isolated communities. The cost of such change should never be borne by these people alone.

The whole Australian community, increasingly, the whole world community, must bear the cost of changes which will deliver a sustainable, interdependent, and sacred world for our grandchildren's children.

Appendix 8

The Climate Bishop

(Lead story in the Environment Business Magazine, November 2006, an edited version of a speech to Environment Business Australia's annual conference by Bishop George Browning the Bishop of Canberra and Goulburn)

Climate change does not mean a choice between economics and the environment. We can—we must—protect both, says Bishop George Browning, convener of the Anglican Church's global Communion Environment Network.

About eight months ago the permanent head of the Department of Environment and Heritage came to my office to explain why the department was going to loosen its environmental requirements for economic reasons. I told him climate responsibility was not about economics, it was about morality. He replied, 'I would expect that of you, but it is essentially about economics.'

Morality or ethics is not simply measuring what is naughty, it is about protecting what is good. A fundamental base for my moral philosophy is that there is no such thing as singularity. Everything is connected. Every form of life is connected, every person is connected. You will not be surprised to hear that one of my heroes is South African Archbishop Desmond Tutu. He famously said: 'I am the sum total of all the lives that have intersected with my own'. Individualism is one of the great heresies of the contemporary world.

Unless we overcome it, we are in great difficulty. You have heard of the butterfly effect: 'when a butterfly flutters its wings in South America, the weather patterns in Europe change'. I am arguing for a morality that takes into consideration the impact of everything we do. I am not a scientist, but I have been convinced by science, I believe the climate change debate is over. We have moral choices in front of us. We either find the courage to act, at little cost to ourselves, or future generations will face the consequences at great expense to themselves.

It has been said there is only one climate sceptic left in cabinet. He and I have had fairly frank exchanges about this matter, particularly following Al Gore' documentary '*An Inconvenient Truth*'. Frustrated by one of his letters, I wrote back saying: 'I challenge you to invite me to bring 100 children into your office and for you to assure them that you are doing all in your power to safeguard their future'. I am still waiting for his response to the letter.

I have written to others in the Cabinet saying I am seriously considering a class action against the government, on behalf of 100 children, for knowingly not acting on the information before them. It is morally wrong for those in power not to act on the information available to them.

People in business must also act, but they will do so within the parameters set by government. Unless or until carbon is priced, the parameters for energy reform are insecure, preventing proper investment. The market must serve society, otherwise it will serve self-interest. Parameters safeguard common good.

Those of us who live in developed countries must also assist those with lower standards of living through shared technology.

I do not mind being called the climate bishop. I am proud of that, but until recently the Church has not funded activity in support of climate responsibility. Because climate change and environmental degradation contribute to poverty it is now recognised that you 'cannot make poverty history' unless you also deal with climate change. Climate change has been brought into the arena of international aid for the first time. It is a reality that unless we deal with the threat of climate change, the poor of the world will become poorer and environmental refugees will swamp migration strategies.

I ask myself most days, what will I do this day for which my grandchildren will thank me. Fronting up to the challenge of climate change will make little difference to my lifestyle, but not fronting up will severely diminish the lifestyle of those who follow after.

Appendix 9

Change needed for our planet
(*The Way I see it*, Canberra Times, *10 July 2004*)

What a wonderful sound rain makes on the roof! However, none of us are under any illusion that this recent 'godsend' is a guarantee of 'normal' weather patterns. No one now seriously disputes the fact of climate change. It is likely that our planet has always been in a constant state of change. What is different is the speed at which it is happening.

No one seriously disputes that in the modern era the human footprint has significantly contributed to the speed at which this change is taking place; or the fact it is having, and will have, an enormous impact upon the lifestyle of future generations of humans and upon the very survival of planetary eco-diversity.

What is hotly disputed is what we should do about it. On the whole, Western governments see the matter through the prism of economic consequences in the short term. The Church, and a growing number of people outside the Church see it as a moral issue.

We do not have the right to a lifestyle at the expense of generations that come after us. We do not have the right to a lifestyle in some corners of the planet at the expense of devastation in some other corners.

Unattended environmental degradation will lead to social disintegration. We do not have the right to value human comfort as a priority demand above the need for environmental sustainability. Indeed, even from a selfish point of view, we know that human beings can only thrive, if the rest of the planet upon which we depend also thrives.

For countless generations human beings have intuitively known that the whole of life is sacred and that we should walk this planet, not with a spirit of exploitation and dominance, but with a spirt of humility, awe, and wonder.

We have already reached a point of moral crisis, if not ecological crisis. Our government is making decisions for what it believes to be the best economic interests of our citizens in the short term, without considering the economic future of our grandchildren who will depend upon sustainable ecological systems. Any serious commitment to true environmental responsibility will only happen if the US, China, and India take a lead.

The ANZAC myth of Australian nationhood is that we made sacrifices for those who were beyond our boundaries. Why is that spirit now so woefully absent that we will only make environmental responsibility a priority if it is in our national economic interest to do so?

The interest of the globe is our interest.

Circumstance will ultimately force us into a way of life that our forebears in faith have long known. Seek dominance and the exultation of individual gratification and we will ultimately be destroyed by our own greed; put the sacredness of life (God) first and everything else will fall properly into place.

Appendix 10

Ecumenical Service to mark Canberra Day

(*St Andrew's Presbyterian Church, Canberra, 12 March 1994*)

When Sally Morgan wrote *My Place*,[93] she touched a chord for all Australians. As an Aboriginal Australian, she gave new insights into her Aboriginal, Australian identity which helped us all to value place.

Every person must cherish a place of their own. Place is an integral part of our common human identity. It is a shared characteristic, that, taken away, destroys our dignity, our humanity.

For this reason, those of us who have security of place are duty bound to work hard to secure 'place' for others. Last year we saw this work in the Mabo legislation which still needs to be converted into reality for the indigenous people of Australia. In recent years Australians have opened their hearts to refugees seeking a home amongst us. This year an appropriate emphasis should be for children who have become victims of their parents' broken relationships. At all times we must be aware of the elderly, who require the dignity of their own space in the latter years of their life.

The gospel reading today spoke of the labourers in God's vineyard (Matt. 20: 1-16), an aspect of that labour is securing a 'place' for all.

93 Sally Morgan. *My place.* (Fremantle Arts Centre Perth, 1987).

For those of us who live in Canberra, this is our place. It is beautiful and spacious. It is endowed with above average amenities. It is a place of which we are and should be proud. It is the place of our homes, schools, favourite walkways, playing fields, shops and theatres.

And yet Canberra can never be only our place. It is the home of all Australians, full of icons that symbolise and give effect to our shared national life.

Canberra has a biblical parallel. When David chose Jerusalem, the Jebusite town, it was a non-place. He needed a neutral place to bring together north and south factions. It came to focus 'presence' for all Israel, and in turn Israel came to believe it focussed the unity and peace of all nations. Why did that dream, or vision, fail to be a reality, both in the past and as tragically in the present? Many reasons: the frailty of human jealousy, the desire to build a power base, loss of vision, racial elitism. Above all it was a failure to understand that Jerusalem, the city of righteousness and peace, could only be so through a vision of empowerment of others.

We now know that God had other plans, Jerusalem the place has become Jesus the person in whom righteousness and peace has been pleased to dwell. He is the new Jerusalem that cannot be spoiled by human sin deceit and pride. He takes that sinfulness, absorbs it to himself, thereby granting new life and wholeness to all.

The first reading today reminds us 'My thoughts are not your thoughts, nor are your ways my ways, says the Lord (Isa. 55: 8-9). God's ways turn ours upside down. Our human inclination is to be the focus. We wish to hold on to power, establish an Empire, preserve our own niche. The more Canberra does that the less of a focus it can be for the rest of Australia. As we celebrate Canberra Day and engage in the exciting festivities of the coming week, what do we, the Christian community, have to offer?

What can we Christians dream for Canberra? In what way can we contribute to national life? Should we dream of the disappearance of denominationalism into organic unity? I think not. God gifts us with differences which should complement one another. We can and should accept one another in one communion and fellowship. It is wrong to deny one another the communion that God has already given us in Christ.

We can dream of a spiritual centre that will not only bridge Church boundaries, but a centre that will cross ethnic and cultural divides as well. A place for all Australians, a place of reconciliation and hope. It is possible to dream of a presence that will not just reflect the past, but point to a future into which God calls us; a future which gladly embraces difference, but binds that diversity into a common unity. This is the reality of God's dream for us, his gift to us in Christ: should we dream less for one another? Now is not the time to speak more specifically of a plan that many are sharing for such a focus on the shores of Lake Burley Griffin. However, God willing, this will be launched later this year and hopefully become a reality by the turn of the century.

We can dream too of Church which speaks in the public forum, not to condemn and disparage, but to challenge, empower and build. A Church which offers leadership through its voice, a voice of prayer and humility.

What word can be said to the wider Canberra community? May I pick up the parallel to which I referred earlier? The dangers and pitfalls that beset Jerusalem are almost bound to befall any city and its people who exist as a focus for others. Human jealousies and personal ambitions for power, a lack of vision, and energy expended on self-perpetuation have been, throughout history, a recipe for destruction.

May we plead for vision in our leaders. Changes in leadership or transfer of power have always been irrelevant if there has been no obvious policy or vision to support such leadership. We are all human and prone to fail personal aspirations, let alone the aspirations of others; but those who lead must be the agents of empowerment for others. It is the claim of the Christian gospel that the only way we can empower is by following the path of humility exhibited in Jesus.

That which applies to leaders also applies to those who serve among them. Most who work in Canberra are public servants, the same standard applies to us. Since arriving in Canberra last year I have frequently heard; 'It is not possible to publicly profess the Christian faith in the public service'. I can think of two reasons why this might be the case. First, because Christians have a reputation for being moralistic, a pain, hypocritical. On the other hand it may be that Christians challenge the absence of vision, personal ambition for power and energy spent on self-preservation.

The first reason is always a possibility, we should be humbly aware of it. Hopefully the second is the truth. In a city whose raison d'etre is public service, the vocation of a Christian can be painful if the community's vocation has been lost. Having become Canberra resident I realise how easy it is to live in a bubble. I need to be reminded that our place is not our place, it is the place of all Australians.

Fulfilling this vision, Canberra can and should be the most spiritually focussed of all cities in Australia. Its vision and ideals take it beyond itself into the nooks and crannies of every other place on this continent. In such a vision we will not only fulfil our vocation, but in the process find blessing and fulfilment for ourselves.

'Then the land-owner went out early in the morning to call labour into his vineyard'.

Appendix 11

Christianity's Australian Character

After many years in residency here, Christianity is seeking citizenship
George Browning considers the emerging Australian Spirituality

(Sydney Morning Herald, 5 July 1994)

When Christianity came to Australia it came with the dogmatic and denominational baggage of the northern hemisphere. Little effort was given to the question, 'What is Gospel on Australian soil?'

In one sense this is surprising because 'celebrating the local accent' has been at the heart of the Hebraic-Christian tradition. Most of the great Hebrew and Christian festivals grew out of the celebration and transformation of local customs.

In another way it is not surprising. The early settlers believed Australia to be a harsh unforgiving land with little to celebrate. The customs and beliefs of foreign lands were imposed upon Australian people (new and old) in ways that were sometimes appalling and had little to do with 'gospel'.

What are the emerging elements of an Australian spirituality?

First: affinity rather than dogma

I have to admit that some of the largest and fastest growing churches in Australia are fundamentalist and driven by dogma which provides the security of black and white solutions to complex questions. However, I do not believe this can or will become the mainline spirituality of Australia, or the way for the majority of people to find depth and meaning.

Increasingly we are developing a real sense of affinity. By affinity I mean a profound sense of meaning and identity that comes from belonging.

Story is important to us: Henry Lawson, Banjo Paterson, Les Murray and Morris West were all important Australian story tellers. The Bible is story; it tells us who we are rather than what is right or what is wrong. When we know who we are, we will know what is right and what is wrong. (Australians are very impatient with dogmatic morality).

Denominational difference often has more to do with power and jurisdiction than truth. Australians will become increasingly impatient with institutions and church leaders who tell them what 'the rules' are if they are plainly rules of empire rather than spirit. A sense of common affinity may encourage communion across denominational boundaries.

Affinity is at the heart of the spirituality of the Aboriginal and Islander people, especially affinity with land. We share the same soil, drink the same water, breathe the same air. Should we be surprised that we are drawn to the same spirit?

Second: Partnership rather than autonomy

For 200 years we have not been able to notch up many Australian triumphs. We are being reminded of the pain and humiliation of the early days of 'settlement'—invasion. We know the ANZAC stories of loss at Gallipoli and the Western front. We are constantly reminded of the ravages of nature. We are aware that our land is more fragile than almost any other, and is easily turned to salt or desert.

We do not need to be reminded that, as an industrialised country, we catch pneumonia when others sneeze. And yet in an extraordinary way we rather revel in this situation. We love the little Aussie battler, we love the sniff of triumph out of the jaws of tragedy. If we have suffered, it has made us who we are. We have learned that in Australia there is little that can be controlled, our style is to be in partnership with one another. Exclusion is not our thing.

Women are rightly growing impatient with church, politics, education and an economy that locks them out.

In politics we are resistant to arrogant tall poppies. A republic is inevitable—but what kind? Churches should involve themselves in the debate, arguing that a republic must reflect our identity, not a model borrowed from another place. One wonders too whether Australia's growing participatory identity will continue to suffer a party-political system for which few Australians have respect.

Because we believe in partnership rather than control, we tend to believe the same of God. A distant God who manipulates strings makes little sense to most Australians. A God with whom we can yarn, who has the same dust in his nostrils, the Jesus of Nazareth, has potentially much to offer most Australians.

Third: Diversity rather than conformity

Jesus said: 'In my Father's house there are many rooms'.

The uniqueness of Australia lies in its openness, its space. In this vastness: from rainforest to desert, alps to tropics, Barrier Reef to grassy plains, conformity can never be imposed. Added to this, the immigration of people from the four corners of the earth means that in Australia we have a gift of diversity which mirrors the rainbow of God's covenant with humanity.

In some respects we are a reluctant nation. We cherish our state and local loyalties. All of this diversity is in sharp contrast with the monocultural origins of most of us. These are some of the emerging signs of an Australian identity and spirituality in a country where an astonishing 80 per cent of the population still say they believe in God, while a much smaller percentage attends a religious place of worship, or observes religious practice.

It is to these and other indicators we will look as we develop a Christian centre in Canberra which expresses a distinctive Australian spirituality.

A centre which is genuinely ecumenical. A centre for the arts, a centre of reconciliation and hope, a centre for celebration and music, a centre for reflection and quiet, a centre for debate and dialogue, a meeting place which acknowledges from whence we have come, but gives us hope for the future into which we journey.

Appendix 12

Archbishop warns US, Israel more terror will come

An article by Laura Tingle (giving me unmerited promotion) in
the Australian Financial Review, *13-14 September, 2003.*

A senior Anglican archbishop has launched a scathing attack on the United States and Israeli governments—and by implication on Australia -over their anti-terrorism policies saying they are built on injustice and will only produce more terror.

In an address to the Anglican Synod in Sydney on Friday night the Archbishop of Canberra and Goulburn, Bishop George Browning said the war on terror 'is doing nothing but producing more terror' and grieved that he was now living in a country surrounded by barricades.

Bishop Browning asserted his right to speak out on other countries' policies and the right of Churches to speak out despite the fact politicians were criticising their interventions. 'What right do I have to speak of other countries and of America in particular?' he said. 'This right comes as a direct consequence of America's insistence upon a globalised world. We can't globalise markets and yet privatise ethics and theology.' Bishop Browning urged 'today's leaders' to 'turn around and go back, you are taking us in the wrong direction.'

'I contend this is the most profound theological issue facing us today, and it will not be put off by politicians telling us it is simply a matter of politics'. Bishop Browning asked of the US: 'How can a country that apparently experiences more [religious] conversions than most other Western countries be so insular, less compassionate, more arrogant?'

'The 'axis of evil' and 'those who are not with us are against us' speeches of [President George] Bush were profoundly disturbing because they portray a view of a world that has religion at its heart, but a religion which seeks to secure its future by eliminating threats, rather than attempting to understand them, live beside them and ultimately redeem them.'

Similarly, he observed that 'in human history no nation has more often been the victim than Israel, most terribly so in the Holocaust'. Notwithstanding this reality Israel will not develop a positive identity by continued humiliation and deprivation of the Palestinian people, but by living generously and compassionately with them as neighbours. He criticised Israel's 'blatant grab for land on which others have built houses and planted olive orchards'.

Bishop Browning, with Canberra's auxiliary Catholic Bishop, Pat Power, reproached Prime Minister John Howard over the government's policies on Iraq early this year during the traditional service to commemorate the opening of parliament.

On Friday night Bishop Browning questioned the 'staggering sums' being spent on security. 'We can build all the security we like, but no security fence will ever be high enough to protect injustice from justice'.